# BUILDING A NATIONAL IMAGE

Bates Lowry

# BUILDING A NATIONAL IMAGE

Publication made possible by United Technologies Corporation

# ARCHITECTURAL DRAWINGS FOR THE AMERICAN DEMOCRACY, 1789–1912

Published on the occasion of an exhibition of the same title shown at the
National Building Museum, Washington, D. C., in the fall of 1985.

Both the exhibition and publication have been made possible by a grant from
United Technologies Corporation, a founding member of the National Building
Museum.

Designed and produced by Derek Birdsall R.D.I.
Edited by Irene Gordon
Typesetting in Monophoto Modern No 7 and Clarendon No 12
by Balding + Mansell Limited.
Color origination by Peak Litho Plates.
Printed on Parilux Matt Cream by Penshurst Press

National Building Museum
Judiciary Square, NW, Washington, D. C. 20001
Walker and Company
720 Fifth Avenue, New York, New York 10019

Library of Congress Cataloguing in Publication Data
Lowry, Bates
    Building a national image.

    "Published on the occasion of an exhibition of the
same title shown at the National Building Museum,
Washington, D. C. in the fall of 1985"—T.p. verso.
    Bibliography: p. 225
    1. Architectural drawing—United States—Exhibitions.
I. National Building Museums (U.S.)   II. Title.
NA2706.U6L68 1985        725′.1′0222        85-18850
ISBN 0-8027-0873-0 (Walker)
ISBN 0-8027-7284-6 (Walker: pbk.)

# Table of contents

The National Building Museum celebrates America's building heritage.
This Corporation is proud to be a founding member of the Museum and pleased
to support the inaugural exhibition.

HARRY J. GRAY
*Chairman*
*United Technologies Corporation*

## Acknowledgments

The genesis of this book lies in the visual documentation program on American art that was begun by the Dunlap Society in 1974 with the aid of a generous grant from the Education Division of the National Endowment for the Humanities. The aim of that project was to help raise the level of teaching and research in the field of American art by providing historians, students, and critics with visual material of high quality not otherwise available. The Dunlap Society chose as a pilot program the documentation of the major buildings in the nation's capital. The results of this investigation were ultimately published on microfiche containing 3,500 visual images related to the history of 27 buildings in Washington, D. C.

In the course of this project the society's researchers uncovered a number of previously unknown visual documents, but nothing so rich as the drawings conserved in the Cartographic Division of the National Archives in Record Groups 121, 66, and 42. At the same time, because of its quest for original visual documents, the society discovered a truly unbelievable wealth of material under the care of the Architect of the Capitol. Here, Florian Thayn, then Head of the Art and Reference Division, Office of the Architect of the Capitol, literally pulled open the drawers containing the vast archive of architectural drawings that documented the history of the Capitol. In addition to these two collections, the Dunlap Society also worked with the better-known and exceedingly important collection of architectural drawings at the Library of Congress where C. Ford Peatross, then Cataloguer of Architectural Collections, always encouraged our explorations of the uncatalogued material.

To bring these invaluable records to the attention of all those interested in and concerned with American architecture the Dunlap Society conceived the idea of sponsoring a series of exhibitions of the drawings. To make such a goal feasible, Karel Yasko, then Counsellor to the Administrator of the General Services Administration for Historic Preservation, commissioned the society in 1977 to prepare an inventory of the more than 50,000 drawings in the National Archives Record Group 121, all of which had originally belonged to the Office of the Supervising Architect of the Treasury. Three students—Pamela Scott, Kresten Jesperson, and Suman Sorg—accomplished this formidable task of creating a finding tool for this record group, which for the first time gave researchers ready access to this material. During this period Ralph Arensberg, then head of the Cartographic Division, and his assistant, Ronald Grim, aided and encouraged our work in every way in this heretofore neglected part of their holdings. They were ultimately responsible for changing the title of the department, which officially became known as the Cartographic and Architectural Branch of the National Archives.

In the eight years between the conception and the realization of this book and exhibition many individuals have made invaluable contributions. From a conceptual point of view the presentation of this—for the most part—unknown material had the enthusiastic support of Barbara Shissler Nosanow, then Director of Education at the National Archives; Joshua C. Taylor, then Director of the National Collection of Fine Arts; Joel W. Solomon, then the Administrator of the General Services Administration; James B. Rhoads, then the Archivist of the United States; and Livingston W. Biddle, then Chairman of the National Endowment for the Arts. All these people furthered the idea of making this material available to students, scholars, and the general public in the belief that an important part of America's architectural history remained to be written.

Support for the project has been provided by a Chairman's grant from the National Endowment for the Humanities, several grants from the Design Arts Program of the National Endowment for the Arts, as well as from the General Services Administration. This assistance maintained key researchers at work on all the issues basic to the investigation of the role of federal architecture. In particular, the Dunlap Society was able to continue to profit from the work of Pamela Scott, who, when faced with a problem previously unsolved, always turned up new material, much of which enriches this book. She possesses the rare creativity that puts an entire issue into a new perspective that invariably illuminates the larger picture. At this same time the society was also fortunate to be able to rely on Edward Zimmer, whose shrewd and careful readings of documents and grasp of the whole historical framework allowed him to make many contributions that clarified areas of knowledge that were previously vague and misleading. Another valuable assistant was Judith Lanius, whose research in the critical literature of the first half of the nineteenth century allowed the author to place the individual work of architecture into a broader context.

During these years of research and preparation the Dunlap Society also benefited from the dedicated services of many student researchers: Andrea Foggle, Pamela Guren, Michael Herschensohn, Elizabeth Meyer, and Patrick Snadon. In the summer of 1978 the project gained immeasurably from the work of two interns from the Winterthur Program in the Conservation of Artistic and Historic Objects, Catherine Nicholson and Shelley Sturman, who worked assiduously on the drawings at the National Archives and completed a preliminary report on the condition of each drawing, with recommendations for the conservation measures that should be undertaken. In 1980 Nancy Aschettino carried out extensive research on the lives and work of the supervising architects from 1866 to 1912, which has greatly increased the knowledge available about this most prolific period in federal building.

Also during this period Patricia Eames directed a team of volunteers who catalogued the drawings selected for the exhibition and provided an invaluable base of information upon which the present book was able to rely. In addition, she undertook several individual research projects, one of which has provided more precise knowledge about the contributions of Ammi B. Young to the formation of a national style.

In writing this book I was able to draft the early chapters dealing with the designs of William Thornton while on the island of Tortola near the ruins of his plantation house and to have written a good part of the manuscript while I was a privileged guest at Sotterly Plantation in Maryland, whose fields and pastures along the Patuxent River have been under continuous cultivation for over two hundred and fifty years. Both environments contributed in some immeasurable way to my formulation of the ideas presented here.

The entire staff of the museum has contributed to the book by their patience and understanding at those times when writing superseded daily problems. Joyce Elliott, the museum's head of publications, kindly read galleys with her usual attention to detail, and Carol Sherwood made herself readily available for processing the manuscript, which she accomplished with impressive skill and intelligence. My heartfelt thanks go to all for their support during this time.

During this recent period, both the book and exhibition have continued to benefit from the generosity and cooperation of staff members at the three federal collections: C. Ford Peatross and Mary Ison at the Library of Congress; Anne Radice, Pam Violante, and Mary Lou Hansen at the Office of the Architect of the Capitol; William Cunliffe and John Dwyer at the National Archives, Cartographic and Architectural Branch.

Norma Jackson and Jan Peden of the Dunlap Society have also continued to offer invaluable services to the project. Fred Klonsky was particularly helpful in obtaining copies of the Burnham correspondence in the library of the Art Institute of Chicago. To Morton and Jean Rose I am grateful for providing me with a quiet haven in which to complete the manuscript.

In this past year the project has benefited from the keen intellect and sensitive eye of Margaret Denton Smith, curator of the exhibition and, in every sense of the word, true collaborator on this book. Her fantastic ability to track down the most elusive reference has led her to uncover wonderful contemporary documents that have added significantly to our understanding of what certain buildings meant to those who designed them. In addition, she has, with firmness yet with grace, controlled incipient bouts of pedantry on my part.

Once again I have been fortunate enough to have Irene Gordon as my editor. Since our first editing experience some twenty years ago her knowledge of the art and literature in almost every field of art history and her uncanny ability to change words without changing meaning have established her as a unique editor. I am grateful that whatever project I find myself engaged in, she is willing to make it more understandable to the reader by undertaking its editing. Those who have come to enjoy this relationship with her share my fear that as her teaching and research absorb more of her time, we may one day have to publish our ideas before she has cast her caring and critical eye upon them.

As both author of this project and director of the National Building Museum I am deeply grateful to Gordon Bowman, Director of Corporate Creative Programs, United Technologies Corporation, whose farsighted belief in the future of the museum led to the support of the exhibition and the publication. To Marie Dalton-Meyer, Manager of Cultural Programs, I express deep appreciation for her sympathetic and constructive understanding of the problems involved in producing a book of such scope. I owe an additional debt to both for having brought the gifted designer Derek Birdsall into this project. His talent, patience, and enthusiasm have provided a handsome format for both the pictorial material and the text.

Finally, I must try to express my gratitude to my wife, Isabel Barrett, about whom it may be justly said, "without whose help this book would never have been written." It has been a joint effort, just as all the projects I have undertaken during our nearly forty years together have been made better—sometimes because of her support in an official capacity as Executive Director of the Dunlap Society, or Head of Documentation and Research Services of the National Building Museum—but most times because her informed and intuitive understanding of the project at hand makes her the best of critics and the one person most capable of helping me achieve what I set out to do.

B.L.

*Figure 1*    Pierre L'Enfant.
*Banquet pavilion designed for the New York City celebration in honor of the Constitution, 1788.*
Ink drawing. Whereabouts unknown.

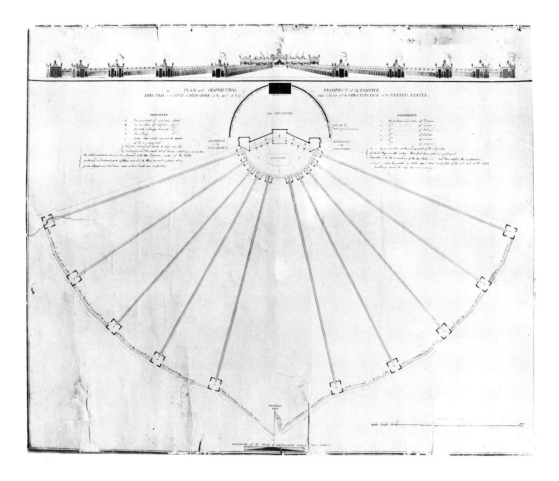

When, in 1788, the city of New York was designated by the Continental Congress to be the capital city of the United States under the new Constitution, it immediately set about to create a splendid building for the meeting of the first Congress and the inauguration of the first president. By providing a setting appropriate for the dignity of these events, the city fathers hoped to persuade Congress that New York City should remain the permanent seat of the central government. As only six months were available for any work to be done it was decided to transform the City Hall, which had been serving the Continental Congress as a meeting place since 1785, into a more magnificent building. To achieve this the committee in charge turned to Major Pierre Charles L'Enfant.

The choice of this French officer was a natural one, for in the years since his service as an engineer in the American cause during the Revolution his talents as a draftsman, surveyor, and architect had come to be greatly appreciated in the young Republic. He was known as one whose advice had been sought by both Congress and General George Washington on the suitability of the various sites proposed at different times over the previous five years for the permanent location of a capital city. And that very summer of 1788 L'Enfant had served the city of New York as the designer of a huge and elaborate banquet pavilion (figure 1) which was the culminating point for a grand procession held to honor the ten states that had already ratified the Constitution and to influence New York State to follow suit.

L'Enfant's natural talents would have earned him a respected role in any society, but the scarcity of such gifts in America at this time gave him an even greater opportunity for fame and distinction. For curiously enough, the American statesmen who had proved so capable in 1776 of eloquently expressing in written form the abstract concepts of liberty, prosperity, and happiness had not been able to translate these ideas into visual imagery. Indeed, some of the same men who had needed only two days to write the Declaration of Independence, when assigned the duty of devising an acceptable design for a national seal could not do so even after six weeks of deliberation. Some six years would pass before a design emblematic of the new Republic would finally be settled upon. Clearly, an artist of the qualities possessed by L'Enfant, who was also a member in good standing in President Washington's circle, would be sought out for guidance in any matter concerning the visual, and symbolic, image this nation should present to a world who found its political existence and unique form of government a matter of astonishment.

The commission for designing the Federal Hall in New York, despite the fact that it was only a hasty remodeling of the existing City Hall, was the most important architectural assignment L'Enfant had yet been asked to undertake. It was an opportunity to demonstrate to the world what the assembly hall of such a new form of government should look like. No models existed for L'Enfant, as no other government had been ordained and established by its own citizens. Although his native countrymen would soon begin to determine how the new political order of France should be expressed architecturally, in 1789 the court architects at

Versailles were concerned only with preparing a temporary meeting place for the first convocation since 1614 of the States-General, a consultative body to the Crown composed of elected members of the church, the nobility, and the middle class. L'Enfant's design for the Federal Hall in New York would not only be judged on its appropriateness as a building serving an immediate purpose, but it also would be seen as the first step in a quest for a national style—for an architecture that symbolized the new nation.

Thomas Jefferson had already identified the architectural form he considered appropriate for a building in which the laws of a republican society were enacted. His designs in the 1780s for the Virginia statehouse were inspired by his admiration for the temple form of the classical past, particularly for the ancient temple he had seen in Nîmes, which Jefferson regarded as a product of Republican Rome. The columnar portico of the statehouse located on a prominent site overlooking the James River (figure 2) gave to Richmond the appearance of a reborn classical city, its architectural imagery matching the revived classical virtues underlying the new Republic. In creating this replica of a Roman temple in America, Jefferson had also intended to affect the future of American architecture by providing his nation's architects with an actual model of a classical building for study and emulation. Jefferson's hope was that his statehouse would inspire other public buildings in the new Republic and create an American architecture solidly based on the classical traditions of Greece and Rome.

In the short time available for remodeling the New York City Hall, L'Enfant could not re-create the image of any specific classical building, even had he considered this the proper direction for a new national architecture. Nevertheless, the training L'Enfant had received in Paris would unmistakably lead him to be sympathetic with the then widely held belief in the superiority of a classical style. Whatever course he might have taken in the creation of a new American architecture, he would be more likely to design within the classical mode rather than adopt—or even invent—some novel style.

Within the six-month period available to L'Enfant for accomplishing this assignment he managed to introduce amazing changes in the architectural presence of the building, all of which may be characterized as variations or inventions within the classical mode. Built originally between 1699 and 1704, the municipal hall had been enlarged in 1763 by the addition of a third story and a central portico (figure 3) strongly reminiscent of similar forms built in England during this period. The adoption of this style was intended to reveal the English as the legitimate heirs of the principles pronounced in both the works and publications of Palladio, the sixteenth-century Italian architect whose canons of design were considered by English architectural enthusiasts to be the apogee of good taste. L'Enfant's elimination of this favorite English motif (figure 4) may perhaps be aligned with the emotions that had led New Yorkers on the evening of July 9, 1776, to haul down the equestrian statue of King George III that stood in Bowling Green. A new nation had to shed the past; it had also to clothe its new identity in a suitable new image.

*Figure 2*    Benjamin H. Latrobe.
*View of the Statehouse in Richmond, Virginia.*
Watercolor, 1796. Maryland Historical Society, Baltimore.

*Figure 3*    Pierre Eugène du Simitière. *New York City Hall.*
Ink sketch, ca. 1769. Library Company of Philadelphia.

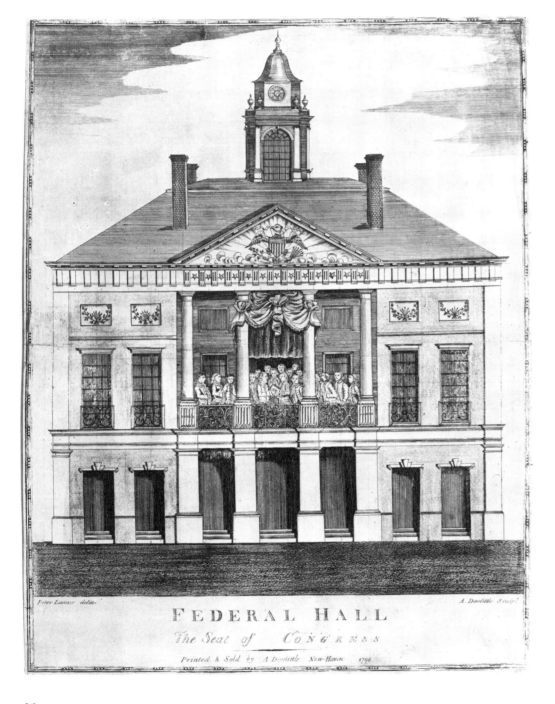

*Figure 4*
*Federal Hall in New York City, as designed by Pierre L'Enfant.*
Engraving of 1790 by Amos Doolittle commemorating the Inauguration
of George Washington.

L'Enfant achieved this by a very adroit restructuring of the original building. At the ground level he enlarged the windows of the two side wings and converted them into doorways that became part of a covered walkway along Wall Street. Visually this passageway created an important volumetric substructure that served as a strong base for the upper portion of the building, which L'Enfant transformed from a two-story element into a single monumental unit by enlarging the height of the second-story windows, thereby ennobling their proportions, and substituting the third-story windows with panels of relief sculpture. Although L'Enfant retained the basic configuration of the building, as well as the earlier lantern, these changes endowed it with a distinctively different appearance.

In addition to these structural changes L'Enfant introduced specific classical elements into his design. He converted the four small columns of the former arcade into heavy Tuscan piers. Above these, as a frame for the second-story balcony, he set four columns of the Roman Doric order. These superposed verticals overpower the horizontal entablature between the two stories and create the visual sense of a massive colossal order rising without interruption from ground level to roofline. Here, in the upper entablature, L'Enfant emphasized the horizontal by a succession of triglyphs, the center ones interspersed with thirteen stars. The pediment, set immediately over these and extending above the roofline, displayed a relief of a large American eagle surrounded by rays, which appears to be bursting from a cloud, carrying thirteen arrows and the arms of the United States. Each part of L'Enfant's design for the first federal building of the United States was an element of classical architecture, but the decorative motifs were all original symbols that spoke of the new American nation.

Contemporary descriptions of the building (which was razed in 1812) spell out these innovations with pride. The writer in the *Massachusetts Magazine* of June 1789, was particularly taken with the way the exterior frieze had been "ingeniously divided to admit thirteen stars" and with the relief tablets in the attic story which displayed thirteen arrows united with an olive branch, an image showing that in this nation only Congress had the power to determine whether the country would be at war or at peace. The writer in the *New-York Journal and Weekly Register* of March 26, 1789, commented especially on the large eagle in the pediment that crowned the building, which had been a matter of tremendous pride and popular acclaim ever since the February ceremony that marked its being hoisted into place. Between that moment and the final removal of the scaffolding on April 22 its display was eagerly awaited and once disclosed caused the building to be acclaimed as "truly august." All of these elements, the *Massachusetts Magazine* reporter commented, "mark it as a building set apart for national purposes."

The same writer carefully described and wholeheartedly appreciated the decorative details inside the building as well: carved trophies using the letters *U. S.* in a cypher surrounded with laurel (to become a standard decorative device in American architecture) were noted in the "Representatives' room," as was the

Within the engraving:

FEDERAL HALL
*The Seat of Congress*
Printed & Sold by A. Doolittle New-Haven 1790

intention of placing a statue of Liberty over the Speaker's chair. The pilasters in the Senate Chamber were "not of any regular order." but were invented by Major L'Enfant especially for the building with capitals "of a fanciful kind" that contained stars and rays amid their foliage and a piece of drapery below suspending a medallion with *U. S.* in a cypher. Although not like any of the ancient orders, they struck the correspondent as having a pleasing effect and an appearance of magnificence. L'Enfant was highly praised for his work and the building was acclaimed by one enthusiastic writer as a "superb edifice . . . superior to any building in America . . . which . . . does honor to the architect" (Torres 1970, p. 328).

Although this Federal Hall served its purpose for only seventeen months, when Philadelphia was chosen as the temporary seat of the national government, its much-lauded design enhanced L'Enfant's reputation and gained for him the continued confidence of President Washington. However, for L'Enfant the New York building quickly became only a first sketch of the appropriate form for America's public buildings. His next charge, this time from the president himself, was to participate in the planning of a completely new capital city for the United States.

Authority for Congress to establish a hundred-square-mile district for the seat of the federal government in whatever state would cede the land was written into the Constitution (Art. 1. Sec. 8). But not until July 1790 was Congress able to agree that the district should be located on the Potomac River. Sites on the Potomac had been considered as early as 1785 and petitions in favor of Georgetown as the site for the city had been put forward several times. However, this final decision was made possible only after the president was able to win over the support of the northern states—who considered the location to be too much in the south—by agreeing to have the national government assume the war debts of the thirteen states. President Washington could now pursue his ambitious and visionary goal: the creation of a new federal city, in a new federal district located in approximately the geographical center of the thirteen states, as an independent political unit belonging to all the states but beholden to no individual one.

Having been given the approval by Congress to select a tract along the Potomac for the federal district, President Washington and his close advisors, James Madison and Secretary of State Jefferson, now had to fix its exact site. As a nearby landowner and as one of the founders in 1785 of the company to build a canal westward along the Potomac, the president brought to the task a personal knowledge of the area under consideration, as well as his training and experience as a surveyor. The other two men also knew the area well, having traveled through it on their way home to Virginia from the meetings of Congress in the north. The president and his two advisors took six months before announcing their decision, which they did on January 24, 1791, in a proclamation that established the boundaries (subject to actual surveys) of the federal district within the two states of Maryland and Virginia. At the same time Washington selected the three commissioners Congress had required for conducting the affairs concerned with

establishing the capital and dispatched Major Andrew Ellicott to make an exact survey of the site described in the proclamation.

Consideration had also been given during the previous six months to where the capital city itself would be located within the hundred-square-mile federal district. In October 1790 the president had come to Georgetown and visited the area around the Potomac for the purpose of fixing the proper situation for what the local newspaper called the "Grand Columbian Federal City," but no final decision was made. The principal landowners in Georgetown volunteered to make over their lands on any reasonable terms if the federal city would be erected in their vicinity, but the president did not accept their offer. Instead he let it be known that he was also considering the area to the east of Georgetown known as Carrolsburgh. The president must already have had some idea during this visit of the size and scale of the city he wished to erect within the federal district, but he did not reveal the full scope of his ambitious plan until the end of March 1791. By that time the landowners of Georgetown and Carrolsburgh were vigorously vying with one another to make sure that the public buildings would be located within their part of the federal district. At the March meeting of the landowners convened by the president in Georgetown he informed them that they would serve their own and the nation's interests better if they would work together, for neither group alone controlled sufficient land to meet the needs of the new city. What was required for a capital city fit for this new nation was all the land controlled by both groups. The next day the landowners agreed to the president's demands, having seen, as Washington noted in his diary for March 30, 1791, "that whilst they were contending for the shadow they might lose the substance."

Washington's skillful negotiations with the landowners allowed a site of more than four thousand acres within the federal district (figure 5) to be used for the capital city. The federal city could now be planned on a sufficiently grand scale—about six square miles—which would allow it to be one-third larger than Boston in area and perhaps, more significantly, to be as large as Philadelphia.

Before leaving Georgetown on March 30, the president officially designated L'Enfant as the designer who would plan the city. L'Enfant had arrived in Georgetown only three weeks earlier to familiarize himself with the terrain but by March 26 he already had prepared a long preliminary description for Washington on how he thought the site could best be laid out. The events that followed L'Enfant's designation as the designer of the city took place with such rapidity, it must be assumed that even before the actual planning began the president and Major L'Enfant had agreed upon many of the major concepts of what this new city should be like. According to an account written by L'Enfant in 1800, he had proposed a plan for the nation's capital city "long before the situation of the district of Columbia was resolved." Even though earlier discussion between the two men on the appearance and nature of a new capital city would have facilitated L'Enfant's task, it nevertheless was an incredible feat on his part to complete the plan within the short span of three months.

During this brief period L'Enfant made a detailed study of the terrain, selected the vantage points for the public buildings, and developed the entire city plan in time to present it on June 22 to the president, who had been away during this period on a triumphal tour of the southern states. Washington apparently enthusiastically embraced the whole of L'Enfant's plan for the city, including its unique diagonal avenues radiating out from the Capitol and the President's House (figure 6) in a manner similar to the designer's 1788 plan for the banqueting pavilion at New York (figure 1). There could not have been any substantial reworking of the plan after L'Enfant's presentation, for a few days later, on June 30, the president presented it to the landowners as the plan by which the city would be laid out. In doing so Washington even assured them that the final plan would be

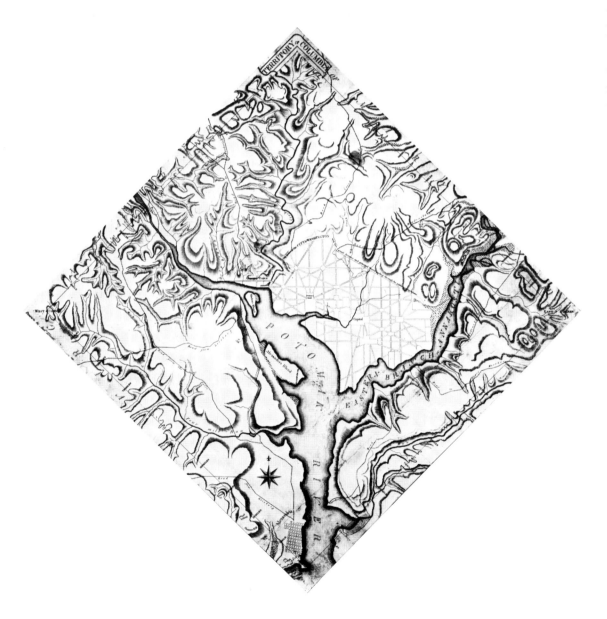

only slightly different, noting that the number of diagonal avenues would be reduced and the President's House shifted slightly to the west. Basically, then, the town plan by L'Enfant, with its amazing sweep of broad avenues, majestic town squares, and enormous public gardens, was designed only four months after L'Enfant had first been sent to lay out the federal city.

Together, Washington and L'Enfant had succeeded in creating an architectural symbol of the new country that would catch the imagination and admiration of the world. News of the great plan for a federal city quickly spread through the world, and early descriptions were lavish in their praise. The *Maryland Journal* of September 30, 1791, describes it as an "inconceivable improvement upon all other cities in the world" and remarks that the great diagonal streets not only produce a variety of charming prospects but also "remove that insipid sameness that renders Philadelphia and Charleston unpleasing." The founding of this new city on such a "liberal and elegant plan" will, the writer believes, be seen by future generations as one of the most important acts taken by President Washington. L'Enfant is given full due, the writer commenting that his presence in the United States at this time is one of the country's most fortunate circumstances. He describes L'Enfant's plan as exhibiting "such striking proof of an exalted genius, elegance of taste, extensive imagination and comprehension, as will not only produce amazement in Europe but meet the admiration of all future ages."

An anonymous account of the city written in French and published in America in 1795 stressed the symbolic importance of the founding of this new city. The author characterizes the idea of a federal city as a vast and grand concept, as a natural way of forever reinforcing the fact that it was through the union of the separate states that the war against Britain was won, and that only by the continued union of the states would the rights of the individual be secure. The author acclaims the federal city as "a temple erected to liberty" that will always attract the "vows and sympathies of all true friends of the Nation." He goes on to say that because of the grand ideals responsible for the founding of this nation, the federal city could not have been designed on a small scale; its streets and public places all had to correspond to the immensity of its destiny, a recognition that was due to the great genius of the president.

The writer is particularly impressed by the symbolic location of the Capitol and the President's House. L'Enfant is credited with making the Capitol the center of the city, just as the city is the center of the nation. Notice is taken of the fact that the site for the Capitol was determined by celestial observations, thereby locating the center of the building on a due north-south axis. This was indicated on the plan (figure 6) by designating the longitude of the Capitol as zero degrees. The writer points out that these sitings also were responsible for the orientation of the entire city. He is also impressed by the number of streets L'Enfant has directed toward the Capitol. The author sees these streets as luminous rays going out from the Capitol to all parts of America, signaling that Congress will always be informed about the true interests of the nation. At the same time, each street is also a symbol of the easy accessibility of the Capitol to each citizen. And, the writer continues, these ingenious allusions are happily enforced by the fact that the Capitol is placed on a hill that dominates the entire city. Such a situation will raise the spirits of the legislator, at the same time reminding him that although it is from here that all the laws go out to the country, this same site will also attract the active inspection of a nation of free men.

The author's interpretation of the placement of the President's House continues in a similar vein. The many streets directed to and from the residence will, on the one hand, keep the president ever aware that he must attend to the interests of all parts of the nation and, on the other, remind him that his actions are clearly and continuously visible. The writer also sees the grand avenue linking these two branches of the government as having been arranged so the president will always have before his eyes the temple in which the laws are made which he must execute.

Whether or not Washington or L'Enfant intended the city plan to convey all the allusions perceived by this writer, it is nevertheless undeniable that a key element of the federal-city plan was the clear reflection of the division of governmental power into three separate branches—the legislative, the executive, and the judiciary—in L'Enfant's location of its principal public buildings. What these buildings should look like was apparently also part of L'Enfant's commission, for the *Maryland Journal* description also reports that the public buildings being planned by this architect and carried out under his direction will be "superb and elegant" and will do honor to the capital of a great and prosperous nation.

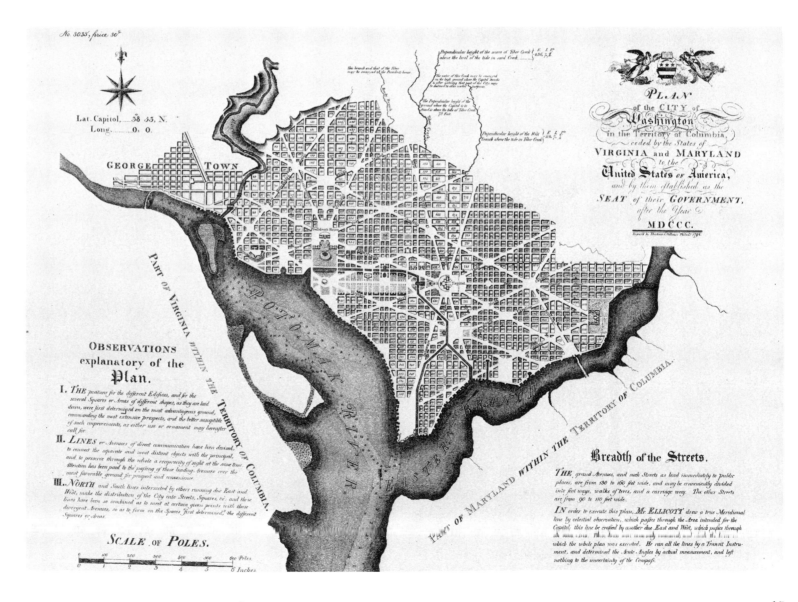

Figure 5
*Topographical map by Andrew Ellicott of the District of Columbia.*
Engraving, published 1793.

Figure 6
*Official plan of the city of Washington.*
Engraving by Thackara & Vallance, published October 1792.

## 2: Washington's Vision for the Capitol

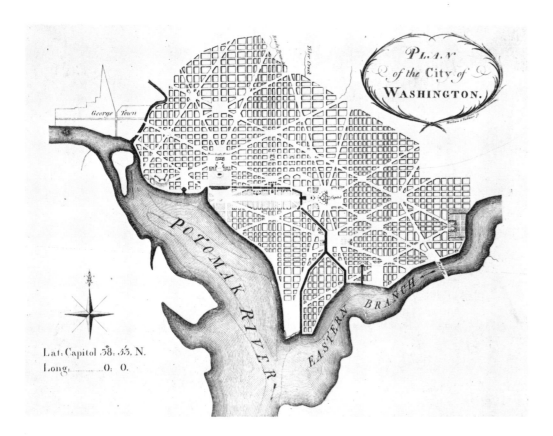

*Figure 7*
*Earliest printed version of L'Enfant's plan for the city of Washington.*
Published in *Universal Asylum and Columbian Magazine* (Philadelphia),
March 1792.

The brilliant performance of Major Pierre L'Enfant during the summer of 1791 as a city planner must have led George Washington to regard him as indispensable for turning his dream of a capital city for the new nation into a reality. According to an account written by L'Enfant in 1800, Washington had been so impressed by L'Enfant's transformation of the New York City Hall in 1789 that he asked him to begin thinking about the appropriate architectural appearance of the "capitol, judiciary and executive buildings." Ever since that request, L'Enfant adds, he had been drawing up plans for these buildings. Indeed, L'Enfant even makes the amazing claim that he only accepted the commission to plan the city because he wanted the chance to design its public buildings.

As late as September 9, 1791, however, Washington, Thomas Jefferson, James Madison, and the three commissioners in charge of establishing the federal city were preparing to solicit such designs through an open competition and had already drawn up the draft of a newspaper advertisement to announce it. Before the notice was placed, however, the president, apparently totally convinced by the genius of L'Enfant, offered to him alone the opportunity of designing the public buildings. Five months later, in a letter to L'Enfant of February 28, 1792, Washington described the decision as having been intended as a "compliment" to him. Such high regard for his services gave L'Enfant the opportunity he had so longed for: the chance to design the first two buildings—the Capitol and the President's House—that would represent the new nation to the world.

Except for the preference President Washington expressed in a letter of July 23, 1792, for domed and colonnaded buildings, and from the design he would later favor, we do not know his ideas for these buildings. He was convinced from the start, however, that the scale of the buildings should be consonant with the grand scale of the city itself. He never waivered in his belief, as he wrote in a letter of March 8, 1792, "that the public buildings in size, form and elegance, should look beyond the present day." Jefferson had already indicated his own preference to L'Enfant in a letter of April 10, 1791, in which he stated unequivocally that when the new legislative hall of the United States was designed he wanted to see it modeled after some classical building that had received the "approbation of thousands of years." Jefferson had already demonstrated this belief by his own design for the temple-like statehouse at Richmond (figure 2). Apparently, some pressure was put on L'Enfant to look to Jefferson's building as a model for the Capitol, for in July 1791, at the instigation of one of the commissioners, the governor of Virginia forwarded Jefferson's original drawings to L'Enfant as a possible source of inspiration. What we know from later events makes it unlikely that L'Enfant was actually seeking such help, but it is difficult to determine exactly what he had in mind for the buildings due to the swift chain of events that ensued from about the time he was entrusted with their design in the fall of 1791 to February 1792 when he was abruptly dismissed.

Today no designs bearing L'Enfant's name exist for either the Capitol or the President's House. That he prepared designs for both these buildings during this period is, however, without question. For by the time he left for Philadelphia in December 1791 he had already determined enough about the nature of the buildings to order work begun at both sites. Surveyor's lines had been staked out at the President's House to guide the excavations for the foundations, and the hill where the Capitol would be built was being leveled so that the building could be laid out. L'Enfant anticipated work to proceed on the foundations of both buildings during the winter of 1791/92 and in a letter of December 16, he gave full instructions to his assistant, Isaac Roberdeau, regarding the number of laborers to be hired and what was to be done.

For their part, the commissioners had been active since late September in trying to hire enough workers to carry out L'Enfant's plans, in building barracks to house them, in purchasing quarries selected by L'Enfant, and in obtaining such materials required for the execution of the design as lime, bricks, and foundation stones. All these activities convey the atmosphere of a bustling, rapidly moving operation which—had it not been for the clash of personalities that erupted during these months—would have provided the tangible evidence so desired by the president that the federal city, now officially called Washington in the territory of Columbia, was coming into existence. Instead, the inability of the commissioners and L'Enfant to work together so impeded progress, that almost two years would pass before the president could lay the cornerstone of the Capitol.

The genesis of the problem lay in the fact that the president and the French officer had already worked on several projects together and developed a mutual admiration for one another. During the spring and summer of 1791 L'Enfant not only earned the growing admiration of the president for his capabilities as a city planner, but he also enjoyed an increasingly close personal working relationship with him. He visited Mount Vernon on numerous occasions to confer with the president on details of the city plan and was free to address his letters directly to Washington. Not unreasonably, therefore, L'Enfant considered himself to be responsible solely to the president and not to the commissioners, particularly after Washington himself had entrusted him with the task of designing the two public buildings. On their part, in their correspondence with L'Enfant and the president during the fall of 1791, the commissioners never failed to acknowledge their awareness of L'Enfant's special status with the president and of his endorsement of the major's abilities.

Two seemingly outrageous acts turned this situation around and led to L'Enfant's being put under the commissioners' jurisdiction. The first event occurred in October 1791, at the time of the initial public sale of building lots in the capital city. For reasons L'Enfant believed to be the better part of astute salesmanship he refused to have the city plan shown to potential buyers. All others involved in the matter considered his behavior exceptionally erratic and a hindrance to the success of the sale. As the president noted on November 20 in a letter to one of the commissioners, it made the sale the equivalent of buying "a pig in a poke."

The second incident occurred on November 20 when, without consulting the commissioners, L'Enfant tore down a house that Daniel Carroll, one of the original landholders, was constructing, because it stood in the way of a new street being laid out in accordance with the city plan. This precipitate action both infuriated and bewildered the commissioners, who saw it as a clear sign of increasingly arrogant behavior by L'Enfant.

During these two heated incidents Washington tried to keep all parties working together harmoniously. Although he recognized that the lines of authority had to be clarified, he was initially reluctant to force L'Enfant to take orders solely from the commissioners. In his letter of November 20 the president had outlined his dealings with L'Enfant on this subject: as early as the beginning of October, during an informal meeting at Mount Vernon, he had "casually" discussed the problem with L'Enfant; subsequently, he adds, he had informed L'Enfant "through a direct channel though not an official one as yet" that he must accept his orders from the commissioners. However, on November 30, after hearing about the destruction of Carroll's house, the president wrote to Jefferson asking him to review the correspondence that had passed among L'Enfant, the commissioners, and himself to judge how far L'Enfant "may be spoken to in decisive terms without losing his services," which, in the president's opinion, "would be a serious misfortune." But, he goes on to say, L'Enfant must be made to realize that "there is a line beyond which he will not be suffered to go" and adds that whatever causes L'Enfant to act this way, "it must be checked; or we shall have no Commissioners."

The next day, after consulting with Madison, Jefferson prepared a draft letter for the president to send to L'Enfant which, he suggests, "may be too severe" but recommends this course of action because L'Enfant's past behavior has shown that he "will not regard correction, unless it be pointed." Washington followed Jefferson's advice immediately, for his own letter to L'Enfant of December 2, made it absolutely clear that although he personally wished him to continue working at the federal city, he could do so only if he accepted the authority of the commissioners "to whom by law the business is entrusted, and who stand between you and the President of the United States." Unfortunately, even after such a stern warning L'Enfant did not recognize when he left for Philadelphia in early January 1792 how seriously his relationship with Washington was deteriorating. He went to Philadelphia prepared to discuss with the president a lengthy and detailed report he had prepared on how the work at the federal city should proceed and to show him for the first time his designs for the public buildings.

With characteristic optimism, as well as some obstinacy, L'Enfant continued to believe himself firmly in control of the work at the federal city. Instead, during the months of January and February a fierce struggle broke out between the commissioners and those L'Enfant had left behind to carry out his orders, and L'Enfant was put in an even worse light than before. Workers were dismissed by the commissioners and L'Enfant's assistant arrested when he continued to put into effect the orders L'Enfant had given him. Although Washington still tried to avoid the ultimate confrontation that would lead to L'Enfant's departure—"I know not where another is to be found who could supply his place," Washington had written on December 18, 1791—his attempts met with no success. Neither the cool, detached approach of Jefferson, nor the more friendly entreaties of Tobias Lear, the president's personal secretary, proved any more effective. L'Enfant steadfastly refused to submit to the control of the commissioners. By the end of February, Washington reluctantly realized that he had to surrender L'Enfant. On February 27, 1792, at the president's bidding, Jefferson wrote to L'Enfant telling him "your services must be at an end." On March 6, Jefferson formally announced to the commissioners that L'Enfant had been dismissed due to insubordination.

In this same letter Jefferson encouraged the commissioners to return to the idea of holding a public competition for the design of the Capitol and the President's House. In a private letter to one of the commissioners written two days later Jefferson claimed that L'Enfant had made no designs for either building, except for those he had "in his head." This declaration is countered by evidence that the president himself had become aware that L'Enfant was displaying his plans for the Capitol and the President's House to colleagues and friends in Philadelphia. In a letter of February 22 the president had told Jefferson, "The plans of the buildings ought to come forward immediately for consideration. I think Mr. Walker said yesterday he (L'Enfant) had been showing the different views of them to Mr. Trumbull." A respected artist and friend of the president, Trumbull may well have

been shown L'Enfant's designs for the public buildings, as he had already gone over the city plan with L'Enfant when seeing him in Georgetown in the spring of 1791 (*Autobiography*, pp. 168–69).

Trumbull, who also worked as an architect, pointed out years later (*Autobiography*, p. 266) that the design of the Capitol adopted by Washington was the same as that "marked on the plan of the city engraved by Thackera & Vallence, in Philadelphia, in 1792," a piece of contemporary, but frequently ignored, evidence. In fact, designs for the public buildings were depicted on the very first publication of L'Enfant's plan for the federal city, which appeared in a Philadelphia journal at the very moment Jefferson was informing the commissioners, and perhaps also the president, that no designs by L'Enfant existed. The engraved plan in the March 1792 issue of the *Universal Asylum and Columbian Magazine* (figure 7) gave the public its first opportunity of seeing what L'Enfant and the president envisaged for the federal city and of gaining some idea about its public buildings. Although the indications for the public buildings on this and subsequent publications of the plan are more symbolic than descriptive, they do allow us to deduce at least the basic character of the buildings planned by L'Enfant.

In the case of the Capitol, the plan shows a circular structure placed on the western brow of the hill selected by L'Enfant as the site for this key building. This architectural form, no doubt intended to support a dome, is flanked on both sides by recessed side wings that expand into a broader front on the east. The President's

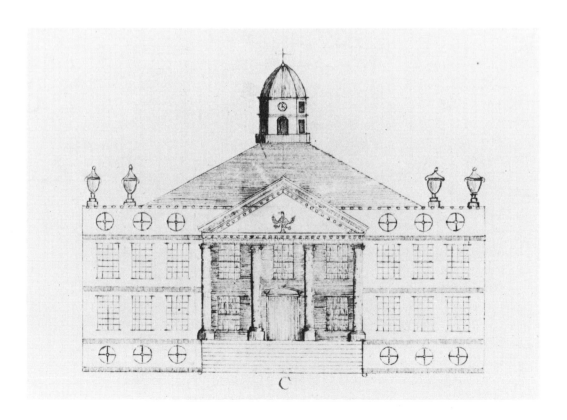

House depicted on the city plan is a palatial complex consisting of a central block and two flanking but separate structures placed farther to the south. Although the information gained from the city plan about these buildings is incomplete and sketchy, it nevertheless supports what other documents suggest, namely, that by the early months of 1792 L'Enfant had in fact prepared designs for the public buildings in fulfillment of his commission from the president. Although it is unlikely that he ever had the chance personally to present these plans to the president—and, in fact, it is doubtful that L'Enfant and Washington ever saw one another again—it cannot be denied that the spirit of Pierre L'Enfant's vision lived on in the dream of George Washington and continued to affect the future architectural image of the capital city.

The commissioners, now freed from the independent presence of L'Enfant, proceeded to announce the competition for the Capitol and the President's House. The submissions were due on July 15, 1792, but responses were few and disappointing. On July 9 Washington himself pointed out in a letter to one of the commissioners that "if none more elegant than these should appear . . . the exhibition of architecture will be a very dull one indeed." In fulfillment of the president's gloomy estimate, no design for the Capitol submitted by the deadline was found satisfactory (figures 8–10), but a design by James Hoban for the President's House was deemed acceptable (see note to plate 10). This decision, however, would soon make Washington aware of how greatly the cause of the federal city had suffered by the loss of L'Enfant.

The president first encountered the problems produced by Hoban's design when he came to the federal city in August 1792 to determine where Hoban's smaller building should be located within the foundation trenches that had been dug according to L'Enfant's directions the previous winter. Two of the commissioners present on that summer day reported in a letter of August 3 to their absent colleague that Washington had had "considerable trouble and difficulty to fix his mind" about where to locate the smaller building but that he had finally decided to place it on the northern limit of L'Enfant's foundation. He did so, the commissioners added, so it would be clearly visible from the diagonal avenues as well as the streets on the east and west, even though this meant it would not be seen "so much so from the Capitol as might be wished." Their observation was echoed some months later by L'Enfant's former assistant, Isaac Roberdeau, who reported to him in June 1793 that work was under way on the President's House, but "the plan not being so deep as yours . . . you cannot see but a corner of it from the Congress House." Obviously, Washington's struggle to fix Hoban's design within the larger building projected by L'Enfant made him acutely aware that its smaller size would result in the loss of one of the key elements of the city plan—the visual, and symbolic, link between the President's House and the Capitol.

As disappointing to Washington as the disruption of one of the principal focal

*Figure 8*  James Diamond.
*Entry in the 1792 competition for the U. S. Capitol.*
Ink drawing. Maryland Historical Society, Baltimore.

*Figure 9*
*Anonymous entry in the 1792 competition for the U. S. Capitol.*
Ink drawing. Maryland Historical Society, Baltimore.

SLIDE

*Figure 10*  Philip Hart.
*Entry in the 1792 competition for the U. S. Capitol.*
Ink and pencil drawing. Maryland Historical Society, Baltimore.

*Figure 11*  Pierre L'Enfant.
*Schematic plan of the U.S. Capitol (detail of fig. 7).*

*Figure 12*  Stephen Hallet.
*Plan of the principal story for the U.S. Capitol.*
Pen and ink with wash and pencil, 1793.
Library of Congress.

*Figure 13*  William Thornton.
*Plan of the ground floor of the U.S. Capitol, based on his successful competition design of 1793.* Pen and ink with wash and pencil.
Library of Congress.

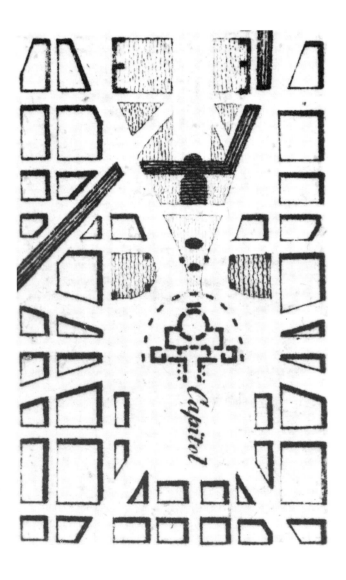

points in L'Enfant's city plan must have been, his concern for the design of the Capitol was even greater, as he always considered it to be the principal public building of the new nation. No design submitted in the 1792 competition having been found satisfactory, the commissioners encouraged two of the contestants—Judge George Turner of Philadelphia and Stephen Hallet, a French architect brought to their attention by Jefferson—to develop their ideas further in order to approach in some degree what the president envisaged. Washington himself met with the two finalists in a special meeting held at the federal city in late August 1792, where, presumably, he specified that the plan for the Capitol must include an apartment for the president and also indicated his partiality for a domed and colonnaded building, both being conditions he had already communicated to the commissioners in a letter of July 23. Judge Turner apparently never submitted another drawing, but in October 1792 Hallet presented a plan radically different from his original entry, which had been inspired by Jefferson's design for the Virginia statehouse. This new design by Hallet did not meet with favor either, but the commissioners continued to encourage him to work on the design and suggested that he discuss it directly with Jefferson and the president.

At about this time another potential contestant appeared on the scene in the person of Dr. William Thornton. A few months earlier Thornton had written the commissioners from his plantation home on the West Indies island of Tortola inquiring whether they would still consider his designs even though he could not meet the July 15 deadline. Whether or not Dr. Thornton was known to the commissioners as the winner of the 1789 architectural competition for the Library Company of Philadelphia, their situation by late July 1792 was such that they encouraged him to send his plans. Instead, Thornton waited until November 9, after he arrived in Philadelphia, to ask again if the commissioners would still receive his design. They encouraged him to send in his plans for their next meeting on December 1, but Thornton still did not act. On December 4 the commissioners expedited the matter by suggesting that, since Thornton was in Philadelphia, he present his plans directly to Mr. Jefferson, who would show them to the president.

Thus, in the winter of 1792/93, the scene of decision-making was transferred to Philadelphia, with only the president and Jefferson involved in the approval process, and only two contestants—Stephen Hallet, whose continued participation had been encouraged and supported by the commissioners, and Dr. William Thornton, a totally new factor. During the months of December 1792 and January 1793 both contestants met with the president, and no doubt also with his advisors and friends. In this arena, Dr. Thornton, a Quaker gentleman of means, education, and social connections, had an edge over the émigré Hallet. Thornton rapidly became an intimate member of the president's circle and was recognized by Jefferson as a gentleman of communal intellectual interests.

By the end of January 1793 Washington had seen new plans by both Thornton and Hallet. Although Thornton's were not yet complete, on February 1, Jefferson wrote one of the commissioners that Thornton's design "so captivated the eyes and judgment of all as to leave no doubt" it was superior, and "among its admirers no one is more decided than him whose decision is most important. It is simple, noble, beautiful. . . ." Jefferson adds, however, that the president's respect for the commissioners' approval prevented him from making a final decision until Thornton showed it to them at their March meeting. On seeing the design, the commissioners dutifully approved the president's choice, and even though Hallet would offer yet another design, the long-sought after form for the nation's Capitol had been found.

What is remarkable about the final designs produced by both Hallet and Thornton under the guidance of Washington is how different they are from the earlier efforts of each architect and how similar they are to one another (figures 12 and 13). Whatever it was that the president offered them as illustration of his own ideas of what the Capitol should look like, it apparently led both architects to design comparable buildings. Even more remarkable, however, is the inclusion in both plans of the form L'Enfant had already indicated on his city plan as the principal feature of the Capitol—a massive, circular room crowned by a dome (figure 11). Both the winning design by Thornton (figure 13) and the final one by Hallet (figure 12) present a ground plan startlingly close to L'Enfant's concept; indeed, the projection on the west front in Thornton's plan is identical to the L'Enfant plan. The conclusion is inescapable that somehow the designs of these two architects, submitted nearly a year later, depend for their basic configuration on a design invented by L'Enfant. Such a derivation for the Capitol design chosen by Washington is exactly what Trumbull claims in his letter to Charles Bulfinch, of January 28, 1818, in which he states specifically that it was L'Enfant who first conceived the idea of a circular room crowned by a monumental dome as the principal feature of the Capitol (*Autobiography*, p.266).

If L'Enfant's ground plan was so influential in the formation of the layout of Thornton's and Hallet's designs, one must also raise the question as to whether their elevation drawings do not also reflect the influence of a design held out to them as a model, particularly in view of the fact that the proposed designs by both architects contain elements inconsistent with their previous work (figures 14 and 15). The principal shift between both Hallet's and Thornton's earlier concepts and what is evident in their final designs is the new emphasis on the building as a solid, uniform block. Whereas both men had accentuated multiple roof shapes in their earlier proposals, in their last designs both emphasize the image of a single unit by providing a balustraded roofline that carefully conceals any such in-dividualized treatment. Aside from this emphasis on a uniform building mass and the similarity of their arrangement of the rooms intended to serve the legislative body, the two designs exhibit very distinct responses to whatever was serving as their source of inspiration.

Remaining documents limit our comparison of each man's approach solely to the design of the west front. Hallet's treatment of this front (figure 17 and plate 2) maintains an almost equal emphasis of all three divisions, the central core of the

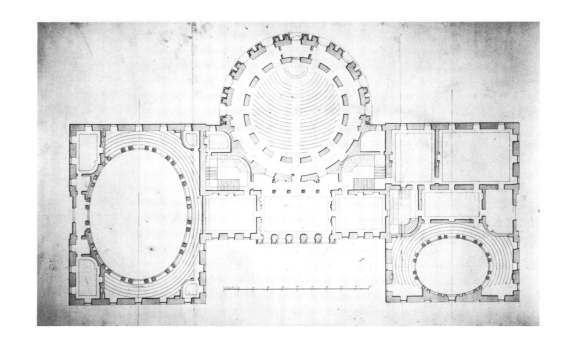

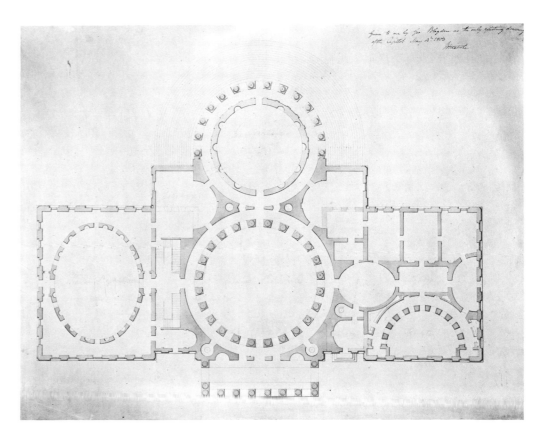

*Figure 14* Stephen Hallet.
*Designs for the front of the U. S. Capitol.*
Ink with wash, 1791 (top), October 1792 (center), January 1793 (bottom).
Library of Congress.

*Figure 15* William Thornton.
*Designs for the front* (above) *and rear* (below) *of the U. S. Capitol.*
Ink and watercolor, ca. July 1792.
American Institute of Architects Foundation.

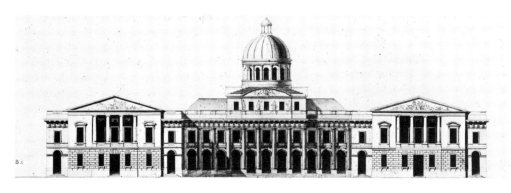

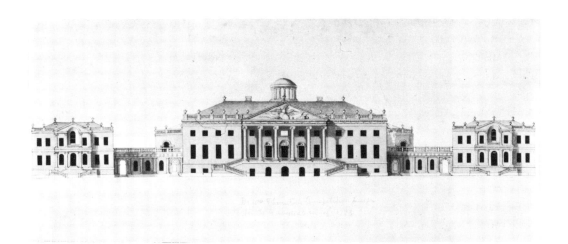

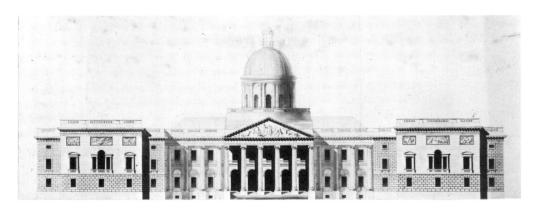

design being only slightly wider than the side wings and projecting from the face of the building a distance equal only to about half the depth of the side wings (figure 12). In addition, the saucer dome Hallet designed for this central unit is too low to provide a commanding central accent to the building. Hallet's treatment of this major area comes across as hesitant and weak, relying on surface decoration for articulating its composition, much in the manner of his earlier designs. As a result, the central section is so layered into horizontal divisions—all equal in height—that the parade of twin engaged columns around the semicircular projection of this front fails to achieve the powerful effect it seeks. Instead it appears crushed between the dome and the highly ornamented lower story, which easily dominates this central section because of the strong light-and-dark contrasts provided by its open archways. At the same time Hallet minimizes the potential impact of this central arcade, which is larger in scale than the side wings, by carrying the same masonry pattern across the base of the entire western front. In essence, the detailing of the central section of Hallet's design is so excessive—the pronounced masonry patterning of the ground floor, the ornamental relief panels, the strongly articulated cornices, as well as the ornamental balustrades—that it becomes less impressive in the overall design than the elevations of the two side wings, whose simple composition provides a majestic counterpart.

Nothing in Hallet's previous work compares with the design of these two side wings whose unadorned surfaces are punctuated only by four horizontal rows of five window and door openings. In his previous designs such a broad expanse of wall was always broken up into a center bay of three openings flanked by recessed walls containing one opening on either side. In his final design the monumentality of the side wings which comes from their simplicity and proportioning is to some degree lessened by Hallet's use of two different kinds of stonework on the lower levels; however, he is in a sense trapped into making such distinctions here in order to carry throughout the whole front the horizontal divisions that he has assigned to the central element. This proposal by Hallet suggests that it is the product of a designer not yet able to digest a new, and unfamiliar, style. The simple mass of the building, evident despite the excessive division of its parts into horizontal layers, and the unbroken wall surfaces of the side wings are distinctly new; the detailing of the semicircular projection, the least successful feature, is closest in spirit to Hallet's prior work.

Thornton's approach to the west front took a very different course in his use of similar component parts (figure 16 and plate 1). First, the central portion in Thornton's design (figure 13) is almost twice the width of each side wing and projects beyond these wings to a distance equal to their entire depth, almost twice the distance of the projecting semicircular unit of Hallet's design. As a consequence, the size of Thornton's central unit alone endows it with an imposing, dominating presence in his composition of the west front, a role more than warranted by the striking architectural features Thornton introduces into this section. The two-tiered, domed classical temple he places here is an impressive

*Figure 16* William Thornton.
*Design for the west front of the U. S. Capitol.*
Ink, watercolor, and pencil, ca. 1793–95. Library of Congress.

*Figure 17* Stephen Hallet.
*Design for the west front of the U. S. Capitol.*
Ink with wash, 1793. Library of Congress.

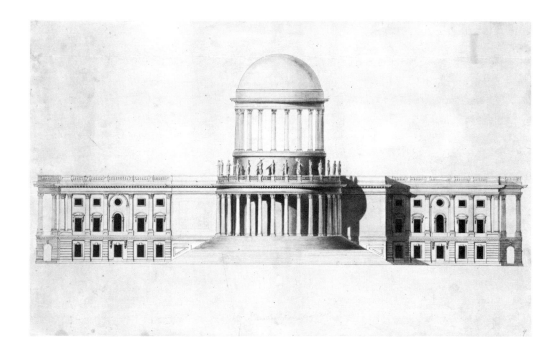

structure enhanced by the vast, circular flight of steps leading up to it, the ring of allegorical statues that enliven its skyline, and the flanking two-story-high walls each of whose flat, unbroken surfaces was to be covered by a single, giant relief sculpture. The design for this domed, circular temple is without precedent in Thornton's work and would seem to be an element picked up from whatever model inspired both contestants. Whereas Hallet has trouble designing the center section, Thornton has difficulty with the side wings. Here his design disintegrates into fussy ornamentation, the surfaces of the wings being divided into many small parts that depend for their unity on a rhythmical grouping of bays defined by pilasters, a type of design fashionable in the earlier part of the century. The scale of the side wings is totally alien to the central part of the composition.

Thus, both Hallet and Thornton alike are incapable of working out a design consistent with what must have been the language of their model—one that contained all the new elements in a unified composition that only partially emerged in each of their conceptions. A harmonious design could only be achieved by joining Hallet's treatment of the side wings with Thornton's delineation of the central part. Just such a design does exist (figure 18) in the form of a small, quickly dashed-off sketch bearing the intriguing inscription "First design of the Capitol," which shows these two features united in a single concept. Although both its technique and the paper appear to date from the end of the eighteenth century, the sketch remained unknown until it was given to the White House Collection in 1971. Both this drawing and another version that exists among Thornton's papers (figure 19) point clearly to the model Hallet and Thornton were following in their attempt to devise a Capitol that would please the president.

These two sketches testify to the existence in Philadelphia in 1792/93 of a daring and bold design for the Capitol that could only have been by L'Enfant. This design had no precedent in any specific antique prototype. Instead, its roots can only be found in the works and drawings of late-eighteenth-century French architects with which L'Enfant would more likely have been familiar than Thornton or even Hallet. Although Hallet had been trained in Paris, his series of designs for the Capitol contain such widely varying stylistic elements, he seems to have been incapable of absorbing the ideals then being set for French architecture. Unlike his work, the type of building depicted in these two sketches would not have seemed out of place had it been proposed as the home of the new National Assembly in France.

Indeed, had the public monuments of both the American and the French republics resembled one another at this moment—before the onset of the reign of terror during the summer of 1793—it would have been deemed the natural consequence of sentiments shared by both countries. Writing on January 4, 1793, to the commissioners of the municipality of Bordeaux in an attempt to encourage workmen to emigrate to America, the city commissioners of Washington describe their role in raising the public buildings as "an honor that swells our ambition, to express in some Degree in the Stile of our Architecture, the sublime sentiments of

*Figure 18    Anonymous design for the west front of the U.S. Capitol.* Pencil and ink sketch, ca. 1793. The White House Collection.

Liberty which are common to Frenchmen and Americans. We wish to exhibit a grandeur of conception, a Republican simplicity, and that true Elegance of proportion which corresponds to, a tempered freedom excluding Frivolity, the food of little minds" (*Documentary History*, p. 21). Although at the time of this letter, President Washington was still searching for a design for the Capitol, only weeks later, he would choose one whose spirit was close to what a work by L'Enfant might have expressed and which matched in good part the description of what the commissioners had described as their own goal.

How detailed knowledge of L'Enfant's designs for the public buildings could have been obtained by either the president or Hallet or Thornton is not clear. There are a number of possibilities, some more innocent than others. Trumbull who seems to have enjoyed friendly relations with all the parties in this affair, may have been an inadvertent agent of transmission. According to Washington's letter to Jefferson, L'Enfant had shown his plans to Trumbull; and according to Trumbull, Thornton had asked him to show his drawings to the president and recommend them, "which," Trumbull reports, "I did" (*Autobiography*, pp. 172–73). L'Enfant himself would complain over and over again, in the numerous petitions he addressed to the Congress seeking to be paid for his services, that while he was away in Philadelphia that winter, his lodgings and his office in Washington were ransacked and all his "papers, drawings and manuscripts" were stolen, as well as "books, a collection of very costly engravings, models of architecture," and plans of his own, most particularly "drawings for the Capitol and the President's House." He also lists preparatory designs for the city canal, bridges, market houses, the great walk and garden (the Mall), and sketches of projects for both public and private buildings. The trunks and boxes containing these papers were never recovered, and as L'Enfant believed the commissioners to be responsible for this theft, he sought compensation for his loss. In other depositions and petitions L'Enfant specifically claims his designs to have been the basis for the work at the Capitol and acidly points out that such work is "not better for departing from the model."

L'Enfant severely criticized the work at the Capitol for being incorrectly related to its site and pointed out that this fundamental error was necessarily compounded in the elevation of the building. Here he is apparently referring to the location of the Capitol, which he had intended to place on the very edge of the western brow of the hill. L'Enfant suggests that in order for the Capitol to be an imposing monument, its size must be increased (only the north wing was visible at the time he made these remarks) by adding to the west front a projecting platform on which lofty double columns should be massed. Above this section he calls for a dome, which must be placed on a plain drum if the building is not to look like a church. Although not all the changes L'Enfant prescribes are easily grasped, the general direction of his remarks makes clear that what he suggests is in accord with the characteristics exhibited in the design proposed by Thornton for the west front (figure 16). L'Enfant is firm in his belief that his designs for the public buildings

*Figure 19* William Thornton.
*Design for the west front of the U. S. Capitol.*
Ink sketch, ca. 1793. Library of Congress.

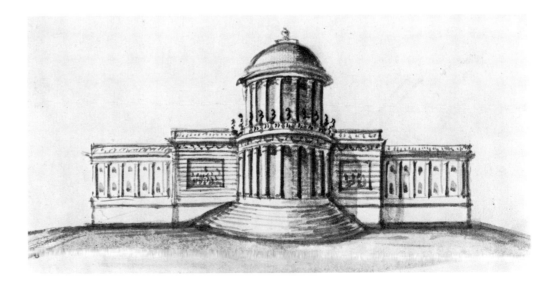

were stolen from him and claimed by others as their own work. He speaks of the work at both the Capitol and the President's House as poor counterfeits of his own designs. The culprit in L'Enfant's mind was clearly Thornton, whom he labels the "so-called" architect.

The design proposed by Thornton for the west front of the Capitol is in a style particularly characteristic of late-eighteenth-century French architecture, as is the plan of the central section (figure 13). The combination of two circular spaces with one projecting beyond the body of the building was a formula not frequently found outside France. The circular projections of the west front were referred to by Thornton as a Temple of Fame placed above a Temple of Virtue, the latter actually being the Conference Room where, on special occasions, both the Senate and House—the makers of the country's laws—would meet with the president—the executor of those laws—in public assembly.

Like other aspects of the design, this arrangement, too, was closely related to the type of legislative building proposed in France during the period immediately after 1789. The French architects—just as L'Enfant at the same time in America—sought a new architectural form to symbolize their new political state. Of the many plans submitted to the National Assembly by a variety of architects, all included as the principal feature a great conference hall where the elected officials and representatives, and the general public, would gather in the presence of the king. Indeed, most of the plans included a special apartment set aside for the use of the king, much like the Executive Apartment that Washington had specifically requested be included in the Capitol. In a description of this feature (which is not visible on any of the plans that remain) Thornton says it was to be placed two steps above the general level of the floor, located immediately adjacent to the Conference Room, and so arranged that the president could enter directly onto the dais without passing through any public corridors.

For a brief period at the close of the eighteenth century the young nation of the United States and the reformed nation of France shared similar concepts of liberty and the sovereignty of the people, and it is fitting that the architectural symbols of these ideas should also have been similar. In both countries, however, the development of the political state moved away from this concept of the relationship between the executive and legislative branches of government, and these shifts also affected the ultimate design of the buildings that came to symbolize each nation.

A Conference Room had been a key requirement of the 1792 competition, and clearly this aspect of the design of the Capitol was determined by ideas prevalent at the time among the president and his advisors with regard to the relationship between the legislative and executive branches. In Hallet's last design of 1793 the great domed meeting hall on the west was destined for this purpose. And it is not unlikely that the circular space indicated in L'Enfant's design was also intended for this role. Regardless of later changes in expression given to such spaces, in the design for the Capitol chosen by President Washington the Conference Room and the Executive Apartment were fundamental features.

The other prominent element of Thornton's design for the central section of the Capitol was the great rotunda on the east, which served as an anteroom or forecourt to the Conference Room. Thornton describes it as being ringed with Corinthian columns thirty-four feet high and covered by a dome. It was to contain in its center an equestrian statue of Washington. The conjunction of these two circular spaces—the high, lofty Temple of Fame and the lower anteroom, each with its individual dome—presented problems in the design of the building that make Thornton's introduction of them patently amateurish. Indeed, future uncertainty about how to deal with these two elements make it clearer than ever that Thornton was not actually cognizant of the ramifications caused by the design he had presented. In 1795 questions were raised as to whether the vestibule was to be covered by a dome or left open; ultimately it was decided that it should, as originally described by Thornton, be covered by a dome.

Although the linking of two circular spaces in a ground plan was an element of French architectural style at the time, architects who used such combinations did not call for each area to be crowned by a different kind of dome. Although not immediately apparent from the strictly frontal, separate elevations of the west and east fronts prepared by Thornton, the conjunction of the low flat dome on the east with the higher temple form on the west would have presented the viewer with an awkward building. Whether Thornton was aware of this we do not know, but the clumsiness of such an approach again suggests that he was working from a model, or designs, he did not thoroughly comprehend. One viewer of Thornton's plans who apparently perceived this fault was the architect Benjamin Latrobe. On Latrobe's first visit to the federal city in December 1798, Thornton proudly showed him the drawings for the Capitol. Latrobe offered to make a perspective drawing presumably to indicate how the two domes would conflict with one another, but Thornton never responded (Latrobe, pp. 114–15).

Latrobe confided to his journal (p. 92) that despite its defect, he must nevertheless record his admiration for "one of the first designs of modern times." In years to come, Latrobe would think less of the design, and he would introduce changes in its plan that both corrected the problem and also reflected a different concept of the relationship between the legislative and executive branches of the government. For now, however, the design of the Capitol chosen by the First Father of the Country was the one prepared by Thornton and the world awaited its construction.

The transformation of Thornton's design for the Capitol into an actual building caused as much trouble for President Washington as had the selection process itself. From the moment he had made his decision in favor of the Thornton design, Washington was plagued by criticisms of it, particularly with regard to its feasibility. Even the city commissioners, who followed his lead and accepted Thornton's design on March 11, 1793, with the judgment that the arrangement of the principal rooms was much to their satisfaction and that they expected its outward appearance would be "striking and pleasing," felt it necessary to point out that some of the smaller rooms might lack light. Since no estimates had been provided, they also were concerned about costs. Although they expressed their belief that the Capitol should "be on a grand Scale and that a Republic especially ought not to be sparing of expences [sic] on an Edifice for such purposes," they nevertheless admitted to some anxiety about how the world would judge them if lack of funds made it impossible to construct such a building (*Documentary History*, p. 24).

Their reservations about Thornton's design must have been even greater than they indicated to the president, for they hired Stephen Hallet, the very architect they had encouraged for the past six months, to evaluate his rival's winning design. As might be expected, Hallet found the plan to be impracticable. He pointed out so many errors so fully that Thornton, in responding to the criticism in a letter of July 16, 1793, described Hallet's comments (unfortunately now lost) as filling "five manuscript in folio volumes." Since the commissioners also consulted two others who were knowledgeable about building matters and who agreed with Hallet's evaluations, the president was so informed on June 23, 1793 (*Documentary History*, p. 26).

In order to resolve the charges brought against Thornton's design, Washington convened a special panel, headed by Jefferson, to examine the issues. From the mass of critical comments put forward, Jefferson and the panel singled out for the president's attention those they felt to be the most serious and bid Hallet to make a plan that incorporated their recommended changes. In a letter to the president of July 17, 1793, Jefferson described the results of the conference as having produced a plan that was considered as Dr. Thornton's but rendered into "practicable form." Despite this assessment the plan drawn up by Hallet after the conference was not acceptable to any of the participants in the conference. His revision eliminated the central rotunda of Thornton's plan, substituting for it the open forecourt and recessed portico he had featured in his own design. Hallet was ordered to redraw this portion of the plan. In passing on to the commissioners his own favorable view of the outcome of the conference in a letter of July 25, 1793, the president remarked that some thought the only reason Hallet had changed the center part of Thornton's plan was "to make it in one essential feature different" from the winning design. The president saw no reason, however, that work could not begin on the foundations for the rest of the building while a solution was sought for the design of this central section. Accordingly, work was begun, and on

September 18, 1793, two years after Washington had entrusted L'Enfant with the sole responsibility for the design of the building, the cornerstone of the Capitol was laid with an elaborate Masonic ceremony. The words of the Grand Master of Masons, Joseph Clark, who delivered the oration, clearly echoed the design. He hoped that the brothers would not only keep "our Hallowed Dome" in good repair, but "adorn it, with the Grand Theological Virtues, Faith, Hope and Charity: and embellish it with Wisdom, Strength and Beauty" (*Columbian Mirror*, p. 2).

During the next nine months such progress was made in laying the foundations, that by June of 1794 the plan for the entire building, from north to south wings and from the great Conference Room on the west to the eastern front, had been laid out on the hill, a job perhaps made easier by the grading begun two years earlier by L'Enfant. Unfortunately, the commissioners again turned to Hallet for help and hired him to supervise the foundation work. Without their knowing, Hallet again substituted his own design for that of Thornton who described the difference between what Hallet had done and what his design called for as having "made square what should have been rounded." This act was the last the commissioners were willing to suffer and Hallet was fired.

Shortly thereafter, on September 12, 1794, the president made Thornton one of the commissioners of the federal city. This position allowed him to oversee the execution of his design without taking on the daily supervision of the work, a role he had refused to fulfill from the beginning. He was content to be known as the inventor of the design, who remained ever vigilant, on guard against any deviation from his conception. Subsequent to Hallet, the commissioners hired George Hadfield, highly recommended by John Trumbull, to supervise the work but he, too, soon had a falling out with Dr. Thornton because he wanted to emend the plan. When the commissioners turned to the president for a resolution of the issue he informed them, on November 9, 1795, that although he had discussed the matter with other experts, he would give no final opinion. He added, however, that unless the Thornton plan was seriously defective he could not "consent to a departure from it," but if Hadfield were right, then he would have no objection "as the present plan is nobody's, but a compound of everybody's." Whatever the decision, he assured them, it would be agreeable to him, thus effectively removing himself from any future role in the decision-making process. The commissioners then rejected Hadfield's suggestions and the president's original choice was again sustained.

Washington may have been somewhat piqued by this affair, for in this same letter he mentions his surprise at learning when last visiting the city that the dome over the rotunda—which "I always expected was part of the original design"— had been eliminated and that the circular lobby was to be open. Such a change was apparently entertained at this period, for in a report to Congress in January 1796 the grand vestibule is described as a feature which "may or may not be covered with a dome." If not covered, it was to be surrounded by an arcade twenty feet high supporting a sixteen-foot-high colonnade. Two years later, however, during the

*Figure 20*   William Russell Birch.
*North wing of the Capitol as completed by 1800*.
Ink and watercolor. Library of Congress.

Adams administration, the main body of the building was described in a House report of March 8, 1798, as being composed of two parts, "a grand circular vestibule to the east . . . and a conference room to the west . . . the first covered with a dome . . . the second with a temple" (*Documentary History*, p. 80).

Such changes in the plan could be considered during these years because actual construction on the Capitol was confined to finishing the north wing in time to receive the Congress slated to convene in the federal city in 1800. Of the vast Capitol on the hill envisaged by Washington, only this one wing would be finished (figure 20), and it would have to serve both bodies of Congress for another eight years before the House of Representatives would receive its own legislative hall. The principal features of the Capitol design chosen by Washington—the central rotunda and the great Conference Room on the west—were not yet constructed, but the commitment to build the Capitol as the president had envisaged it was made even deeper by the death of the Father of the Country in 1799.

Thus, the year 1801—when Thomas Jefferson was elected president—saw a renewal of Washington's belief that the construction of a federal city, and the Capitol, were critical for the world's perception of the state of affairs in the new nation. Not until 1803, however, was Jefferson able to convince Congress that the construction of the public buildings should be continued. Jefferson appointed Benjamin Latrobe to direct this new building program, thereby making him responsible for carrying out Hoban's design for the President's House and Thornton's for the Capitol. In the case of the former, Latrobe was able to introduce many

*Figure 21*    Benjamin H. Latrobe.
*Proposal for the completion of the U. S. Capitol.*
Ink, watercolor, and pencil, 1817.
Library of Congress.

*Figure 22*    Alexander Jackson Davis.
*Plan of the principal story of the Capitol as completed in 1829 by Charles Bulfinch.*
Ink and wash, ca. 1834. Library of Congress.

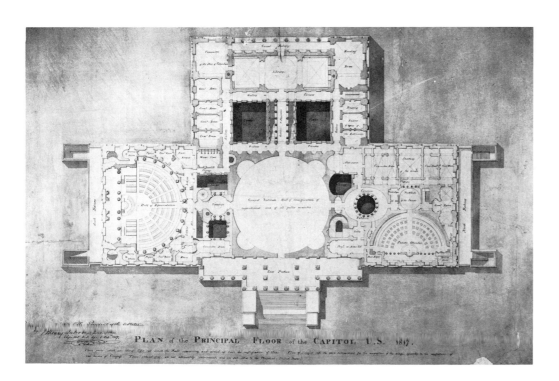

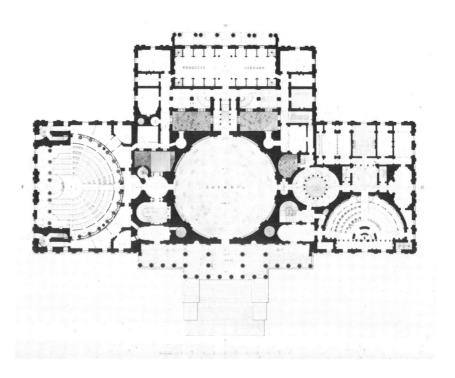

elements of his own invention (plate 10), apparently without controversy, but in the case of the design for the Capitol he was hampered by Thornton's continued vigilance even though the office of the commissioners had been discontinued. But Latrobe was even more thwarted by the sacrosanct character the design chosen by Washington had achieved since his death.

Over the next nine years Latrobe would erect the south wing for the House of Representatives and extensively remodel the Senate wing. By the end of this period he had created two of the most admired legislative halls in the world (plate 8), but he had been unable to complete the building. As Congress no longer would appropriate funds to continue the work, the central section with the great circular vestibule on the east and the temple form of the Conference Room on the west had yet to be begun. Latrobe was deeply disappointed, for he had from the beginning of his appointment made plans and designs for the completion of the building. In 1806 he had drawn up a new plan (plate 6) which would have materially altered Thornton's design. Latrobe dropped the idea of the circular Conference Room and temple on the west, reduced the size of the central rotunda, and increased the size and importance of the portico on the east by extending it across the entire central section and providing it with an impressive flight of steps (plate 5). Latrobe's design essentially exchanged the importance of the two fronts, that on the east becoming more clearly established as the principal one.

By the removal of Thornton's Temple of Fame from the west front Latrobe converted the low Roman dome over the rotunda into the primary crowning element of the design. Still later, at the moment when the next stage in the construction of the Capitol would focus on the central section, Latrobe prepared another design (plate 7). This would have restored to the building some of the monumentality lacking from his earlier plan by vastly increasing the size of the dome and by adding a colonnade along the front of a greatly enlarged west-front projection. The dream Latrobe expressed in these plans must have made his inability to alter the design by Thornton extremely frustrating. He could never convince Jefferson to move away from the design accepted by Washington, but had to content himself with the general admiration his work at the Capitol gained for him. Latrobe must have taken particular pleasure in the letter Jefferson wrote him on July 12, 1812, when his work on the Capitol was at an end, in which Jefferson describes the Capitol as "the first temple dedicated to the sovereignty of the people, embellishing with Athenian taste the course of a nation looking far beyond the range of Athenian destinies" (Hamlin 1955, p. 292).

After the burning of the Capitol by the British during the War of 1812, Latrobe was called back again, this time to supervise the work of restoration. Although for a brief period a move was underway to rebuild the Capitol on a flat area closer to the President's House, sentiment for the original site prevailed. Latrobe offered a plan (figure 21) comparable to the one he had prepared in 1810–11, and in 1817 it was accepted by President James Monroe. Now Latrobe would have the opportunity of

*Figure 23    View from the White House along Pennsylvania Avenue toward the U. S. Capitol.*
Engraving, ca. 1839.

seeing his own design for the Capitol put into execution and the Thornton design finally supplanted. With the adoption of this design only a truncated version of the building that Washington, L'Enfant, and Thornton had visualized as projecting from the brow of the hill would be built.

Latrobe had the satisfaction of having his design approved, but he did not succeed in carrying it out. The reconstruction work necessarily concentrated first on the legislative halls (plate 9), and Latrobe's work on these areas was made difficult by Congressional suspicion that he was extravagant and a dictatorial supervisor. Finally, in November 1817, an increasingly unsympathetic president led to Latrobe's resignation. It became the responsibility of his successor, Charles Bulfinch, to complete the central part of the Capitol. He did so over the next eleven years, during which he carried out Latrobe's design in most respects although he shortened the projecting west wing (figure 22) and substituted a weak central portico for Latrobe's boldly scaled colonnade. The massive Roman dome proposed by Latrobe was transformed by Bulfinch into a higher but less impressive crowning. Despite these departures from the more striking designs of both Thornton and Latrobe, the finished building was nevertheless an imposing edifice and dominated the federal city (figure 23) much as the original dreamers—L'Enfant and Washington—had foreordained.

The hill site L'Enfant had selected for the Capitol made it impossible for a building of any type not to be a conspicuous landmark. Nevertheless, the Capitol as finished by Bulfinch lacked the monumental domination of the hill that the original L'Enfant-Thornton building would have achieved. In a sense, the hill that L'Enfant saw as a pedestal awaiting a monument had yet to be occupied. The Bulfinch Capitol, by being farther removed from the brow of the hill, with a dome not as high and a treatment of the west front not as dramatic as the original, temple-like form proposed in the Thornton design, did not in actuality live up to the graphic renderings. Perhaps this more modest architectural image more accurately reflected the state of the nation at the time, but it no longer spoke of that future greatness of the Republic envisaged by George Washington.

Ironically, almost at the very moment when the completed Capitol projected more the image of a small Republic than a vast empire, the new nation was actually forging ahead to the size its founding fathers had foreseen. The disparity between the modest image and the country's newly achieved standing among the nations of the world would soon become apparent to those who strongly believed that a nation's architecture should reflect the greatness of its achievements. In time this belief would lead to a complete re-design of the Capitol in order to make it a truly appropriate national symbol. Initially, however, plans to alter the Capitol were considered only in response to complaints about poor ventilation, bad acoustics, inadequate lighting, and, ultimately, overcrowding. Various solutions to these problems had been proposed over the years between 1830 and 1850, but none had been executed.

As the official in charge of public buildings during most of this period, Robert

*Figure 24* Robert Mills.
*Plan proposed in 1846 for the extension of the U. S. Capitol.*
Published in Owen, 1849.

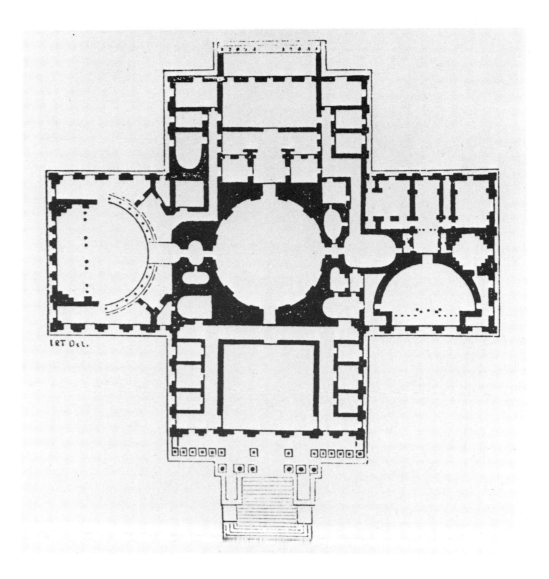

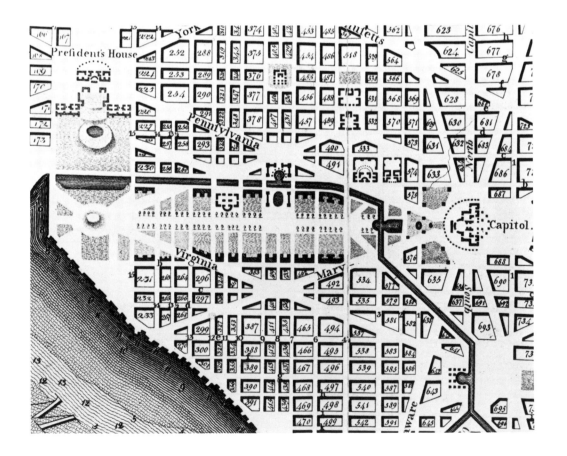

*Figure 25*
*Central section of the official plan of the city of Washington* (detail of fig. 6).

Mills was the architect often consulted about these problems. In 1846 he had proposed a design that, by adding an extension to the east front (figure 24), would not only provide the needed extra space, but would also cure what was considered to be a major fault: its "lop-sided appearance," which came about because the dome over the rotunda was not located in the center of the building. In 1850 the Senate Committee on Public Works, under the leadership of Jefferson Davis, endorsed a subsequent design by Mills for enlarging the original building and moved to have it adopted by Congress. Apparently, however, there was no agreement on how the Capitol should be enlarged, for instead of adopting the Mills plan recommended by its committee, the Senate voted to hold an open competition. As part of the terms of this short, two-month competition, Congress reserved the right to amalgamate features from any of the entries into a single design.

The need for enlarging the building without displacing Congress permitted only a limited number of solutions. New wings could be added alongside the original north and south wings, although this would produce such a long, low architectural mass, the impact of the central dome would be radically diminished. A significant westward extension was not possible due to the drop-off of the terrain. The flat plain east of the building was the most logical site for an expansion, but any addition here would severely alter the appearance of the east front, which already had begun to accumulate the sanctity of tradition.

None of the entries submitted in the competition were found to be satisfactory. Thus the committee, following the system already forecast in the terms of the competition, asked Mills to draw up a design incorporating the best features from all the submissions. None of the existing designs by Mills for this extension precisely match the description of the one actually adopted by the committee in 1851 (*Documentary History*, pp. 446–47). Two of his designs, however, include a much-enlarged central dome surrounded by a colonnade and a large semicircular portico on the west front (plates 11 and 12). Both of these features recall similar ones in the Thornton design and, had they been implemented, would have increased the dominance of the western front of the building looking toward the President's House.

Any possibility that Mills might be chosen to work on the extension of the Capitol was ended, however, when President Millard Fillmore exerted the authority granted him by Congress and on his own selected a new architect and a new design for the Capitol. Thomas U. Walter, whose entries in the competition had called for a vast addition toward the east, was sworn in as Architect of the Extension of the Capitol in June 1851; by July 4, 1851, the cornerstone was laid for the new design (plate 14). What the president had ordered Walter to build, apparently without consulting Congress, was two large wings on the north and south ends of the existing building—attached to it by connecting corridors (plate 13)—which substantially increased the space for the legislative bodies.

The enlargement of a building to provide more space or improved services need not necessarily be viewed as affecting its symbolic image, but by 1850 the Capitol had become the national symbol that Washington and Jefferson had foreseen. Even in the popular imagery of the day the building had come to be interpreted as a symbolic linchpin in the union of the states. Indeed, the decision to enlarge the original Capitol was interpreted in just this light. The cornerstone ceremonies of July 4, 1851, were carefully patterned after those of 1793. After a procession from the City Hall, President Fillmore laid the stone with the same trowel that had been used by President Washington, and the same Masonic rites were carried out. The Grand Master of Masons, B. B. French, saw the construction of the new building adjoining the old as a reflection of the admission of new states—Texas, California, and New Mexico—into the Union, joining with the old, becoming one and the same. The Senate Chaplain in his invocation called the Capitol the cornerstone of the Union, which held the states together (*Capitol Centennial Celebration*, pp. 136, 132).

Daniel Webster, then Secretary of State, concluded the ceremony with an oration that set out the symbolic significance of the event even more specifically. Extending the Capitol building was, he proclaimed, an extension of those beliefs in democracy manifested when Washington stood on this spot fifty-eight years before, and Webster developed the link between the two occasions by calling up a vision of what Washington would say were he present at the occasion. The dominant theme of these imagined remarks by the first president was the importance of preserving the Union, "cemented as it was by our prayers, our tears and our blood." Webster promised to heed Washington's words and to allow no "ruthless hand" to "undermine that bright arch of Union and Liberty which spans the continent from Washington to California." The extension of the Capitol was seen as the extension of the nation, the continued union of the states, and the reaffirmation of the Constitution that protected the freedom and rights of the individual.

The work at the Capitol took on an even greater importance, both structurally and symbolically, when the decision was made in 1855 to replace the low wooden dome by Bulfinch with a great cast-iron dome designed by Walter (plate 24). Although his design contained features suggested earlier in several of the Mills designs—the colonnaded drum and the crowning statue of Freedom—and was not unique in the choice of cast iron, its form and profile were completely original and on a far more massive scale than anything previously suggested. The new dome (plate 25) would be approximately twice as high as either the existing one or the one that had crowned the Temple of Fame in the design proposed by Thornton, although it still would be located farther back from the brow of the hill. Nevertheless, the decision to build a new dome for the "people's palace," as the reporter Noah Brooks would refer to the building in 1863, reinstated the Capitol as both a monumental architectural statement and a powerful national symbol.

At the same time as these changes were restoring to the Capitol the importance L'Enfant and Washington had given it as centerpiece of the city plan, a new symbolic reading of the plan itself was introduced. In an address before the Art

Union Association on March 31, 1859, the mayor of Washington, James G. Berret, hailed the plan as a "beautiful and grand conception of Washington" that was a "monument to the first true representative Republic (resting directly on the will of the people) the world ever saw." It was, he claimed, "a carefully matured plan, calculated, through the symbolic character of its conception, more intimately to cement and bind together this brotherhood of States, however indefinite its extension." Because of this design, the mayor declared "our great warrior, statesman, patriot, has, to my mind, won the title of *artist*."

Washington's leading idea, he said, was the fact that the "broad Avenues are just fifteen in number, corresponding to the 'Old Thirteen,' with Vermont and Kentucky admitted after the adoption of the Constitution, and before the completion of the plan." Another principal feature was the way Washington named the avenues "commencing at the north, with New Hampshire, the most northerly State, and proceeding south, the avenues, as nearly as their irregularity will permit, are named in the order of the States, ending with Georgia, the then most southerly one, half being north of the Capitol and half south of it." The names of the three avenues that vary from this plan—Massachusetts, Pennsylvania, and Virginia—had an added symbolic meaning for the mayor. As they are "nearly double the length of the others, and spanning the city from the northwest to the southeast borders some four miles in length," the mayor believed Washington had chosen their names with special care. He ventured to enter the thoughts of Washington as he

sat brooding over this beautiful conception of his genius, and hesitating as to the baptism of the most northern and longest of the avenues, his great heart thought of the theatre of the first blood shed in the deadly strife—of Lexington, of Concord, of Bunker Hill, and of Charlestown, where he first assumed the office of Commander-in-Chief . . . and, with a hand trembling with emotion, he christened it "MASSACHUSETTS." Pennsylvania, just midway between the three States, touches the Atlantic and the lakes, thus making it the Keystone of the "Old Thirteen." In happy coincidence with that idea, the name of that State is given to the noble avenue which cuts directly through the *centre of the Capitol and the President's House*, thus symbolizing the idea which has distinguished Pennsylvania as the "KEYSTONE" of the arch. The third of the long avenues, named after his own Virginia, aside from the distinction of her sons and the splendor of her achievements, was entitled to it on that account. . . . Is it venturing too much to conjecture that the distinction given to Virginia and Massachusetts beyond the other States, in bestowing their names upon the south and north of the longest avenues, may have also been intended to be typical of their containing the landing places—Jamestown and Plymouth—of the first emigrants from the Old World?

The mayor concludes his address by urging that the pediments of the center and the new wings of the Capitol be filled with sculpture reflecting the symbolism of the city plan. He proposes that the sculptures already prepared by Thomas Crawford for the north pediment be installed instead in the center pediment, where they would symbolize "the material interests and progress of the country, the central and tallest piece being Liberty, with her cap." For the south pediment the mayor

*Figure 26    Thomas U. Walter's design for hoisting the statue of Freedom to the top of the Capitol dome* (detail from drawing by Auguste Schoenborn, 1863). Architect of the Capitol.

*Figure 27*
*Capitol dome under construction.*
Photograph, 1860.

suggests that the appropriate design "would be the landing of the first Emigrants at Jamestown, in Virginia, and for the north one, the landing, fourteen years later, of the first Emigrants at Plymouth, in Massachusetts. What could be more in keeping with the leading idea in the conception of the plan of the city . . . than such a symbolization of the landing of the first emigrants at the South and the North, the two joined together, as it were, in the centre pediment, by Crawford's noble types of material progress—the complement of strength and union—with the crowning token of Liberty 'NOW AND FOREVER' in the centre." Since the entire composition faced the great statue of Washington by Horatio Greenough, which had been placed on the eastern grounds of the Capitol in 1844, it was only fitting, the mayor proclaimed, that the figure of Liberty would thus "[gaze] with intent regard and triumphant air . . . directly on the Father of his Country, who, sitting in majestic and solitary grandeur," could contemplate "the perfect fruition of his desires."

For six years the cast iron columns, capitals, and entablatures making up the colonnade of the dome were hoisted into place on the Capitol. The great iron ribs of the cupola, silhouetted against the sky, began to foretell the final shape (figure 27). But the bonds of the Union were broken before the dome could be completed, and the fears of men like Daniel Webster and Mayor Berret were realized. The fundamental concept of the Constitution, of a central government based on the will of the people, was now in peril. For a brief period at the outbreak of hostilities

between North and South work was suspended on the dome. But in the spring of 1862, at the urging of president Abraham Lincoln, Congress voted to complete the work. Leaving it incomplete, Senator Foot of New Hampshire said on the Senate floor, would be "a humiliating confession, to the country and to the world, of a national weakness and imbecility, of a national impoverishment and bankruptcy. . . . We are strong enough yet, thank God, to put down this rebellion and to put up this our Capitol at the same time." When the Union was restored, he added, it would be fitting to celebrate the occasion by "crowning the American Capitol with the statue of the Goddess of Freedom" (*Documentary History*, p. 802).

This crowning did not await the restoration of the Union but was held in December 1863. The reporter for the Sacramento *Daily Union*, Noah Brooks, wrote of the excitement the event produced as precisely at noon the last section of the twenty-foot statue was lifted upward and hammered into place (figure 26) above the "airy dome of the people's palace." A salute by the artillery of the 22nd Army Corps given to commemorate the event was described as an expression of respect for "this material symbol of the principles on which our Government is based."

To turn the symbol into a reality required a plan by means of which the rebellious states, once defeated, would be brought back into the Union. That same month Lincoln presented a course that would allow the re-unification of the states on a humane and charitable basis and would carry into reality what the Capitol symbolized. Fifteen months later, in his last inaugural address, delivered on March 4, 1865, before the newly completed east front of the Capitol, Lincoln sought to gain support for his position in a solemn message that invoked malice toward none and charity for all in binding up the nation's wounds to achieve "a just, and a lasting peace." Five weeks later, soon after the surrender at Appomatox, the president made what would be his last public address, in which he again urged that the Union be restored without reprisal against those who had been led into rebellion and punishment meted out only to their leaders. By pardon and amnesty Lincoln hoped to achieve a swift reconstruction of the Union, but his death on April 15, 1861, prolonged the process of recovery. Nevertheless, the icon makers of the day (figure 28) were quick to recognize that Lincoln had preserved what President Washington had forged—a political entity whose power and authority sprang directly from the will of its citizens—and had also, by his commitment to complete the Capitol, brought to fruition the architectural ideal of the first president (figure 29).

What the new building meant to the citizens of the day was expressed some years later by a *New York Times* reporter in speaking of New York City's need for a magnificent new post office. "No person of this Republic," he wrote in 1868, "has ever regretted the amount the nation has expended in the erection of the Capitol. None tread beneath its matchless dome, but feel the pride of country in the thrill of patriotic fervor following the proud reflection that no where upon the earth's surface can its proportionate and stately grandeur be equaled."

APOTHEOSIS OF LINCOLN & WASHINGTON.

*Figure 28.*
*Commemorative card published after assassination of President Lincoln in 1865.*

*Figure 29*
*U. S. Capitol, viewed from the west.*
Photograph, 1877.

## 4: Public Architecture and the Well-being of the State

The symbolic importance of public architecture that served the Republic was not limited solely to structures in the capital city but was attached to public buildings erected anywhere in the nation. In the first half of the nineteenth century ideas about what these buildings should look like were much discussed in the American press and literary magazines, as well as on lecture platforms around the country. The intense interest and concern given these architectural matters stemmed directly from the recognition that the United States had a unique opportunity, unavailable to European nations, to create a new architecture. But it also came about because of an even deeper and more firmly held belief that the proper kind of architecture could produce tangible benefits for society. In particular, public architecture of high quality was believed to strengthen the attachment of the people to their government and even to promote higher intellectual and moral standards in the citizens who lived among these buildings. Out of these beliefs came many arguments urging the new nation to reap such benefits by encouraging public buildings of the highest quality.

An anonymous essay that appeared in the *Analectic Magazine* of 1815 made the case that nothing "contributes more powerfully towards elevating the reputation of any people, than the grandeur of public edifices" (p. 374). The benefit derived from such displays of public magnificence, the writer notes, binds the citizens together, "imparting 'an hour's importance to the poor man's heart,' and enabling him for a time to forget the inferiority of his condition, and feel a community of interest with his wealthier neighbour" (p. 375). What the author has in mind is "a noble hall for the purposes of legislation or of justice [which] is the immediate property of the people, and forms a portion of the patrimony of every citizen" (pp. 374–75).

This democratizing virtue of public architecture surfaced in many essays. In 1830 the author of *Views in Philadelphia* insisted that since no individual had the wealth to erect large buildings, national pride had to be gratified by the magnificence of public edifices—the common property of the nation—in which "every citizen has his due share alike of the burden and the glory" (unpaginated).

A similar sentiment was expressed about the same time in a series of important articles published in four consecutive issues of the *American Journal of Science and Arts* from October 1829 to July 1830. Here the anonymous author proposes that objects of architectural beauty could provide "a common bond of union among us; something to make us feel that we are members of one great community . . . and attach us more powerfully to our fellows, and to the country" (p. 107). He warns, however, that to evoke such associations, public buildings must be erected not just for the present but for the "intelligent and keen-sighted population" of our future. If we wish them to respect our memory and our laws and institutions we must build objects to "heighten reverence . . . not provoke their ridicule. How," he asks, "would our feelings for our Declaration of Independence be affected, if the Congress which voted it, had voted also the erection of a capitol, by a silly architect, and if this now stood among us the object of our contempt?" (p. 228).

*Figure 30*
*Business card of architect James Dakin, ca. 1833.*

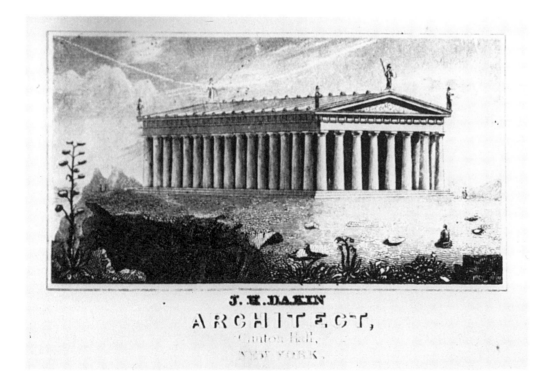

J. H. DAKIN
ARCHITECT,
Canton Hall,
NEW YORK.

In his article that appeared in the April 1844 issue of the *North American Review* the architect Arthur Gilman sought to impress on the readers the important role architecture played in a society by reminding them that architecture has been regarded as "among those causes which affect the character of an age, and exert a prominent influence over the moral and intellectual habits of a people" (p. 436). How such a beneficial influence operated in society had already been described in the 1829/30 series of articles in the *American Journal of Science and Arts* where the writer explained that if the public buildings in a town are of high quality they will in turn act as models for the private dwellings. Because the "principles of good taste" that will be applied to the design of the outside of the dwelling will also be followed inside, they will bring about a rapid improvement in the "cleanliness, good order and regularity" of the households. Such better surroundings, the author assures us, will have a strong and beneficial effect "on the mind, as well as on the moral character of the occupants" (p. 109). The writer further proclaims that the great architecture America would produce would draw "a bright halo around the name of our country" making "us a better and a happier people" (p. 26).

It was also believed at this time that all the patriotic, intellectual, and moral blessings good architecture was capable of bestowing on a society were more likely to occur in America than anywhere else in the world. The principal reason for this belief stemmed from the conviction that the arts truly flourished only during a state of liberty and freedom. The artist, historian, and playwright William Dunlap makes this point in an essay of February 1836 published in the *American Monthly Magazine* where he argues that although at first glance the arts may appear to flourish during periods of despotism, it is only because they already had achieved a high level of perfection during an earlier period marked by "previous progress and triumphs of republicanism." For example, "The age of Alexander had been preceded by Grecian democracy; that of Augustus by the glories of republican Rome" (p. 116). The anonymous author writing in the *American Journal of Science and Arts* also pointed out that distinction in architecture always occurred when the form of government was republican, citing Greece, Palmyra, Florence, Genoa, and Venice as examples. The American republic, he believed, should feel encouraged that "this form of government seems to be best fitted for the success of architectural effort" (pp. 15–16).

In addition to the belief that the arts benefited from the form of government that existed in the United States, it was also held that the arts profited as well from the "natural good taste and the unprejudiced eye of our citizens," as they were characterized about 1850 by the architect Robert Mills in a brief manuscript outline of a work he was planning to write about his career. Many writers during the first half of the nineteenth century discovered special characteristics in the American people which, they prophesied, would favor the growth of the visual arts in the new nation. As early as 1815 the anonymous writer in the *Analectic Magazine* singled out the "faculty of sight" as a power possessed by the native citizens of America to a greater "degree of accuracy and perfection" than in any other country. He adduces as proof of this power the national skill in gunnery "from its simplest form as it appears in the quickness and accuracy of eye and certainty of fire of our million of marksmen, up through every form of artillery," and derives further corroboration from the surprising ability of Americans to judge precisely "heights and distances, of the extent of a field, the size of a room, or the shape of distant objects." But the evidence he finds most supportive of America's unique faculty of sight is "the wonderful and otherwise unaccountable spontaneous growth of the art of painting among us." What other nations, such as Great Britain and France, labored for years to achieve in the visual arts "suddenly sprouted up of themselves on this side of the Atlantic" (pp. 363–64).

In place of a natural superiority of American eyesight, the author of the 1829/30 articles in the *American Journal of Science and Arts* substitutes the superiority of the analytic power of the American people. For this writer Americans have a "strong susceptibility to objects of mental pleasure" because "we are a reading community" and are thus always in search of more information. Because Americans are also a traveling people they have an "abundant opportunity for comparing places" and "are gradually forming a pretty correct judgement, as to the beauties of a landscape or a town. . . ." This is shown, the author believes, by "the crowds that gather to the deck of a steam or canal boat, as a fine point of view, or a handsome village, is approached and is heard in the murmur of approbation among little groups of such travellers." The author is so impressed by these characteristics, he avers that in no country but America "is a striking object" analyzed more quickly or its value "more correctly estimated" (pp. 101–2).

Whether or not the American public actually possessed the level of good taste in architecture and the other arts ascribed to them in the first half of the nineteenth century, it is obvious from the literature that they were exposed to a great deal of talk about architecture and exhorted to make judgments about the buildings of their day. Indeed, the writer of the 1829/30 series of articles on architecture in the United States informed his readers that they had a responsibility to become knowledgeable about architecture since only when there was a demanding public did the artist work at his best. He averred that this had been as true for the Greek artists in the time of Phidias as it was in the current republic (p. 100).

The memoirs and letters of the day contain innumerable comments on buildings being erected, and some display a keen sense of appreciation for the visual effects of these structures. That new buildings excited local pride and admiration is revealed—unwittingly—in the travel account published in Edinburgh in 1833 by the dour and pedantic Scottish traveler Thomas Hamilton. Although the purpose of his comments was to denigrate American taste in architecture—"There is nothing in which the absence of taste in America is more signally displayed than in their architecture"—he nevertheless conveys the enthusiasm Americans had for their new buildings when he refers to their clamorous demands "on the admiration of foreigners, in behalf of buildings which it is impossible to look upon without instant and unhesitating condemnation" (Hamlin 1944, p. 96).

At the same time the critics were expressing belief in the public good brought to the nation by buildings of high quality they also attempted to define what was appropriate for the Republic. As the author of the 1815 article in the *Analectic Magazine* admitted, although public edifices were an appropriate way for a republican government to display its munificence, such display must accord with "the general simplicity of republican institutions." Otherwise, "like the show and pomp of private luxury, they are of a selfish nature . . . and reflect little lustre on the state by which they are bestowed" (p. 374). Lawmakers, too, were aware that architecture must embody the republican spirit of the nation. The discussion on the floor of the House of Representatives on March 13, 1824, concerning the appropriations for continuing work on the Capitol prompted Congressman Cushman of Maine to try to characterize the quality America's public buildings should have. "Of all governments," he said, "a republic ought to appear with sober pomp and modest splendour. Not the dazzling radiance of a throne is here reflected; but the mild lustre, the serene majesty, of the sovereign people" (*Documentary History*, p. 260). Six years later, the author of *Views in Philadelphia* tried to give the abstract qualities of republican virtue a more definitive correlation in architecture: "If there be any analogy between public works and the public spirit which achieves them, we may naturally look for the simplest style of architecture in that nation, which above all others, has assumed as the basis of its institutions, the utmost simplicity in all the forms of its government" (unpaginated).

During the early years of the nineteenth century critics, architects, and laymen alike were convinced that the architectural goals the new Republic should strive for in its public buildings were those exemplified by the ancient Greek republic (figure 30). By following the same principles American architecture could be assured of reaching a comparable level of quality. Some critics even called for a direct imitation of specific monuments of that republic's Golden Age. The Parthenon on the Acropolis (figure 31) and the smaller Theseum in the Agora below were at the top of their lists, although other monuments could also serve as inspiration. Knowledge of these prototypes came primarily from prints or books, particularly from *The Antiquities of Athens* the four-volume publication by James Stuart and Nicholas Revett issued in London between 1762 and 1816, which reproduced measured drawings of the major buildings and their ornament.

The critical attitude endorsing the Greek style as the model to be followed is succinctly stated by Philip Hone in his diary entry of February 14, 1838. "How strange it is," he wrote, "that in all the inventions of modern times architecture alone seems to admit of no improvement—every departure from the classical models of antiquity in this science is a departure from grace and beauty" (p. 302).

Hone's comment had been prompted by a visit to Philadelphia and his seeing once again the Second Bank of the United States (figure 32), the much admired work designed twenty years earlier by William Strickland modeled after the Parthenon. The bank had become one of the most acclaimed architectural

*Figure 31*
*Parthenon, Athens, 447–438* B.C.
Photograph, ca. 1890.

embellishments of the new Republic, widely praised for its perfect handling of the principles of Greek architecture as expressed in its highest form—the Doric order. It stood as the exemplar for other American public buildings and stirred the kind of emotional attachment to its image that the elegiac comment by Hone attests to. It was for many critics of the time the most beautiful building in the land and received high praise from foreign visitors. Strickland's banking house also was the first example in the world of the adaptation of the Greek temple form to a building serving a practical purpose and it opened the way for myriad subsequent applications of the temple form to buildings whose uses were far removed from those of a sacred shrine.

The Philadelphia bank was the headquarters of a national banking system chartered by Congress in 1816 to help restore order to the financial affairs of the country. Commerce had suffered greatly after the congressional charter of the first national banking system, devised by Alexander Hamilton in 1790, had been allowed to expire in 1811. Although chartered by Congress, the bank was basically a private corporation made up of shareholders, of which the federal government was a principal one. Nevertheless, the public perceived the bank as a federal entity, and thus the almost thirty branch banks opened around the nation between 1817 and 1836 represented the first widespread introduction into the states of the Union of public buildings associated with the central government.

The branch offices of the Second Bank strove, each within its particular circumstances, to achieve the architectural image set by the parent bank in Philadelphia. Although many of the branch banks were far simpler, all were adorned with at least one classical element—a pediment, column, or pilaster—that linked them to the Philadelphia building. The original design for the branch bank in Boston was noted by the *City Record* of November 5, 1825, as having been "intended to be an imitation of the purest example of the Grecian Doric Order, with two porticoes; but the scite [*sic*] which was finally obtained required a different arrangement." The design (figure 33) adopted by its architect Solomon Willard was, instead, what the newspaper calls "the primitive form of the Grecian temple," which has two Doric columns set between the projecting side walls of the building. The entire structure, including the carved cornice, was made of granite, which the newspaper characterized as a "refractory material." The shafts of the columns were four feet in diameter and twenty-four feet high, each made of a single piece of granite. The appearance of the bank, the journalist adds, was "intended to be of a severe and masculine character becoming a National Edifice of the young Republic."

Although after the withdrawal of federal support, the Second Bank was converted into a state institution with a Pennsylvania charter in late 1835, the style it had made so identifiable with banks continued to be the one most favored by the banking industry throughout the Republic. One of the buildings closest to the Strickland model was the bank in Erie, Pennsylvania, designed by William Kelly in 1837 (figure 34). Although conceived on a smaller scale, it, too, presented a

SLIDE

*Figure 32*  William Strickland. *Second Bank of the United States, Philadelphia, 1817–24.* Engraving, n.d.

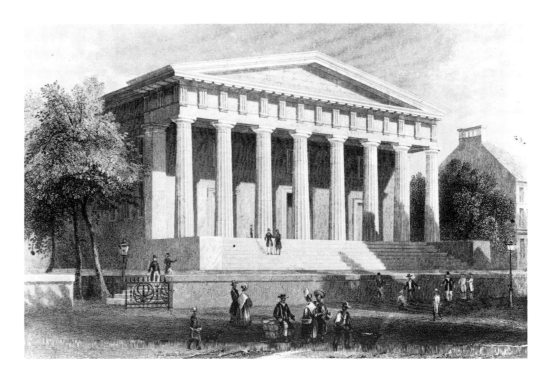

*Figure 33* Solomon Willard.
*Boston Branch of the Second Bank of the United States, 1824–25.*
Engraving, 1825.

*Figure 34* William Kelly.
*Erie Branch of the Bank of Pennsylvania, 1837–39.*
Photograph, ca. 1935.

handsome portico of Doric columns modeled after those of the Parthenon. The marble columns were quarried and carved in Dorset, Vermont, and were sent to Pennsylvania through the new conveniences of transportation: south by the Champlain and Hudson Canal to Albany, then westward via the Erie Canal. By 1849 both the Philadelphia and the Erie banks had been purchased by the federal government to become U. S. custom houses, with no need to transform their exterior appearance to display their new role. The efforts of both architects and patrons alike to make buildings that would excite the imagination of the local citizens surely would have been gratifying to the author of the 1829/30 articles in the *American Journal of Science and Arts* who had called for examples of noble architecture to be set among the nation's towns.

The city that was most successful in creating an architectural image of the Republic during this period was Philadelphia, which could boast of more fine examples of architecture than any city in America. Not only was it the home of the greatly appreciated Second Bank of the United States, but it also had nearby the Merchants' Exchange built in 1832–34 (figure 35) by the same William Strickland. Here, however, he does not follow a single Greek building as prototype but exhibits a freer and more creative use of Grecian forms and a more mature understanding of the design principles of Greek architecture. Strickland joins to the main rectangular body of the Exchange a gracefully curved colonnade that serves as a base for an imposing circular lantern, patterned after the Choragic Monument of

Lysikrates, a much-admired Greek work frequently reproduced in prints at that time. Strickland's building provided a memorable and elegant entry into the heart of Philadelphia's commercial area and made an instant impression on visitors arriving at the city's waterfront.

Farther away from the center of the city, occupying an area completely unencumbered by other buildings, rose a more recent architectural wonder, thus providing proof of the concept that one fine architectural specimen would lead to the creation of others. The set of buildings designed in 1833 by Thomas U. Walter for Girard College was greeted upon its completion in 1847 as a perfect example of the successful evolution of an American style based on Greek prototypes (plate 27). The colonnade and temple form of the principal building were conditions of the competition set by its building committee, a member of which was Nicholas Biddle, the president of the Second Bank of the United States and the first American actually to have traveled in Greece visiting the classical remains. The will of the founder, Stephen Girard, had also specified the type of buildings to be selected and spelled out the exact dimensions for the principal building. Walter displayed tremendous ingenuity in working within these confines to create an impressive classical temple that also provided a series of rooms that suited the purposes of the school. In addition, his grouping of the adjacent dormitory buildings, gate lodges, and entrances gave to the Corinthian temple of the principal building a sense of grandeur that such equally classically inspired but less happily located buildings as the Second Bank of the United States could never achieve. The complex of classical buildings that Walter provided for the orphans who would occupy these premises not only met the requirements of the donor and the building committee, but also satisfied their aspirations for providing buildings whose character would have a positive effect on their inhabitants. "What is the use of the *marble palace*? what the value of the fluted column and gorgeous capital?" asked one of the orators, Joseph R. Chandler, on the occasion of placing the crowning stone on the main building in 1847. His answer was that such buildings would affect "the minds of the young," ultimately making them "living temples of moral truth" as important to the society of which they would be part as the "splendid building in which they shall be reared" will be the "pride and beauty of the city in which it stands" (*Final Report*, Building Committee, Girard College, pp. 34–35). Girard College remains one of the highest achievements in American architecture of this period and was appropriately used as the frontispiece to the history of architecture published in 1848 by Mrs. L. C. Tuthill—the first such book to include a consideration of buildings in the United States.

In addition to the happy commingling of buildings erected in the classical style in Philadelphia, other impressive civic buildings were being built in this style around the country which gave visual, tangible evidence of the nature and development of a national style. Such buildings were so singular, or so dispersed, within the urban fabric that their impact on the public was greatly heightened and may, indeed, have led to the exaggeration of their qualities that so annoyed the

*Figure 35*   William Strickland. *Merchants' Exchange, Philadelphia, 1832–34.* Photograph (by John Moran?), ca. 1865.

SLIDE

Scottish visitor Thomas Hamilton in 1832. Because of their uniqueness, however, these individual works, though representative of an American style, did not conjure up the ideal townscape desired by the aestheticians and architects alike. With the exception, perhaps, of the building complex of Girard College, the vision these buildings sought to achieve could only be captured in a painting, such as the work painted by Thomas Cole in 1840 entitled *The Architect's Dream* (figure 36). The size and scale of the buildings pictured here and their classical style reflect accurately the aspirations of the written criticism of the time; but the painter was able to go beyond simple description to evoke a vision of a majestic setting for a noble form of government.

Although some critics and architects unquestioningly accepted Greek architectural forms as the ideal models to be followed, others tried to determine just why this should be the case. Even though they might agree that the Greek Doric order was the finest possible model for the public architecture of the United States, they still sought to understand the reasons for its superiority. Such an investigation was undertaken in the 1829/30 series of articles on American architecture published in the *American Journal of Science and Arts*. Here the author argues that because there were so many Greek buildings in so many distant places which all possessed the "same grand and noble character," their success could not be attributed to "a lucky hit" or to the labor of one man. And as "every column, every block of marble . . . seems to have received its form from some master in the art," there must have been "certain principles well known and extensively practised" to produce "this constant and extensive effect." These principles cannot be, he argues, simply a matter of proportions, shapes, or forms, for although these are universal in Greek works, the "Romans adopted them and failed, and so have the moderns." What is the secret, he wonders, that would explain why a Greek edifice, even in its ruins has a "speaking character, a majesty, a power" in its expression which "Roman buildings never had, and to which modern architecture makes no approach" (p. 15).

The author finds the answer to this question in the "grave but beautiful" Doric order which, he states, was used not only in the Parthenon, but also in every superior structure built in Greece or its colonies. From this single order he extracts the secret of Grecian perfection which, after a detailed examination, he concludes rests solely in "its simplicity" (p. 18). He is not speaking, he warns us, of the simplicity inherent in Egyptian architecture, which is admirable but which lacks entirely the "strong mastery over the soul" experienced in Greek architecture. Greek architects, he concludes, achieved this effect because they possessed "a taste so well disciplined" that they were able to judge instinctively the beauty of forms (pp. 19–20).

How, he asks, could such a disciplined taste have been acquired? He proposes that the Greek architect must have begun by studying solid forms in nature. As he matured he studied ever more complicated forms, but always with an eye for their

*Figure 36*    Thomas Cole.
*The Architect's Dream.*
Oil on canvas, 1840. The Toledo Museum of Art (Gift of Florence Scott Libbey).

underlying simplicity. This training led to his developing an instinctive perception by which he could begin to make his own "expression in solid forms." Once confident in his powers he could claim his work as original, without any obligation to another (p. 23). The truth of this conclusion is difficult to accept, the author confesses, because all Doric temples appear so similar that the architect of one could not help but appear to "follow in the footsteps of others." In fact, however, this similarity only proves, the author asserts, that all objects of "true beauty" share the same qualities: "great simplicity and great finish" (p. 23).

Once an architect mastered these principles he was able to make beautiful anything he was called upon to design, not merely a Doric temple. The Romans failed as architects because they lacked this discipline of taste, as did the Christian church builders, for whom "failure was inevitable," particularly in the case of St. Peter's which was simply "a labored quarry above-ground" (p. 25). Only by achieving the same discipline of taste and the same simplicity as the Greek architects, the author believes, would America produce a noble architectural style, and he welcomed the excitement the challenge would provoke. "The prize as well as the race is placed before us," he wrote, adding that America had every reason to believe that it would succeed (p. 25).

Other writers during this period did not ponder why following Grecian architectural principles would lead to a superior style but boldly questioned the truth of the initial assumption. As early as 1814 a writer in *Port Folio* wondered if the admiration and approval of classical architecture was not simply the result of habit. The writer agreed that Greek architecture possessed an intrinsic beauty that should be emulated, but he is not at all sure that this should be accomplished by copying its forms. The author cites the Virginia statehouse, designed by Thomas Jefferson, as an example of the problems that can occur when a building intended for a different function must nevertheless be contained within an ancient temple form. He first points out how the arrangement of the rooms within the building requires users to enter it from the sides rather than from the front and then notes that the temple form of the building nevertheless dictates that the entrance must be perceived as being at the front. Therefore, he comments, "the real entrance is without a shelter," and the apparent one provides no access (p. 568). Such practical observations and criticisms about a public building that had been recognized as an innovative model for American architecture when Jefferson designed it underscore the recurring search in this period for the appropriate mode in which the Republic should be represented.

In the 1840s an increasing number of architects and critics began to agree that the unquestioning application of Greek models to American buildings was not necessarily the best path to follow. Indeed, some became convinced that it was even morally wrong to adopt forms originally intended for a temple to serve the purposes of a banking establishment or an institution of higher learning. The enthusiastic adoption of Greek prototypes for buildings throughout the nation had, on the one hand, led to an American style of architecture that crowned the

*Figure 37.*
*Berry Hill (Halifax Co.), Virginia, ca. 1835–40.*
Photograph by Huestis Cook, ca. 1890.

humblest home with a pedimented doorway and transformed others into full-scale imitations of ancient models (figure 37). On the other, it intensified the debate over what a truly American style of architecture should be.

As early as 1836 William Dunlap had proposed that "the great experiment of a national democratic government . . . is now gazed at by the world, and the people of all nations are standing on tiptoe, eager for the race in which we are leaders." Dunlap believed that the United States would be the "leaders in the arts, as well as in political institutions" (p. 120); it was the destiny of the new Republic to form a new style of architecture.

Gradually, a consensus was arrived at which held that an American style should indeed be created by following the principles of Grecian architecture, but that this American style should at the same time devise new combinations of the classical forms. The works of Bramante and Palladio, the two chief architectural masters of the Italian Renaissance, were put forward as models to be taken as guides, because the buildings these architects designed already had introduced "endless new combinations" of architectural forms derived from classical prototypes (*Dial* 1843, p. 115). The following year Arthur Gilman, in his article in the April 1844 issue of the *North American Review*, cried out against the "Procrustean bed" of Greek architecture that was forcing all buildings to conform to its principles. The great mistake that had been made so far in the development of American architecture, he maintained, was its attempt to follow the monuments of Greek architecture as its sole model. As the author of the *Dial* article of the preceding year had done, Gilman suggests that the proper models might be those whose form was already the result of observation and assimilation of classical precepts, that is, the Italian "palazzo style" (figure 38).

At the same time that some critics were encouraging American architecture to profit from the lessons to be learned from such respected interpreters of classical monuments as Palladio (figure 39) and Bramante (figure 40), others were questioning the need to follow any models of the past. In the *United States Magazine and Democratic Review* of August 1843 Horatio Greenough wrote an essay fresh with new ideas about the right kind of architecture for America. Here Greenough argued for introducing into the design of buildings the same principles followed in the building of the great clipper ships. "Could we carry into our civil architecture," he wrote, "the responsibilities that weigh upon our ship-building, we should ere long have edifices as superior to the Parthenon for the purposes that we require, as the *Constitution* or the *Pennsylvania*" are to the ancient Greek sailing ships (p. 208).

Applying these principles to architecture, he suggests, would result in buildings being designed from the inside out rather than "forcing the functions of every sort of building into one general form." No longer could a designer "huddle together a crowd of ill arranged, ill lighted and stifled rooms" and by "masking the chaos with the sneaking copy of a Greek façade, usurp the name of architect." Architecture designed according to his way Greenough classified as "organic;" its products

*Figure 38.*
*Verospi Palace, Rome.*
Engraving from Le Tarouilly, vol. 1, 1840.

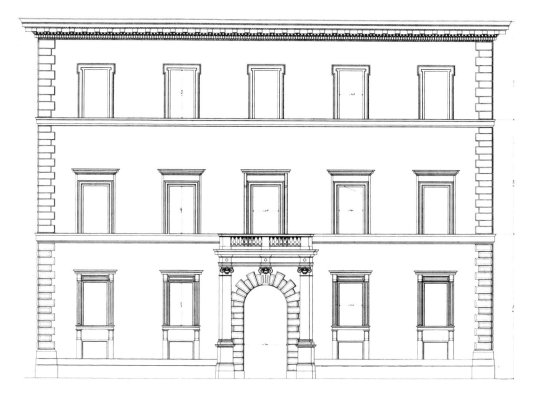

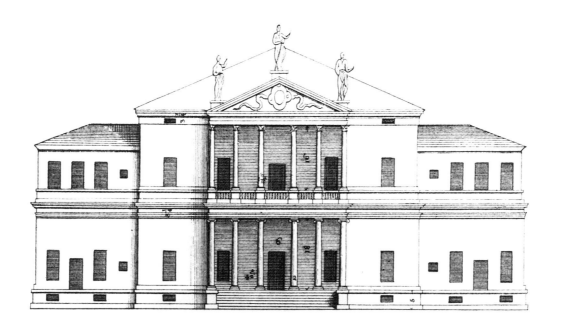

*Figure 39*  Andrea Palladio.
*Villa Cornara, Piombino, Italy, ca. 1560.*
Engraving from Palladio, ed. 1738.

SLIDE

*Figure 40*  Donato Bramante.
*Cancelleria Palace, Rome, begun ca. 1485.*
Engraving from Le Tarouilly, vol. 1, 1840.

being a bank with the "physiognomy of a bank," or a church that "would be recognized as such" (pp. 208–9). Working to give each building its proper form and expression, the architect would not be copying specific models of the past, but would be discovering the "fundamental laws of building found at the basis of every style of architecture." In a final reference to the classical past Greenough reaffirms that the Greek masters can indeed teach us, but in an apt analogy he qualifies just how the Greek antiquities should be used: "As a Christian preacher may give weight to truth, and add persuasion to proof, by studying the models of pagan writers, so the American builder, by a truly philosophic investigation of ancient art, will learn of the Greeks to be American" (p. 210).

One architect who clearly thought in this way was Robert Mills, whose major public buildings are marked both for their classical appearance and their originality. Fortunately for the future of the capital city, Mills became the architect responsible for fulfilling some of the ideals of L'Enfant's plan. The early part of the nineteenth century had seen so little progress in achieving the vision of President Washington and L'Enfant for the nation's capital, that Charles Dickens could aptly describe it in his *American Notes* of 1842 as a "city of magnificent intentions." Yet at this same moment, under the aegis of President Jackson, work was under way on three major projects designed by Robert Mills. Andrew Jackson proved to be as visionary as George Washington in advancing the idea that the public buildings of the nation's capital should be erected on a magnificent scale, and Mills proved a respectful and worthy follower of L'Enfant.

One of their most ambitious projects was the construction of an all-masonry, arched bridge to replace the wooden Long Bridge originally authorized by President Jefferson to connect the capital city with a road to Alexandria, Viriginia. President Jackson and his cabinet ceremoniously crossed the bridge when it opened in October 1835. Some sixteen years later, in his address delivered at the laying of the cornerstone of the extension of the Capitol, Daniel Webster would hail this bridge built of "arches of ever-enduring granite" as an example of President Jackson's desire to create a symbol "of the firmly cemented union of the North and the South" (Webster, p. 26).

In 1836 construction began on a new Treasury Building after a design by Mills which called for a structure some four times as large as its predecessor and featured a monumental colonnaded front (figure 41). That same year Mills was also responsible for supervising the construction of a new Patent Office Building, which again was a building designed on an enormous scale and which would provide the capital city with its first example of a colossal Doric portico (figure 42). Raised high above a basement story and approached by a massive flight of stone steps, this portico dominated the skyline of Washington during most of the nineteenth century.

A fourth undertaking in this ambitious federal building program directed by Mills was begun in 1839. Mills's design for the General Post Office Building—the first marble building in the capital—represents an original adaptation of classical

*Figure 41* Robert Mills.
*Treasury Building, Washington, D. C., begun 1836.*
Lithograph, ca. 1840.

elements to a new building type (figure 43). Like the rest of Mills's buildings the Post Office had no origin in a specific antique prototype, but its design was developed from Mills's knowledge of the vocabulary of classical architecture and his ability to invent new forms according to its principles. Whether or not his work would appear to the essayist in the *American Journal of Science and Arts* as the result of a disciplined taste that had rediscovered the Grecian secret of quality, the creativity of Mills's approach to designing architecture in the classical style could well qualify him as having invented the first American style.

It seems altogether appropriate that the architect whose designs were fulfilling the dreams of the city's founder should also have been chosen in 1833 as the designer of the Washington Monument. Although work on the latter would not be completed for forty years and, with the exception of the bridge over the Potomac, none of the other buildings begun by Mills would be completed until after the Civil War—and by then all under the direction of other architects—his activities as Architect of Public Buildings ensured that the original vision of the capital city would be realized. How critical his role was in furthering L'Enfant's original concept of the city can be seen in a lithograph published in 1852 (plate 28) showing Washington as it would appear when Mills's designs for the Washington Monument, the Treasury Building, the Patent Office, and the General Post Office became a reality.

*Figure 42*   Robert Mills.
*Patent Office Building, Washington, D. C., begun 1836.*
Lithograph, ca. 1836.

*Figure 43*   Robert Mills.
*General Post Office Building, Washington, D. C., begun 1839.*
Lithograph, 1848.

SLIDE

Before 1845 the federal government had erected only a few public buildings outside the capital city in which to carry out its constitutionally assigned duties of levying customs, operating a postal system, enforcing federal laws. Those buildings that the government had actually commissioned rather than leased for these purposes were small or without architectural significance save for two major exceptions: the custom houses in New York City and Boston.

The Custom House in New York had been constructed between 1834 and 1842 following the design by one of the nation's first architectural firms, the partnership of Ithiel Town and Alexander Jackson Davis. Their design, using as a model a Greek temple in the greatly admired Doric order (plate 30), called for porticoes composed of colossal columns to be placed at each end of the building above a high ground story. The prominence given to the basement level lifts the building above the street to give it a commanding presence within the existing urban setting. At the south front (Wall Street) the building was approached by a monumental stairway. Along the flanks the columns usually found down the sides of a Greek temple were replaced by massive projecting pilasters which conveyed the feeling of a Greek temple while avoiding the expense of constructing the required columns on all four sides.

The Greek temple form proposed for the Custom House was to be combined in Town and Davis's original design with a dome, a hallmark of Roman architecture. The combination of these two ancient classical forms was a scheme highly favored by the architects of this time, although purist critics of the day rejected such a solution since it combined features from two different moments in the development of classical architecture. Because of this critical hostility and a lack of agreement on how the design should be executed, Town and Davis's original plan was altered to conceal the dome beneath a more "proper" slanting roof. Upon its completion the New York Custom House was the most magnificent architectural representative of the federal government outside the capital city.

The impressive embellishment the federal government was adding to the city of New York immediately led its northern competitor, the port of Boston, to demand a similar commitment. Boston had no intention of being bested by New York when it came to the munificence of the Republic. Accordingly, in 1835 a select group of the Boston commercial community petitioned Congress to appropriate funds for constructing in their seaport a building equal or superior to the New York Custom House. Their request was promptly heeded by the Massachusetts delegation and three months later the full Congress authorized a new custom house for the city of Boston.

An act of Congress was required for the construction of a federal building because the Constitution assigned to the legislative branch the sole power for erecting such "needful buildings" as the federal government would come to require. The type of building and the method of their construction were matters the Constitution left to the determination of future Congresses. This broad mandate could be interpreted by Congress in any manner it pleased, at one extreme

*Figure 44*    Ammi B. Young.
*U. S. Custom House, Boston, 1837–47.*
Engraving, 1856.

authorizing a federal building to be "of such dimensions as may be required," at the other setting a moratorium on the addition of any buildings to the public inventory. Once authorized, appropriations by Congress for public buildings then became the responsibility of the secretary of the treasury, as part of his obligation to supervise the spending of all monies appropriated by Congress. In this particular area of responsibility, the secretary had to oversee the securing and letting of contracts for building materials, an area potentially rich in political patronage, as well as approve the appointment of a local representative to superintend the project, a decision also subject to political influence. Indeed, any aspect of establishing an outpost of the federal government was potentially subject to pressures from Congress or the Administration. At this time, where federal buildings would be located or how large or elaborate their design would be were not issues insulated from political pressures.

In the case of the Boston Custom House, the first step taken by the secretary of the treasury was the selection of a local board of commissioners, made up of those civic and business leaders who had initiated the original petition plus those whom the administration wanted to reward. It was the duty of the commissioners to select the site and design of the new building, as well as to supervise its construction, all subject to the approval of the secretary of the treasury (who, in this instance, actually visited Boston to inspect potential building sites). An open competition was held, and in 1837 the local commissioners chose the proposal submitted by New England architect Ammi B. Young (figures 44 and 45). After their choice was approved by the secretary of the treasury, the commissioners also chose Young to supervise the construction of his design. Like his fellow architects of the New York Custom House, Young chose to present the federal building in the guise of a Greek temple and, again like their original design, crowned his temple with a Roman dome. He, too, used a high ground story to raise the building well above street level but, unlike the scheme by Town and Davis, Young used Doric columns on all four sides and placed projecting porticoes along the flanks of the building. The location of the porticoes on the long sides and the use of columns on all four sides gave the lower, "temple" part of Young's building a strong visual impact, which made the low Roman dome appear to be a logical and proper crowning of the building, rather than the unhappy conjunction that was the case in the Town and Davis design for New York. Although also criticized by the purists for mixing Greek and Roman styles, Young's solution was generally applauded, and the dome gained great fame, particularly because it was the first stone dome erected in the United States. The majestic appearance of the exterior of Young's building was matched by the magnificence of the great rotunda of the banking hall (plate 29) which was reached by an impressive stairway leading from the street level.

Like the dome, all parts of the building were constructed in granite quarried in the nearby hills of Quincy, where the inventions of Solomon Willard—the designer of the Bunker Hill monument—for cutting and moving blocks of enormous size

*Figure 45* Ammi B. Young. *U. S. Custom House, Boston, 1837–47.* Photograph, ca. 1870.

enabled Young to endow his building with qualities of permanence that were as readily visible to the eye of passers-by at that time as they are today. The fluted shafts of the monolithic columns, the sharply carved triglyphs and mutules beneath the pediment, and the incised ornament of the interior all required a degree of skill in stonecarving that at that moment was perhaps available only in the area around the Quincy quarries. The amount of time required for such work was amazing: the carving of one newel post alone for the central stairway is recorded as requiring 789 hours. In its design, its materials, and its perfection of detail the Boston Custom House set the model for what a public building of the Republic should accomplish for both the central government and the town in which it was erected. One of the first buildings visitors saw as their ships sailed into Boston—the "Athens of the North"—the new custom house stood as a monument to the strength and glory of the young nation.

The New York and Boston custom houses were the beginning of what rapidly became a burgeoning program of replacing earlier, smaller custom houses with grander and larger buildings. During the 1840s Congress made appropriations for additional custom houses not only to meet the growing demands of thriving port cities, but also because the increased custom revenues justified the cost. As more and more projects came into being, the system of control followed by the secretary of the treasury up to that time began to falter, and its flaws became only too evident, and painful, to the occupant of that post. How cumbersome the process had become of exercising final approval in Washington of decisions made by local commissions can be seen in the events surrounding the construction of a custom house in Savannah, Georgia.

The process began in March 1845 with a congressional appropriation for the purchase of a site. Over the next two years a steady stream of letters descended on the secretary of the treasury from the citizens of Savannah expressing their concern over the choice of the architect and the location and size of the building, issues which were also actively pursued by the Georgia congressional delegation. Because of these efforts the secretary agreed to have the site for the new structure shifted away from the area originally chosen—described in a citizen's petition of June 1845 as being near "a number of Sailor Boarding Houses, grog shops, and a neighborhood very unsuitable"—for the intended building. However, their request that the eminent local architect Charles Cluskey be allowed to design the building was not granted. Despite glowing recommendations from Savannah made as early as May 1845, the secretary chose John S. Norris as architect because, he explained, Norris's plan could be built for the money Congress had appropriated, whereas Cluskey's could not. When Norris's appointment was officially announced in January 1846, the secretary was immediately petitioned by hundreds of outraged Savannah citizens to reverse his decision. Describing Norris as "an architect from New York"—even though he was currently at work on another custom house in nearby Wilmington, Georgia—they complained that by this appointment of someone from outside their own community the central government was misrepresenting the "capacity of our people." Their petition concludes with the hope that after due reflection a decision will be made with "a proper regard for the rights and interests of our Citizens generally" as well as with a "single eye to the advancement of the arts in every section of the Country, by exciting a spirit of emulation in the Mechanicks particularly." A year later, in February 1847, well after Norris had begun work, a letter of complaint was sent by numerous citizens of Savannah to President James Polk, protesting the injustice done to Cluskey, who had been "superseded by an individual from New York" (National Archives, R.G. 121).

The citizens' petitions for the need for a larger building, strengthened by the pressures of the congressional delegation, met with greater success, and in March 1847 the secretary of the treasury agreed to suspend the ongoing work on the custom house until additional appropriations then in the course of passage were adopted. Norris had made a larger, alternate plan the preceding summer and had carried out the foundation work so that it could easily accommodate an enlarged building. At the same time the secretary was attempting to satisfy the local citizens and the Congressmen over these issues he also was required personally to approve such matters related to the building process as whether or not a boat could be purchased rather than hired to haul sand, or a wagon bought to cart stone. All such decisions required his written approval.

Despite all these problems the outcome was, at least for the citizens of Savannah, a happy one. Reporting on the cornerstone laying in July 1848, the *Savannah Weekly Georgian* hailed the New York architect's talents, saying his design would produce the most "beautiful and substantial building between Washington and New Orleans" (figure 46). The secretary of the treasury, however, continued to be embroiled in matters concerning the architect's compensation as late as 1854, two years after the completion of the building.

In New Orleans during these same years the problems inherent in the requirement for the secretary of the treasury to supervise the construction of a building by working with a local commission and a local architect became so difficult, it became apparent that some other system had to be devised. The New Orleans project became particularly onerous for the secretary because of feuding within the community which quickly escalated to political infighting in Washington. From 1845, when Congress first appropriated money for plans for a new custom house, to 1852, when a plan was finally set, no less than three men occupied the local position of superintending architect. The troubles indicated by these shifts were the results of a complex mixture of practicality and politics.

One principal problem arose from the location of the new building on a plot of ground marking the southern limit of the Creole district of New Orleans. This community had actually donated the site to the federal government for this purpose, and they clearly perceived the building to be an embellishment for their section of the city. The original design by A. T. Wood adopted in 1847 (plates 31–34) amply fulfilled their expectations with its grand central banking hall and the imposing stairways leading to it. When, after the abrupt dismissal of Wood in 1850, the subsequent superintending architect, James Dakin, suggested that this great banking hall would be better located on the side of the building facing away from the Creole community, they viewed this proposal as an attempt to transfer to the adjoining section of the city the commercial advantages, as well as the public embellishment, they had anticipated would come to their own community. Passionate debate and protest immediately ensued, and the Creole community quickly passed a resolution addressed to the secretary of the treasury expressing its fierce opposition to changing the location of the banking room and to any other changes in Wood's original design.

A few months later Senator Pierre Soule introduced an amendment to the federal general appropriations bill for 1851–52 prohibiting any changes in the design. Instead, the Senate passed an amendment requiring that the president himself appoint the architect, with the advice and approval of the Senate. However, when in March 1851 President Millard Fillmore nominated James Dakin, the architect who had proposed the changes, the Senate rejected him. The next day the president nominated James Gallier; the Senate approved, but Gallier declined. In September, Dakin resigned.

In October an interim appointment of a superintending architect was made and Wood was appointed to be an advisor to the project to guarantee the fulfillment of his original plan. In November, however, the secretary of the treasury summoned an impartial board of examiners to consider Dakin's proposed revisions of Wood's original design. After a month-long hearing the board reached the conclusion that all the changes proposed by Dakin were indeed desirable. In December, President Fillmore once more submitted a nomination to the Senate for the position of local superintending architect, but it, too, was rejected after running into objections from Senator Soule. Finally, some two months after receiving the conclusions of the impartial board of examiners, the secretary of the treasury ignored their unanimous advice and decided to proceed with the original Wood plan. Not until 1856—eleven years after the initial appropriation—was any part of the building ready for occupancy (plate 35), and it was not finally completed until well after the Civil War.

The many problems concerning the construction of new buildings which had embroiled previous secretaries of the treasury in endless controversies were apparently well known to the new secretary appointed by President Franklin Pierce in 1853. For shortly after taking office, Secretary James Guthrie set up a new division in his department entitled Construction Branch of the Treasury and appointed as its head Captain Alexander H. Bowman of the U. S. Army Corps of Engineers. Ammi B. Young, who had been brought into the department in 1850 as supervising architect, probably because of his work on the Boston Custom House, was named to be his assistant. Together, these two men would put into practice a

*Figure 46* John S. Norris.
*U. S. Custom House, Savannah, Georgia, 1846–52.*
Photograph, ca. 1900.

system for designing and constructing public buildings on a national scale that had no parallel elsewhere in the world.

At the time of the founding of this new office the United States owned only twenty-three custom houses, with an additional fifteen in the course of construction. The ongoing work at these sites now fell under the direction of Bowman and Young, who would also be responsible for supervising the construction of an additional forty-six new buildings in the course of the next three years. That the fledgling office could support such a vast increase in the government's building operations was due primarily to the fact that the control over all aspects of site selection, materials, and construction, as well as the design of all buildings, had been transferred from local commissioners, whose actions were subject to the approval of the secretary, to a single, central bureau directly under his control. Concentration of these activities ensured the success of new management systems instituted by Captain Bowman which required regular progress reports on construction, as well as detailed accounts on the disbursement of funds from the local site superintendents appointed by the secretary. In his first annual report (1854), he noted how advantageous it was that the preparation of all plans, specifications, estimates, and contracts were carried out within one office. Perhaps

in an attempt to mollify whatever resentment was aroused by the end of the practice of allowing local citizens to have a voice in these matters, he also observed that since the buildings were being designed with "frequent discussion with those who occupy them," they were more likely to suit their purpose better.

The new Construction Branch in the treasury greatly increased its efficiency not only because it possessed the power to control all the construction activities of the federal government, but also because of the uniform practices introduced by Bowman and Young in the preparation of the working drawings and specifications for a building. In the case of the specifications prepared for each building—which spelled out the type and grade of materials required, the quality of the workmanship demanded from all the trades, and exactly how particular sections of the building must be assembled—the bureau, followed the example introduced by Young in 1852 for the Cincinnati Custom House and adopted a uniform system for prescribing these standards. As the bureau began applying these identical specifications to all its buildings, a common level of performance for the work on a federal building was established regardless of where it might be located. The system vastly simplified the preparation of contract documents and enabled the central control process to become effective.

Bowman also introduced another measure of quality control by having the bureau itself contract directly with the manufacturer for the purchase of the wrought-iron girders and beams that, at his urging, the government was now requiring in all its buildings. The ironwork for the floors and ceilings in the Post Office at Wheeling, West Virginia, for example, were ordered by the bureau from the Trenton Iron Works in New Jersey, from whom the ultimate contractor for the building would have to purchase them. In the case of the Custom House at Sandusky, Ohio, the Construction Branch not only ordered the material but also arranged for the wrought-iron beams and girders to be delivered to a wharf on Lake Erie.

These steps toward effectively controlling the quality of federal buildings were enhanced by Young's creation of a standard type of design for buildings that served the same governmental function no matter where they were located. Young had already initiated this practice in 1852 when he prepared almost identical designs for custom houses in Cincinnati, Ohio, and Norfolk, Virginia. The benefits of creating a uniform building type that could be duplicated at different sites were enormous, and they were made even more so by Young introducing at this time the practice of publishing the elevations, plans, and detailed working drawings as lithographic prints, thereby significantly reducing the amount of time spent in tracing the working drawings in order to provide copies needed by the contractors, manufacturers, and field supervisors. Bowman apparently saw the usefulness of Young's system, for it became standard operating procedure in the new office and was a key factor in its incredible performance in such a short period.

Bowman and Young's innovations enabled them to design and issue specifications on thirty-five new buildings during the years 1855 and 1856, more than double the number of completed buildings the office had inherited in 1853. The practice of issuing all the working drawings as lithographic prints became fundamental to their operation the moment they were put into general use. In 1855 seven buildings of identical design were planned for Buffalo and Oswego, New York; Newark, New Jersey; New Haven, Connecticut; Chicago, Illinois (plate 37); Milwaukee, Wisconsin; and Wheeling, West Virginia. For each of these a set of nine working drawings was prepared which controlled the building's structure and appearance. The arrangement and function of rooms within the buildings were varied to meet local requirements or preferences, but all other aspects of their design were identical. In fact, of the nine working drawings, six were so identical they could be printed from the same lithographic stones. Thus, the stone bearing details for the interior of the Wheeling Post Office (plate 36) was also used for the other six buildings; the only change required on the lithographic stone was the substitution of one location for another. The following year an identical design was used in three other cities: Detroit, Michigan; Cleveland, Ohio; and Dubuque, Iowa. Again, almost all the lithographic plates detailing the design of shutters, doors, staircases, newel posts, and post boxes were identical, many in fact being the same plates used the previous year for buildings of this type.

For the thirty-five new buildings the bureau was responsible for in this two-year period, only fifteen different designs were prepared. Six of these were unique designs for buildings in six different cities. Of the remaining nine design types, however, one was used at ten different sites; three types were used in three different locations; and five types were applied to buildings in at least two different cities. The fifteen designs created by Young are all similar in style, if not identical in details. For smaller buildings, such as the custom houses built in Gloucester, Massachusetts, and Petersburgh, Virginia (plate 38), the decorative details on the exterior were minimal, but the proportions, scale, and overall design are the same as that of the larger buildings in Chicago or Wheeling (figure 47). Another variant was his design for the post office of Rutland, Vermont (plate 39), which was repeated in that same state at Windsor. Here, by the introduction of decorative ironwork transoms and cast-iron imitations of intricately carved stonework around the openings, Young offers a more decorative design. Although he creates variants within the nine basic design types, his building style remains consistent and easily recognizable. No longer, however, does Young depend solely on pure classical prototypes for his buildings. His new work marks the beginning of his adaptation of the Italian-palace style which some critics of the day were advocating and examples of which were readily at hand in the library of the Construction Branch, which contained books liberally illustrating the Italian buildings. For the many Roman palaces Young had access to the publications of Le Tarouilly (figures 38 and 40), for those in Tuscany, to an 1815 work by Grandjean de Montigny (figure 48).

Young's move from the classic revival style to one more akin to the Italian-palace style seems to coincide with the formation of the treasury department's

*Figure 47*  Ammi B. Young.
*U. S. Custom House, Wheeling, West Virginia, 1856–60.*
Photograph, ca. 1860.

*Figure 48*
*Gondi Palace, Florence.*
Engraving from Grandjean de Montigny, 1815.

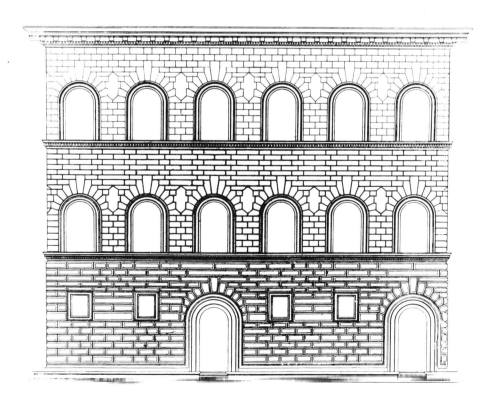

*Figure 49* Ammi B. Young.
*Front elevation of the U. S. Custom House, Cincinnati, Ohio.*
Lithograph, 1852.

*Figure 50* Ammi B. Young.
*Front elevation of the U. S. Custom House, Bath, Maine.*
Lithograph, 1853.

Construction Branch in 1853. Only the previous year Young's twin designs for the Cincinnati (figure 49) and Norfolk custom houses were descended from his earlier work in the Greek Revival style. Their vocabulary of temple fronts, columnar porticoes, and refined classical detail is also found in his design of 1850 for the custom house in Charleston, South Carolina, or his earlier courthouse at Worcester, Massachusetts, of 1842. But the very first two buildings he designed as a member of the new central construction bureau are distinct departures from this familiar style. A single design adopted by Young in 1853 for the modest custom houses at Wilmington, Delaware, and Bath, Maine (figure 50), appears to be a tentative essay in the development of his new personal style.

Young's adaptation of an Italianate style would appear to have been in response to the challenge of developing a standard building type which, with slight changes, could produce buildings of different appearance. The search for such a style may prototypes imposed on his work. His amazing outburst in this new style in the period 1855–56 exudes the feeling of discovery and freedom that often characterizes an artist's delight in a new means of expression. Young's Italianate buildings maintained a classical grandeur for the federal image while responding to charges made by some critics that a democratic form of government ought not to be

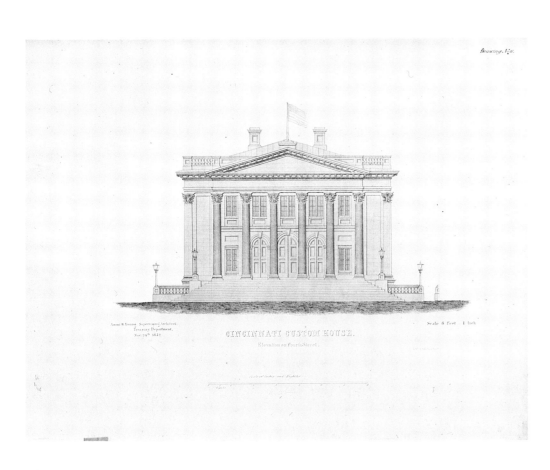

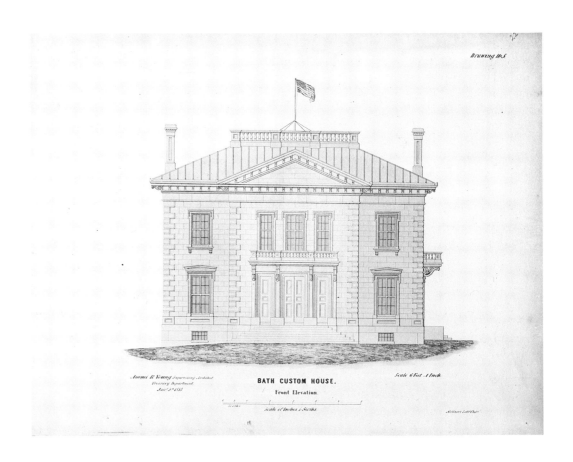

represented by ostentatious, expensive buildings such as the monumental, classical custom houses of Boston and New Orleans. He had invented a new type of federal building which provided the government with an image of solidity and seriousness of purpose by its sober and classical austerity and was also a decorative and pleasing addition to the community much appreciated by the local citizenry. As the Dubuque *Daily Times* remarked on January 25, 1861, about its new custom house (figure 51), "It will ever be the pride of our citizens to point it out to the stranger as a monument of beauty and strength."

After the burgeoning design program of 1855–56 the need for new building designs dropped sharply as the office endeavored to complete the ones already started, most of which were finished in a substantially shorter period of time than previous federal buildings. As Young had little opportunity to design new buildings during the next four years, we are denied the possibility of charting the evolution of his new style. But in 1860, near the end of his tenure in office, a post office/courthouse was authorized for Philadelphia which gives us an idea of how Young's use of this style had matured. The description accompanying the lithographic prints produced for this building (included in a bound volume from the Supervising Architect's office now in the National Archives, R.G. 121) gives a succinct statement of his approach to the design of such buildings:

The style and architectural character adopted for the building is Italian, with Grecian details. . . . The exterior of the entrance story has a columnar ordonnance, suggested by a study of the Palace Massini [*sic*], Stradda della Valle, Rome, over which, on Chestnut street, are two stories, and on Library street one story of Fenestral Italian ordonnance, crowned by an appropriate cornicion, similar in many respects to that of the Faranese [*sic*] Palace at Rome. The fronts on Chestnut and Library streets are somewhat elaborately ornamented; but, at the same time, there has been kept in view a severe chasteness of character, preventing, as it is believed, an overloading of the parts and giving them a pleasing effect to the eye; while the flank towards the custom-house is so managed as to add to the importance of the two fronts, and at the same time, assuming sufficient character in itself to make it a chaste and appropriate architectural composition.

Young's description of his intention in the design of the Philadelphia post office not only identifies the sources of his inspiration in the Roman palaces, but also reveals his sensitivity to the setting of the building and its relationship to the surrounding spaces and structures. He was particularly aware that his building in the new style would be located near the famed example of Greek Revival architecture, Strickland's Second Bank of the United States (then in use as a custom house). The flank facing the custom house was designed by Young not only in relationship to the two fronts of his own building, but also with respect to its more chaste neighbor.

Young was aware, too, of the proximity of his building to Independence Hall and developed as the central ornamental feature of the entrances to the post office a large, candelabra-like lamp standard (figure 52) that included a replica of the Liberty Bell. His use of this national icon as a decorative element was in one sense

*Figure 51*  Ammi B. Young.
*U. S. Custom House and Post Office, Dubuque, Iowa, 1857–66.*
Photograph, ca. 1880.

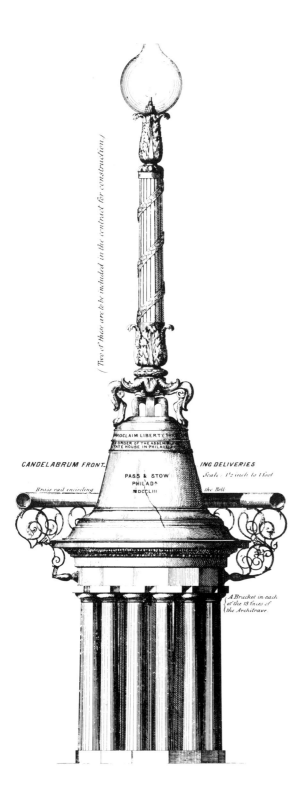

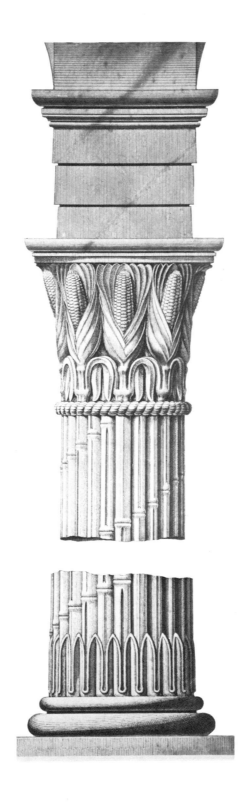

*Figure 52* Ammi B. Young.
*Design of a candelabrum incorporating a replica of the Liberty Bell*
*for the U. S. Post Office and Courthouse, Philadelphia, 1860.*
Lithograph, 1861.

*Figure 53* Benjamin H. Latrobe.
*Design of the corn column for the U. S. Capitol, 1806.*
Engraving from Brown, 1900–1903.

comparable to L'Enfant's use of specifically American symbols in his 1789 design of the Federal Hall in New York City, or to Latrobe's invention of capitals utilizing such American plants as tobacco, cotton, and corn (figure 53) for the Capitol. But the acclaim that had greeted these American inventions was not long sustained. Already by the middle of the century critics no longer considered such national references the way in which a distinctive American architecture could be created. What is different about Young's adoption of such a national symbol as the Liberty Bell is his use of it only as part of an independent decorative object, not as an element in the basic architectural decoration of the building, which was strictly limited to classical and Renaissance ornamental motifs (plate 40). This same distinction between architectural ornament and decorative furnishing is evident in the work in progress at the Treasury Building during these same years, which came under Young's jurisdiction as supervising architect. Here, in a purely classical structure the design for the chandeliers, as well as various types of wall brackets, carry references to the American Indian. Designed by J. Goldsborough Bruff, a draftsman in the Office of the Supervising Architect who had perhaps actually observed such scenes when he briefly left the office to seek his fortune in the 1849 gold rush, they include such native subjects as a campfire scene and a buffalo hunt (figure 54).

The elaborate decorative detailing Young lavished on the candelabra of the Philadelphia Post Office (plate 41) gives us a clear idea of his love and gift for ornamentation, but it also underscores the restraint he practiced when using it as part of an architectural composition. No decorative element is allowed to distract the viewer's attention from the overall mass of the building and the clarity of its parts. Like his Renaissance and classical models, rich ornament enhances and complements the basic architectonic forms. In a design such as the Philadelphia Post Office, Young seems to have captured the essence of the Grecian principles of architecture—the combination of a purity of solid forms with the delicacy of ornamental motifs based on nature—and created thereby an architectural imagery that could well fit the cry of some critics of the day for a style that was truly American.

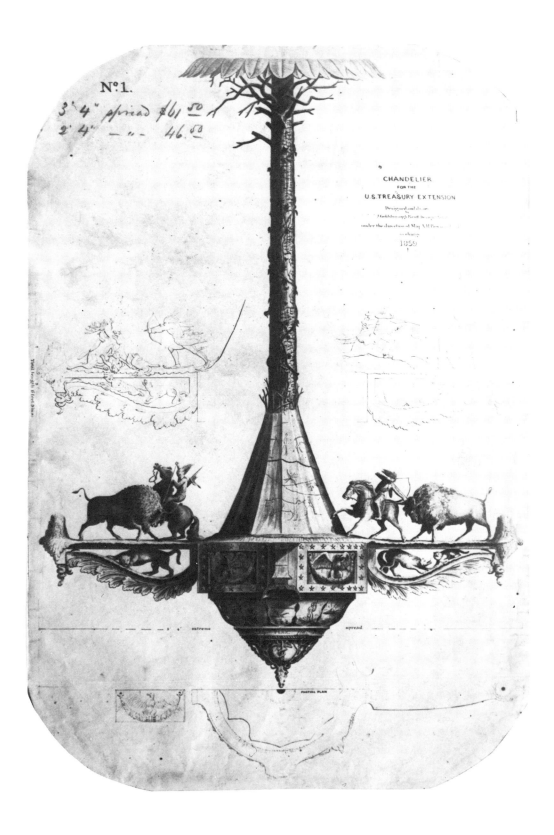

*Figure 54* J. Goldsborough Bruff.
*Design of a gas chandelier with buffalo hunt for the U. S. Treasury extension, 1859.*
Whereabouts unknown.

Between 1866 and 1897, the years following the close of the Civil War, the federal government built nearly three hundred new buildings throughout the Union. By the end of this period the Office of the Supervising Architect—formerly the Construction Branch—of the Treasury Department was responsible for eight times as many buildings as it had been at its inception in 1853. As a result of this incredible increase in the number of buildings authorized by Congress, almost every large municipality, as well as small towns with particularly effective congressmen, had acquired an official, distinctive building whose presence led to glowing expressions of patriotic pride. The appearance of the federal buildings constructed during this period was in sharp contrast to those erected in the preceding years of the century. The severe classicism of the 1830s and the Italian Renaissance palace style that had been practiced by Ammi B. Young were abandoned. In their place designs following specific historical periods were adopted, or were created by combining motifs from a variety of epochs or nations. The result was a panoply of federal buildings stretching across the nation whose sole common bond was that they all owed their parentage to a single office in Washington. That their design was so varied was due in part to the fact that during this period a far greater number of supervising architects occupied this office than before, and their work was more apt to resemble the multifarious styles that characterized the private architectural practice of the day. But it also clearly reflected that during this period both agreement and conviction were lacking on the proper form to be given to a public building that represented the federal government.

Ironically, just at the moment when pent-up demand for the resumption of building projects suspended during the Civil War was at its highest and the need and desire for new buildings was daily being voiced in Congress, the Office of the Supervising Architect abandoned the standard building types so successfully introduced before the war by Alexander Bowman and Ammi B. Young. Alfred B. Mullett, the supervising architect appointed in 1866, firmly rejected the principle that buildings destined to serve the same purpose, no matter where they were located, should be built according to similar designs. In his first official report, of 1866, Mullett explicitly stated that he endeavored to avoid "the repetition of style and design so common heretofore, that, while exhibiting a poverty of idea, has retarded instead of encouraged the cultivation of correct taste and a love of art, without effecting the slightest saving, except in the labors of the designer." Mullett's rejection of a standard building type applied not only to the basic plan of the building and the composition of its exterior design, but also to all the ornamental detailing of its interior. His new designs, he hoped, would be "found to be more in accordance with the principles of architecture than those formerly prepared" (S. A. T. Report, 1866, p. 189).

Mullett aimed to design each building according "to the material adopted; the wants of the officers and the public; to the peculiarities of soil and climate, and the necessities of the various localities." He also endeavored "to attain the greatest permanency of construction" at the least expense. A consequence of this approach was the abandonment of the previous practice of using the same or nearly identical designs for buildings in different locations, which had allowed the working drawings to be reproduced on lithographic plates. Instead, Mullett's new direction required that the central office provide innumerable drawings in ink and in watercolor to ensure that the construction of the actual building, under the direction of the site architect, followed the original, approved design.

This control required that detailed drawings be prepared for every aspect of a building's construction. Not one detail could be left to the discretion of the local supervisor of the work, who in many cases, as Mullett frequently complained in his annual reports, had received the position as a political favor and felt no need to be overzealous in its execution. Accordingly, under Mullett the office set an unbelievably high standard for the quality of the architectural drawings prepared for a building, from the views of the entire buildings (plate 43) down to detailed drawings for the ironwork (plate 46). From these original ink and watercolor drawings as many tracings were made as were needed for the field supervisors and the contracting officers. Blueprints appear to have been used only rarely at this period, so that the number of draftsmen employed by the Office of the Supervising Architect increased each year as both the number and size of the projects increased. Such growth was possible because the cost of the drawings was assigned to the specific project, thus not requiring a separate appropriation from Congress to cover the salaries of the draftsmen.

The extent to which control by Washington was maintained by these drawings is demonstrated by the number of original watercolor drawings extant for the construction of the New York post office. A staggering eight hundred drawings concerned with every aspect of its construction still remain, including drawings prepared for every course of granite laid for the four-story building. Each drawing identifies the quarried block with a number and shows where it is located in a particular stone course and how it is to be clamped to its neighboring stone. Equally detailed are the drawings for the ironwork of the building, from the wrought-iron columns of the lower three stories, which allowed Mullett to create a completely open space within the self-bearing masonry perimeter walls, to the complex design of the ribs supporting the crowning mansards.

The drawings for the custom house in Portland, Maine, exemplify how the nature of the decorative detailing Mullett wanted to achieve was communicated to those responsible for executing it (plates 44–47). The quality of the drawings is so The drawings for the custom house in Portland, Maine, exemplify how the encourage the same level of craftsmanship in the workers who executed the stone- and ironwork. The draftsmen who prepared such drawings certainly conceived of them as works of art in themselves, from the placement of the elements on the sheet to the rendering of how individual pieces were to be joined. To a present-day viewer some take on an existence of their own as abstract works of art, each charged with an independent energy.

Although Mullett preferred the individuality of his buildings to the standard building type instituted by Young and Bowman, the body of work he produced during his eight-year tenure as supervising architect is nevertheless clearly marked by the prevalence of certain architectural elements which subsequently became identified as hallmarks of the federal style. Although one of Mullett's first designs after taking office in 1866, the U. S. Branch Mint in Carson City (plate 43), was much in the tradition of the building type developed by Young, another of his designs of the same year, the custom house and post office in Springfield, Illinois, displayed what would become one of Mullett's favorite design elements: the mansard roof. Mullett used this type of roof over and over in his designs, and his buildings became characterized by their elaborate skylines achieved by an aggregation of curved mansard roofs, dormers, cupolas, and lanterns, all inspired by the elaborate designs of the buildings erected in Paris during the Second Empire, particularly the new additions to the palace of the Louvre (figure 55).

*Figure 55*   L.-T.-J. Visconti and H.-M. Lefuel. *New Louvre, Paris, 1852–57.* Photograph by Edouard Baldus, ca. 1860.

*Figure 56* George B. Post.
*Western Union Telegraph Building, New York, 1873–75.*
Engraving from *New York Illustrated*, 1874.

Another characteristic of Mullett's style was the projecting wall surface achieved by stepped vertical offsets, or created by layering the wall with an abundance of porticoes, balconies, and stairways, or by surrounding the windows and doors with ornate embellishment. These complemented one another to create a building alive with light and shadow on the lower mass of the building's block and a variety of silhouettes above. Mullett's buildings, however, never relied on a flamboyant use of ornament, nor did he abandon the classical style to mitigate or articulate their mass, as was the practice of the architects designing the commercial structures going up in New York City in the 1870s. In contrast to their richly ornamented and architecturally novel fronts, such as the Western Union Telegraph Building of 1873–75 by George B. Post (figure 56), the government buildings were at once more simple and more imposing.

Mullett was able to develop his style to the fullest because his term of office coincided with the desire, and need, for ever-larger federal buildings. In addition to the mammoth State, War and Navy Building in Washington, D. C., gigantic courthouses, custom houses and post offices were begun between 1867 and 1874 in Philadelphia, Chicago, Saint Louis, Cincinnati, Boston, and New York (figures 58 and 59). Although Mullett designed each of these buildings, not all were completed according to his initial plans, as the construction work extended far beyond his term as supervising architect. He was nevertheless responsible for establishing the federal presence in major cities of the country in highly visible, bold, and striking buildings. The post office in New York City was the building Mullett believed would establish his reputation as an architect of note, for, as he remarked in his letter of resignation in 1874, the position "paid such little recompense that no one would take it except for the chance of enhancing his reputation" (National Archives, R.G. 121). Thus, with the New York building almost complete, Mullett could resign assured that he had gained his objective.

The particulars of the quest for a design for the New York building certainly strengthen Mullett's belief that the building would be recognized as his masterpiece. The search began in 1867 with an open competition, in which two-thirds of the entries were based on seminal works recently constructed in Paris in the new French style (figure 55), the dominant element of which was the convex mansard roof already favored by Mullett. The overwhelming majority of the fifty-one entries described in the *New York Times* of June 7, 1867, were said to have mansard roofs and "balloon and pyramidal pavilions" similar to those of the Louvre and Tuileries palaces in Paris. No single design was chosen as the winner of this competition; instead, five entrants were asked to prepare an amalgamated design. In March 1868, the result (figure 57) was described by the architects in an accompanying report as being designed in "the pure French Renaissance style." At this point the House of Representatives officially requested the secretary of the treasury to give detailed cost estimates of the amalgamated plan. He passed the task on to Mullett, who prepared a lengthy, highly critical report dealing essentially with technical matters, but concluding that there need be no change in

*Figure 57*
*Amalgamated design for the U.S. Post Office and Courthouse, New York.*
Ink drawing, 1867. National Archives.

*Figure 58* Alfred B. Mullett.
*Design for the U.S. Post Office and Courthouse, New York.*
Ink drawing, 1868. National Archives.

the type of exterior design proposed by the five architects. In addition, he submitted a proposal of his own (plate 53) which closely resembled the amalgamated design.

Over the next year there were disagreements between the five architects and Mullett, political infighting over the site, which had already been purchased in 1867, and contention over who would have administrative control over actual construction. At some point Mullett apparently was put in charge of the whole project and produced further designs of his own (figure 58, plates 54 and 55), which were a departure from the earlier amalgamated design. The principal difference between the two rested in the way Mullett made the central pavilion of the south side into an active, baroque composition, which he achieved by breaking up the wall surface here into a number of clearly defined vertical elements each successively recessed from the central pavilion (figure 59). Since each vertical unit is given its own terminating roof element, a far more elaborate skyline resulted than that proposed in the amalgamated design. Two sharply pitched pyramidal mansard roofs flank a large balloon mansard, which in turn encompasses a smaller balloon mansard whose elaborate dormer window crowns the pediment that tops the central pavilion. In its final form Mullett's design exhibits his inspiration from the Second Empire style structures of Paris (figure 60), which in this case enabled

Figure 60    Gabriel Davioud.
Fontaine Saint-Michel, Paris, 1860.
Photograph, ca. 1875.

him to use a potentially awkward site in a manner that produced a triumphant sequence of richly ornamented wall surfaces that flowed rhythmically from the central pavilion on either side.

A *New York Times* reporter who visited the roof of the new post office on October 29, 1873, was incredulous at the panorama that spread before him. The Trinity Church spire no longer dominated the skyline of the city, he observed. Except for the efforts being made both by "the diminutive groups" working on the Brooklyn Bridge and by the "tradesmen hammering away" on the Western Union Building, he wrote, "the builders of the new Post Office might congratulate themselves as being without rival in the field of colossal architecture." Although the mass of the New York example would soon lose the dominance it once had on the Manhattan skyline which can be seen in an 1876 view from Brooklyn (figure 61), in other cities the monumentality of Mullett's buildings assured them a long life as the architectural symbols of the central government.

Another dramatic shift in the appearance of federal buildings took place in 1875 when William A. Potter succeeded Mullett as supervising architect. Well known for his buildings designed in the Victorian Gothic style, particularly those erected at Princeton University, Potter immediately adopted this style for his designs of custom houses, post offices, and courthouses destined for various parts of the country. Suddenly public buildings reminiscent of civic structures in Rouen, Antwerp, or Bruges graced such American towns as Evansville, Indiana (figure 62), Covington, Kentucky (figure 63), and Fall River, Massachusetts (plate 56). For the citizens in these communities the buildings of their national government now took on a medieval guise.

By introducing the medieval style into the design of federal buildings, Potter reversed an attitude that had strongly resisted the application of this style to buildings representing the Republic. Although from time to time designs in styles other than the classical had been proposed for public buildings, they had never met with success. Some of the designs entered in the 1867 competition for the New York post office, for example, were described in the *New York Times* as being inspired by the Byzantine architecture of Venice, the Moorish style of the Alhambra, and by the Gothic cathedral of Notre-Dame in Paris; however, the designs selected as the basis for the ensuing amalgamated one (figure 57) were all variations on the French classical or Renaissance styles. In 1846 James Dakin had submitted a building in the Gothic castle style to the competition for the New Orleans custom house, but he must have been dissuaded from this approach by the local commissioners, for in the following year he submitted a design in the Greek Revival style. In the 1850 competition for the custom house in Charleston, South Carolina, the local commissioners did choose a Gothic castle design, by E. C. Jones, as the winning entry. However, their choice was rejected by the secretary of the treasury, and a classical plan by Ammi B. Young, similar to his Boston custom house (figure 45), was adopted.

Only one exception to the steadfast rejection of every non-classical style for

*Figure 61*
*View of Manhattan during construction of the Brooklyn Bridge.*
Photograph by Joshua H. Beal, 1876.

*Figure 62*  William A. Potter.
*U. S. Custom House and Post Office, Evansville, Indiana, 1876–79.*

*Figure 63*  William A. Potter.
*U. S. Courthouse and Post Office, Covington, Kentucky.*
Design published in the *S. A. T. Report*, 1875.

federal buildings had occurred before Potter's incumbency. In the early 1840s, when Congress was still determining what type of national institution should be set up to accord with the generous bequest of James Smithson, the two architects most associated with the classical style—Robert Mills (figure 64) and Alexander Jackson Davis (figure 65)—both proposed buildings in the medieval style for the new institute. Although Davis also proposed an impressive, domed classical building, all the designs subsequently entered in the formal competition of 1846 were in the medieval style. The winning design by James Renwick was cast in the English medieval style called Norman (plates 57 and 58). Although in part this concentration on the medieval style might have been due to the semi-collegiate character of the Smithsonian Institution, the adoption of it was due principally to the strongly held belief in the virtues of the medieval style by Congressman Robert Dale Owen, the chief supporter of the Smithsonian and, ultimately, the most influential member of the committee charged with choosing the building's design.

Owen was firmly convinced that the medieval style offered greater opportunities for developing a truly national American style because it was more practical than the classical modes. He particularly objected to the rigidity of the classical style, pointing out that in following a temple plan, the architect was forced to arrange the rooms within its rectangular straightjacket, whereas the irregular and flexible plan of the medieval type allowed the architect to arrange the rooms according to the function they were to serve—an observation made as early as 1836 by an

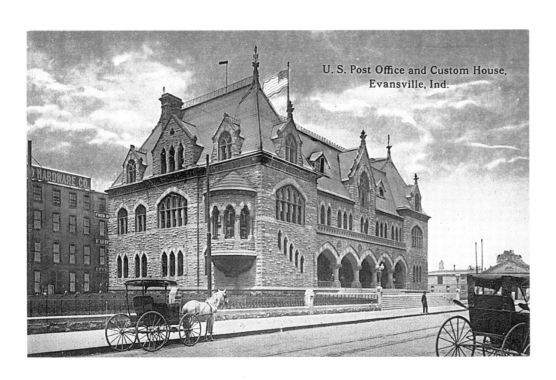

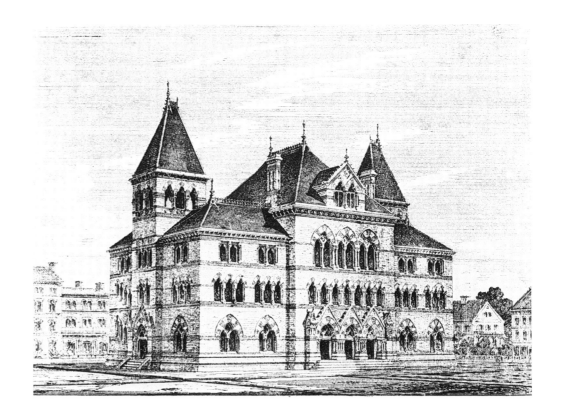

anonymous writer in *North American Review* (p. 363). As Owen put it, a building in the medieval style could be designed from the inside out. Such buildings, he observed, could easily be added to, and they allowed better heating and ventilating systems than did the Greek or Roman temples, which never had sported chimneys on their roofs or suffered window openings in their walls.

In Owen's terms, then, the basic superiority of the medieval style rested in its utilitarian aspect as well as its practical, for he considered it cheaper to build than the classical style. However, he confessed that another of its charms was its variety. Unlike Greek architecture, which he characterized as being made up of identical parts, medieval buildings depended more upon ornament inspired by nature, where no leaf in a forest is a "servile" copy of another. These arguments, plus the force of Owen's personality and his cunning manipulation of the selection process, resulted in this singular alien note being struck among the classical buildings of the capital city.

Although Owen succeeded in his goal with the Smithsonian building, some thirty years would pass before the medieval style would invade the classical realm of federal building. That this prolonged rejection of the non-classical was not solely the result of aesthetic choice but was also due to associations the medieval style awakened is dramatically revealed by Horatio Greenough's responses during a visit to the capital city. While walking along the Potomac one night the sight of the Capitol in the moonlight made him reflect on how it recorded "the labors, sufferings, and triumphs of the champions of freedom; of free thought and belief; of free speech and free action." Suddenly his vision was interrupted by the dark form of the Smithsonian: "Tower and battlement, and all that medieval confusion, stamped itself on the halls of Congress, as ink on paper! Dark on that whiteness—complication on that simplicity! It scared me." It threatened, it was monastic and thus too closely associated with the theological doctrines and politics he had observed in Rome. Although his fears were somewhat allayed by looking more closely at the building and discovering that it was not a solid fortress, he still could not recover from his alarm. The towers and steep belfries continued to make him uneasy and he wondered, "Is no *coup d'etat* lurking there?" (Greenough 1851, pp. 17–18).

Such associations had faded from the public's mind by the time Potter introduced his medieval courthouses, post offices, and custom houses into the American cities of the 1870s. Indeed, associations between a particular historic style and the moral and political character of the period or nation in which it had been produced were no longer so clearly drawn. What form of architecture was appropriate for the American republic was no longer a question much debated, nor was any one architectural style considered inherently superior to any other. How difficult it had become for architects to predict what might be considered an appropriate form for a federal building—even in the capital city of Washington—is amply attested to by the protracted difficulty encountered in the choice of a design for a building to house the Congressional library.

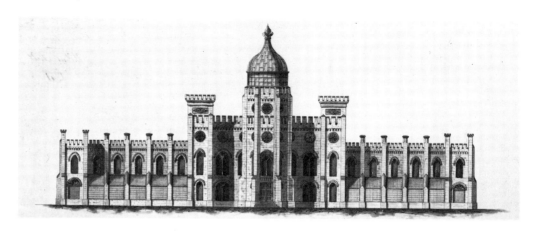

*Figure 64*  Robert Mills.
*Design for the Smithsonian Institution Building.*
Ink drawing, 1841. National Archives.

*Figure 65*  Alexander Jackson Davis.
*Designs for the Smithsonian Institution Building.*
Ink drawing, ca. 1840. The Metropolitan Museum of Art, New York.
(Harris, Brisbane, Dick Fund, 1924).

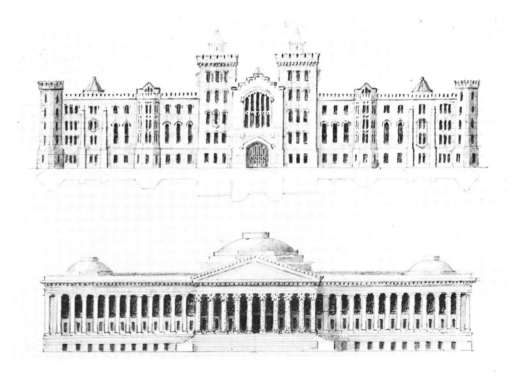

The search for a suitable building for the library started simply enough in August 1873 with the announcement of a competition for the design of a fireproof building to be built on Capitol Hill with a reading room at its center and a capacity for two million volumes. The exact dimensions were given, and it was also expressly stated that if the design included a dome, it must be lower than that of the Capitol. Twenty-eight entries were submitted. The winning entry, by the architectural firm of Smithmeyer & Pelz of Washington, D. C., was a design in the Italian Renaissance style without a dome (plate 59). The runner-up was Adolph E. Melander of Boston, whose entry was a far more decorative, classical style building with a low dome (figure 66) and an elaborate art gallery (plate 61). The extreme differences between these two winning designs are perhaps indicative of the lack of certainty on the part of the selection committee and foretell the long, sixteen-year struggle that was about to begin over what the correct design should be.

If the fourteen projects preserved today are truly representative of those submitted, there were basically three styles favored by the entrants, each of which was a variant on a classical style. In addition to those cast in the Italian Renaissance style of the winning design, others followed in the path of Melander and featured a more decorative treatment of a classical building, with a dome and extensive sculptural ornament (plate 60), while some favored the popular French Empire style, which in at least one case showed a remarkable originality in its presentation of the characteristic elements (plate 62).

None of the entries had favored a medieval, Moorish, or other exotic style for the library. Given this apparent unanimity of approach, the subsequent events in the search for a design are both startling and revealing, and they demonstrate how rapidly the concepts of what was a proper model for public architecture in America were changing. The very next year one of the three judges of the competition, Senator Timothy Otis Howe of Wisconsin, decided, after an inspection tour of the national libraries of Europe, that the winning entry was not grand enough for the United States and persuaded Congress to reopen the competition. His personal choice was for a design in the "Victorian Gothic" style.

Former competitors as well as new entrants took advantage of the re-opening of the competition. One of the new entries was by Alexander R. Esty of Framingham, Massachusetts, who offered a design in the now apparently preferred medieval style (plate 63). For the next twelve years Smithmeyer & Pelz submitted design after design to meet the shifting demands of the Senate committee, beginning with their "Victorian Gothic" design of 1874 (plate 64) and followed over the years by a thirteenth-century Gothic plan and a Romanesque design. When the medieval style was abandoned by the senators because it appeared too expensive, Smithmeyer & Pelz then produced designs in the French, German (plate 65), and "Modern" Renaissance styles, as well as variations on their original Italian Renaissance design. Finally, in 1885, Smithmeyer & Pelz prepared a far more elaborate development of their original 1873 design (plate 66). This was approved by Congress in 1886 and construction finally began. Not until 1889, however, did

*Figure 66*    Adolph E. Melander.
*Design entered in the 1873 competition for the Library of Congress.*
Heliotype.

Congress approve the final design (figure 67), which by now was closer in spirit to the much-admired Opera House in Paris (figure 68) by Charles Garnier, built between 1861 and 1875, than to any of the long series of designs that Smithmeyer & Pelz had produced to reach this point.

These shifts in the preference for different styles which marked the sixteen-year search for the design of the Library of Congress also characterized the work carried out at the same time by the Office of the Supervising Architect. After the brief eighteen-month tenure of William A. Potter (January 1875–July 1876), the office was held sequentially for the next decade by James G. Hill (August 1876–September 1883) and Mifflin E. Bell (November 1883–July 1887), both of whom designed federal buildings in such a variety of historical styles that the character of these public buildings became an expression of the individual, personal style of the architect in office rather than the result of a widely held philosophical belief.

The editor of the *American Architect and Building News* recognized this development in his comments in the issue of July 30, 1887, on the appointment of William A. Freret as the successor to Bell in the Office of the Supervising Architect. Although the salary is small, the editor pointed out, only a few years in the position will give its occupant "a permanent place in architectural history" (p. 45). He prophesies that when the history of the architecture of the United States is written, its subject matter will be derived primarily from the buildings erected by the federal government, "so that, to the future historian of American Art, the succession of the Government Architects will be nearly as important as that of the

*Figure 67*   Smithmeyer & Pelz.
*West front of the Library of Congress, 1886–97.*
Photograph by Richard Cheek, 1976.

*Figure 68*   Charles Garnier.
*Opera House, Paris, 1861–75.*
Photograph, ca. 1890.

kings of England in a British secular history" (p. 45). He foresees such a history of American architecture by the year 2000 as having chapters headed "The Mullett Era," "The Bell Style," or "The Freret Transition." His choice of title for the Freret era was ironically apt, for Freret held this office for only one year (1887–88) and was followed by a succession of four architects during the next seven years: James H. Windrim (1889–90); Willoughby J. Edbrooke (1891–92); Jeremiah O'Rourke (1893–94); William Martin Aiken (1895–97). Altogether the direction of the enormous building program of the federal government changed hands nine times during the period 1866–97, clearly exceeding the rate of succession of monarchs in any period of British history, as well as greatly expanding the possible style citizens might expect to find imposed on any federal building erected in their community.

As the designs of federal buildings during this period increasingly became the personal expression of the supervising architect, their quality fluctuated according to the talents of the incumbent. The standards set by the medieval buildings of Potter were not often matched by his successors who designed in that style.

Approved under Act of March 3rd 1875.

ELEVATION ON BROADWAY.

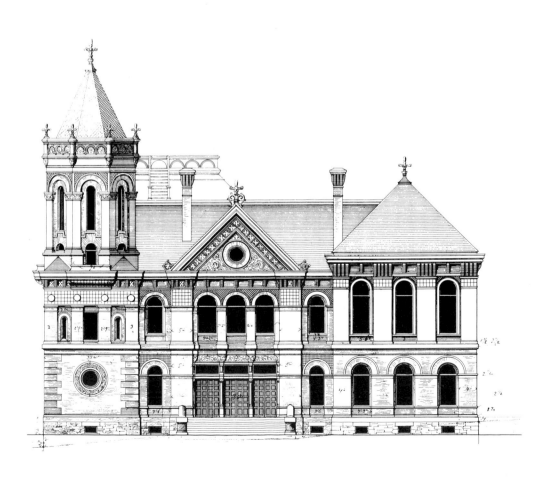

Potter's work in Evansville (figure 62), Covington (figure 63), and Fall River (plate 56) were models of their kind, reflecting his keen sensitivity to the delicate tracery of ironwork, the subtle shadings of polychromatic stonework, and the geometry of exposed wooden framework demanded by the Victorian Gothic style (plates 67–69). In his instinct for fine decorative detail and sense of harmonious proportions, Potter was a worthy forerunner of Henry Bacon, whose design for the Lincoln Memorial would bear these same hallmarks. The seven supervising architects who followed Potter showed less understanding of the balance between structure, space, and decoration that makes Potter's work so distinctive. They relied primarily on an elaborate use of rare and costly materials and a high quality of workmanship to endow their historically derived designs with an impressive appearance.

Of the more than two hundred and fifty buildings erected by these architects between 1876 and 1897 the predominant style was some form of medieval architecture to which each architect gave his own interpretation. One favorite form was the fortress-castle style, as found in Freret's 1889 building for Troy, New York (figure 69), and Windrim's post office in Sacramento, California, of 1890 (plate 76). Two other designs of 1889 by Freret display a more fanciful approach to the castle style, one for Bridgeport, Connecticut, and the other for Vicksburg, Mississippi (figure 70), the latter looking as if its inspiration had come from the cubic forms of the Anchor blocks that were a favorite instructional toy for children of this period. A more robust and serious approach to this form had been taken in 1886 by Bell who combined the fortress idiom with a later palace-type building to create the imposing post office for San Antonio, Texas (figure 71).

Another popular model, used especially in smaller towns, was an imaginary type of Romanesque civic building, already successfully initiated by Henry Hobson Richardson as an appropriate building type for a library. Edbrooke particularly favored this form, and his post office buildings for Lewiston, Maine, Fremont, Nebraska, and Lafayette, Indiana (plate 77), show him to be a competent designer of small compact buildings, although his designs are less successful when forced into a larger scale, as in Omaha, Nebraska and Washington, D. C.

Apart from using the medieval style—a choice also much in favor for state and municipal buildings across the country—various of the supervising architects at times used some adaptation of the classical Renaissance style. Hill did this in his 1882 design for the courthouse and post office of Jackson, Mississippi (plate 70), in which, in his typical fashion, he brings together a diverse series of ornamental motifs not frequently found together, but which in this instance are not unhappily married in the overall design. Bell used classical elements, particularly monumental porticoes, pediments, and crowning sculptural figures, with a flamboyant disregard for the design of the rest of the building, as in his 1884 design for the post office of Louisville, Kentucky (plate 73).

Although no single style characterizes the work of any of the supervising architects during this period, their use of one architectural feature did give a

*Figure 70*   William A. Freret.
*Design for the U. S. Courthouse, Post Office and Custom House, Vicksburg, Mississippi.*
Ink drawing, ca. 1888. National Archives.

*Figure 71*   Mifflin E. Bell.
*U. S. Courthouse and Post Office, San Antonio, Texas, 1888–90.*

*Figure 72*    William A. Potter.
*U. S. Custom House, Post Office, and Courthouse, Nashville, Tennessee.*
Design published in the *S. A. T. Report*, 1875.

*Figure 73*    Mifflin E. Bell.
*U. S. Courthouse and Post Office, Pittsburgh*, 1881–91.

*Figure 74*    Mifflin E. Bell.
*U. S. Post Office, Brooklyn, New York*, 1885–92.

common look to many of the new buildings going up across the country. Potter had introduced the motif of a central bell tower in his 1875 design for the post office in Nashville, Tennessee (figure 72). Standing high above all other buildings, the tower quickly became a symbol of the national government. From that moment on subsequent architects relied on the bell tower as the centerpiece of their design, whatever the style, and the citizens came to recognize it as marking the site of the nation's business. Hill, who succeeded Potter, used it two years later in his 1880 design for the Pittsburgh post office, which was later redesigned by Bell with an even higher central tower (figure 73).

Another favorite design incorporated a tower in the corner of the structure, as in Bell's post office in Brooklyn (figure 74). Variations on the tower design were used even for smaller buildings, as in Windrim's post office in Sacramento (plate 76) and O'Rourke's post office in Taunton, Massachusetts (plate 80). As impressive as many of these buildings were, it is revealing to see how such a master architect as Richardson handled the same basic design. Whether or not the citizens of Pittsburgh were aware of the differences between their new federal building (figure 73) and their County Courthouse designed by Richardson in 1884 (figure 74), today

the Richardson solution appears to have produced a far more powerful and dramatic building. In contrast to all the other tower designs, which gain their height by piling up a succession of different architectural features, such as turrets, arcades, balconies, cornices, the Richardson tower, with its continuous turret-like corners and limited articulation of mass, surges up from the ground in a single, swift uninterrupted thrust.

A miscellany of styles or combinations of styles characterize many of the buildings carried out in this massive construction program. Buildings such as Bell's post office in Fort Wayne show the influence of Northern Renaissance buildings, as do Aiken's buildings in Clarksville, Tennessee (plate 82), and Paterson, New Jersey (plate 83). Hill's 1883 design for a post office in Minneapolis (plate 71) suggests a new direction in the search for an American style by matching the ethnic make-up of Minneapolis with a northern European style of architecture. Other designs of this same period reveal no single historical or geographical source but simply combine individual architectural elements into new and unusual compositions, as in Bell's post office of 1884 in Hannibal, Missouri (plate 72).

Although some of the designs adopted for the federal buildings during this time appear to be so original they might be looked upon as constituting an independent national style, they are in fact not different from those being produced in private practice for homes, railroad stations, banks, and even factories, which displayed the same variety of historical derivation. Among the succession of supervising architects operating during the period, only the work of Freret can be said to offer a uniquely personal style, as can be seen in his Moorish design for the courthouse and post office in Houston, Texas (plate 75), or in the fanciful designs for the buildings in Bridgeport, Connecticut, and Vicksburg, Mississippi (figure 70). Despite his brief tenure, his distinctive style stands out in sharp contrast to the work of the other supervising architects, thereby underscoring how typical their work was of the architectural designs being followed in all types of buildings at this particular moment in the rapid conversion of America's natural world into a built one. America's cities and towns displayed rich and varied scenes, of which the citizens were extremely proud. When the nation arrived at its centennial, its architectural image encompassed works from almost every past civilization. There was no longer an impassioned need to search out a single American style; by the number and size of the buildings the central government had erected during this time its tangible existence had been well established.

A circumstance that arose in 1892 soon changed the satisfaction with which the recent buildings had been received by Congress and the public. Because of this occurrence the supervising architect of the time, Willoughby J. Edbrooke, would —unwittingly—become as influential for the future development of the nation's building program as William A. Potter had been with his introduction of the medieval style two decades earlier. Edbrooke would be thrust into this critical position by the events surrounding the design of the United States pavilion for the World's Columbian Exposition that was to be held in Chicago in 1893.

*Figure 75*   Henry Hobson Richardson. *Allegheny County Courthouse, Pittsburgh, 1884–88.* Photogravure, 1898.

*Figure 76*    James H. Windrim.
*Design for U. S. Government Building, World's Columbian Exposition
of 1893, Chicago.*
Ink drawing, 1890. National Archives.

*Figure 77*    Willoughby J. Edbrooke.
*Design for U. S. Government Building, World's Columbian Exposition
of 1893, Chicago.*
Ink drawing, 1891. National Archives.

The directors of the fair had had the foresight to turn to Daniel H. Burnham, one of the city's most prominent architects, to create a board of architectural advisors that would set the guidelines for the plan of the entire complex and the appearance of the major buildings. Burnham succeeded in having some of the country's major architects join the advisory board—Richard Morris Hunt and George B. Post of New York, Peabody and Stearns of Boston, Van Brunt and Howe of Kansas City—but his efforts to have the supervising architect, James Windrim, join them were fruitless. Burnham first wrote to Windrim on December 24, 1890, urging him to join the other architects at their first meeting, scheduled for January 1891, so that the government's building might "be considered artistically together with the others of the group of which it forms an important part." Instead, Windrim simply sent Burnham sketches of the building he intended to erect. In a return letter, of January 2, 1891, Burnham described them as "beautiful and fitting," but again urged Windrim to attend the meeting, in order to "lay them before the others" so "that the work of all may be an harmonious whole." And, Burnham added as a lure, "The gentlemen selected are those you will take most pleasure in meeting."

Windrim did not attend the meeting, at which the advisory board made the major decision that in order to achieve a harmonious effect, all the buildings grouped around the Court of Honor should maintain a uniform cornice line and be designed in the classical style. Windrim's design for the federal building (figure 76) fell far short of this goal, being essentially a repeat of the United States Pavilion at

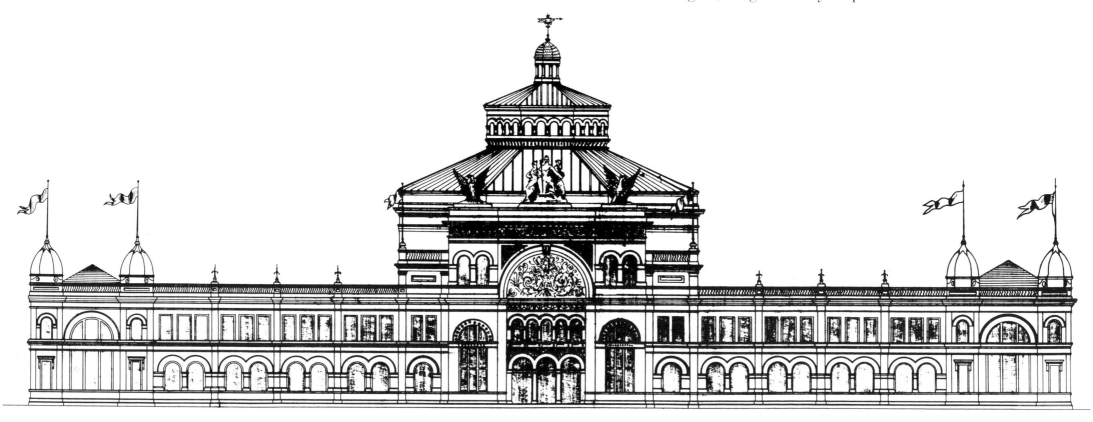

the 1876 Centennial Exposition in Philadelphia. The advisory board must have regarded Windrim's building as completely out of keeping with the ideals established by the group, for when Burnham next wrote to Windrim, on February 2, he informed him that Hunt had reported that he had "urged you to change the form of the building," and Burnham asked if anything like that could happen. On February 7 when Burnham again wrote to Windrim, he mentioned that he had received some indications that although a change could be made in the form of the government building, "you did not wish to do so." Burnham tried to encourage Windrim to change his design by observing that he felt "this to be the greatest chance for architecture ever known on the continent," and he hoped all would be done "to insure the noblest lines and proportions." On February 9 the persevering Burnham again tried to get Windrim to join the advisory board at its next meeting by declaring, "This will be a meeting memorable in the annals of architecture, and we feel that its dignity, and that of your position, demand your participation in this national event."

Windrim neither accepted Burnham's invitations nor changed his design. Some two months later he left both the problem and the Office of the Supervising Architect to his successor, Willoughby J. Edbrooke, who apparently was ordered to produce a government building that would accord with those grouped around the Court of Honor. Curiously, Edbrooke did not consult with Burnham about the new design he was preparing. Instead, Burnham first learned about it from his morning newspaper, when the *Chicago Tribune* published it on May 16, 1891. Although Burnham immediately wrote to Edbrooke, pointing out that any changes in the building had to be approved by him, there is no record of any such confirmation. Burnham later stated specifically that neither Windrim nor Edbrooke took part in the work of the advisory committee (Burnham and Millet, p. 23). Edbrooke's building was on its own.

Edbrooke's new design (figure 77) re-established the link between the classical style and federal buildings. Its impact, however, was far greater than a single example would warrant, for when the Edbrooke building was seen at the Chicago fair in conjunction with all the other buildings of classical design, critics were unanimous in decrying it as a dismal failure. Even more, it was considered to be "mortifying" that amid all the great classical buildings erected by private architects, the official government entry displayed such a lack of knowledge of the classical principles of design. In the great White City erected by the shores of Lake Michigan there was no room for mediocrity. The federal government's first step back into the classical world was a disaster that critics would not allow it to forget. Ironically, this building ultimately became the agent that would reinstate the classical mode as the sole, proper style for the public buildings of the United States. The brief flirtation with medieval, Moorish, and other exotic styles would soon be ended.

*Figure 78*
*Court of Honor with Administration Building by Richard Morris Hunt,*
*World's Columbian Exposition of 1893, Chicago.*
Photograph by Frances Benjamin Johnston, 1892.

The great Chicago fair held in 1893 to celebrate the four hundredth anniversary of the discovery of the New World by Christopher Columbus filled Americans with a heightened awareness of both their uniqueness as a new nation of the world and of their special destiny as a political body whose power came solely from the consent of its people. How much the Republic had grown and prospered over only a little more than one hundred of those years was clear evidence of the success of the system. The accomplishments of the nation's industrial and agricultural workers were so well documented in the fair's exhibition halls, and the future wonders and blessings of inventions such as electricity were so dazzlingly displayed that all who visited these demonstrations could only come away with a vision of the brilliant prospects of the nation's future.

That this message was so ringingly transmitted to the visitors at the Chicago lakefront was due, however, not so much to what was actually displayed at the fair, as to the bewitching architectural setting, resembling a marble city of antiquity, in which the exhibits were presented (figure 78). The brief seventeen years since the great Centennial celebration of 1876 in Philadelphia had not produced so many advances in technology or agricultural production, which might account for the far greater impact the 1893 celebration had on the nation. What was different between the two events was the fact that the architects of the Chicago fair had not simply designed a fairground in a park, but had created a fantasy city to be strolled through, both during the sunshine of the day and the novel floodlighting at night, to be photographed, to be widely disseminated in innumerable expensive and cheap souvenir books, and above all to be remembered. The Great White City at Chicago was imprinted instantaneously and firmly on the mind of America as a paradigm of how a city should look. Although not necessarily noted at the time, the White City was in truth a full-scale, three-dimensional realization of the kind of city envisioned by L'Enfant for Washington. Its buildings were conceived according to a common classical vocabulary and arranged according to a grand urban plan. The overall plan dictated both the relationship of each building to the other, as well as their arrangement on the broad avenues and along the waterways adorned by monuments that re-created vistas of ancient cities of ideal splendor similar to the illusions evoked earlier in the century by the paintings of Thomas Cole (figure 36). It was as if one hundred years later L'Enfant's vision had been reborn, and the designers realized what the great capital city of the Republic should look like. Although most of the buildings were constructed of impermanent material and would soon be gone, the force of the idea and the emotional impact of the appearance of these buildings was so strong that classical architecture as the correct symbolic expression of the political values of the nation once again became dominant in the minds of its citizens and a particular group of its architects.

The architectural mirage of an ideal city had been conjured up by the board of advisors that had determined the architectural regulations that specified a uniform cornice height for the buildings around the Court of Honor, a decision that in itself posited a classical garb for the principal buildings of the fair. This direction was far more the result of the thinking of the eastern architects on the board, particularly of the first Beaux-Arts–trained American architect, Richard Morris Hunt, than it was of Burnham, the designer, with John Wellborn Root, of some of the most innovative high-rise buildings in the nation during the past decade. Yet Burnham immediately perceived the virtues of following a classical canon for individual buildings in order to achieve order in the appearance of large urban areas. From this time on, Burnham's architectural efforts would be as directed to achieving the "City Beautiful," as they would be to the design of individual buildings.

Those who fell under Burnham's spell and agreed to work under incredible pressure to produce the buildings for the exposition all subscribed in varying degrees to the principles of classical architecture as it had been codified in what was known as the Beaux-Arts style. This style was born in Paris in the mid-nineteenth century with the work carried out to complete the vast palatial complex of the Louvre and the Tuileries (figure 55) on which Hunt, the first American to study at the Ecole des Beaux-Arts, the official French school of architecture, had worked as an inspector of construction in the 1850s. During the period of its greatest influence, the precepts of this school were the predominant influence in the design of buildings all over the world. After Hunt, many American architects took at least part of their formal training there, and its educational principles and practices were emulated in American architectural schools for nearly half a century after the 1893 fair.

Although considered to be an extension of a classical tradition that began with Greek and Roman architecture, the Beaux-Arts style actually was characterized by a more ornamental approach to architecture than is found in the chaste and severe examples of classical antiquity. Indeed, one of the hallmarks of this style stemmed from early-seventeenth-century French architecture, which was characterized by an emphasis on the contrast between the color and materials of the wall surface of a building and the highly elaborate stone framing of windows and doors (plate 90). Also favored was the French style of the last half of the eighteenth century, which featured all-stone buildings employing diverse classical motifs (plate 92) and encompassing distinctive and flowing divisions of interior space. The Beaux-Arts style was also more concerned with elaborate sculptural embellishments (plate 94), palatial stairways (plate 93), and immense chandeliers (plate 91) than it was with archaeologically correct adaptations of the architecture of Greece or Rome. In any case, by the time of the 1893 fair, all these elements had become accepted as embodiments of a classical style and were accepted as such with no regard to questions of authenticity. By this broadening of the concept of what might be considered "classical," the style gained considerably in its ability to project a sumptuous image and to heighten the sensuous appeal of the original classical orders.

Despite these enrichments, the attitude on the part of the Office of the Supervising Architect of the Treasury remained dure. Willoughby J. Edbrooke appears to have been sufficiently swayed by his experience of working in the classical style for the 1893 fair to depart from his special preference for the Romanesque style to produce a distinctly different kind of design for the Kansas City post office (plate 78); and one of his last designs as supervising architect was for the modest post office in Fargo, North Dakota (plate 79), which marks a complete reversal from his earlier works. Nevertheless, he was firmly convinced, as he says in his final report as supervising architect, that "those of the public buildings of the United States which were intended to be and are monumental in character . . . compare most favorably with, and in some instances excel, many of the finer structures of European countries" (*S. A. T. Report*, 1892, p. 10).

His successor, Jeremiah O'Rourke, was openly defiant of any new move to a Beaux-Arts style for public buildings. His own contributions during his term of office (1893–94) reflected his opposition to this new direction in his preference for either a medieval style or a Picturesque one for his buildings, depending upon their size (plates 80 and 81). William Martin Aiken, who succeeded him, was also a follower of the Picturesque style, as his design for the post office in Clarksville, Tennessee, demonstrates (plate 82). This design was designated as being of German Renaissance origin, while his fanciful design for the post office in Paterson, New Jersey (plate 83) was considered to be Dutch Renaissance, perhaps a reference to the first colonists of that state. Aiken endorsed following the regional colonial style when building in towns of the original colonies, as at New London, Connecticut, or Spanish colonial for cities in the west, such as his 1896 post office and courthouse for San Francisco (figure 81). But these continued efforts by the Office of the Supervising Architect to resist the classical style brought into favor by the Chicago fair were battles in a lost cause. The official philosophy of what a federal building should look like was not compatible with the ideal set by the fair.

The role of the nation's supervising architect in setting the style for America's public buildings had been unretrievably weakened by the bleak presence of the gray, black-domed building representing the United States government among the gleaming white classical buildings of the Chicago cityscape. Why Edbrooke did not follow the dictate of the fair's board of advisors, that all buildings should be white, is not known, but his decision must have haunted him for years afterward. For the building he designed, which he thought "to be in keeping . . . with the national dignity of the Exposition" (*S. A. T. Report*, 1891), was met with disdain and was seen as clear proof that the official architecture of the United States was incompetent. This public failure was so commented upon in the press and so spotlighted by the detractors of the supervising architect's office, it quickly became the lightning rod for the campaign against the Office of the Supervising Architect which had been under way for most of the preceding twenty years.

Beginning with the annual report of William A. Potter in 1876, each of the succeeding occupants of the Office of the Supervising Architect up to 1890 had been incredibly forthright in saying that some method other than reliance on a single architect should be devised for selecting the designs of the public buildings of the

United States. Each in his own way invoked the dilemmas faced by a supervising architect who had no time to be involved with the design of buildings because so many were being authorized by Congress and who, because his position was by political appointment, was subject to pressures stemming from considerations other than architecture. Each also made the point that the country would gain added dignity and beauty in its public buildings if it were served by more than a single architect.

During this same period several legislative initiatives had been taken to open the design of public buildings to the private sector. None was successful until after the experience of the 1893 fair. In that very year, the clear contrast between the private and the public practice of architecture, with the favorable opinion much in favor of the former, led to the passage of the Tarsney Act, which permitted the secretary of the treasury to seek designs for public buildings through open competition. Although the battle to open up to the private sector the eminently lucrative field of the design of public buildings had been won, there remained the problem of convincing the secretary of the treasury actually to exercise the option Congress had made available.

On the one hand, the battle was waged in a series of letters that passed among Daniel H. Burnham, president of the American Institute of Architects; the secretary of the Institute; the secretary of the treasury; and the incumbent supervising architect, Jeremiah O'Rourke. The exchange became so bitter, the secretary of the treasury concluded the correspondence on March 12, 1894, by informing Burnham that his letter was so "very offensive and ungentlemanly . . . this Department will have no further correspondence with you upon the subject [of the Tarsney Act] . . . or any other subject" (*American Architect and Building News*, April 7, 1894, p. 12). On the other hand, snipings at the official government architects were frequent in both the daily newspapers and the architectural press. For example, in the same issue of the professional journal that published the heated correspondence, Glenn Brown presented (pp. 2–9) a detailed comparison of the costs of erecting a building by independent architects with those incurred by the federal government, revealing the distinct savings realized by the former.

One of the costs emphasized in Brown's article was the preparation of drawings by the supervising architect's office. Since the specific expense of these drawings was hidden in the total appropriation made for each building project, the actual cost was not easy to ascertain, although some years before, William Freret had pointed out how much cheaper it had been to commission drawings from private sources (*S. A. T. Report* 1888, p. 6). Brown's estimate that the drawings cost twice what a private firm would spend for working drawings is probably close to the mark, as the need for extremely detailed drawings had always been a concomitant of controlling the construction of a building from the central office in Washington. Private firms did not in any way work on the same scale as the federal operation. Already under Mullett, drawings were needed to indicate the makeup of every course of stone laid for the walls of the New York post office or to detail the assembling of each piece of cast-iron framework of the roof. Drawings made in the Washington office controlled every phase of construction, from where hoisting derricks should be located to how concrete foundations should be laid (plate 84).

Drawings of this type continued to be made during the entire period between 1866 and 1897, and the greater variety of styles that were dictated by the succession of architects, the more detailed a rendering of the ornamental work was required (plate 85). In addition, the introduction of the elevator (used for the first time in a federal building in Mullett's New York post office) required increasingly detailed drawings dealing with the mechanical systems of a building. The use of electricity had produced a particular problem for the supervising architect's office due to the peculiarities of the appropriation system which placed the funds for lighting federal buildings under the control of the chief clerk in the secretary of the treasury's office. During the years 1885 and 1891 the supervising architect described the difficulty of this arrangement, pointing out that it would be more practicable, and certainly more economical, to know in advance whether or not the building would depend upon gas or electricity for its lighting. Precisely when the system was altered so that such design and construction considerations came under the control of the supervising architect's office is not clear. When this did occur, however, instead of developing the capacity for the design of these elements in house, the office increasingly assigned the design of elevator systems and electrical fixtures to private firms (plates 86 and 88). However, as in the case of the post office in Charleston, South Carolina (plate 87), the supervising architect continued to design the decorative framework in which these elements were to be introduced.

In order to sustain this system of control as the number of buildings increased, an ever-growing corps of draftsmen was required, as well as more highly qualified site inspectors. As critics pointed out, the local inspectors were almost always political appointees with no knowledge of construction management, whose only interest in the job was to prolong it so as to continue being paid. In 1892, Edbrooke had tried to establish a roving crew of supervisors, each of whom would be responsible for a specific part of the building—plumbing, foundations, drainage, etc.—and gradually these posts were placed under civil service and filled by professionals. Nevertheless, the vulnerability of the central office was becoming more and more apparent.

Although the statistics presented in Brown's article appear reasonably accurate and often staggering—he demonstrated that government buildings cost 60 percent more than comparable private ones—his arguments were not always persuasive, particularly since he includes the Capitol of the United States as the work of "private architects." However, his statistical tables lent such an air of authenticity to his argument, his article must have been a body blow to those trying to resist the weakening of the central bureau of construction in the Treasury. Other voices were raised, among them that of the respected critic Montgomery Schuyler, who urged that America be allowed to profit from its ablest architects in the design of its public buildings (1894B). Hostility in Congress toward the Office of the Supervising Architect remained constant during this period, and although the Tarsney Act had yet to become operative, in certain instances Congress passed appropriations for specific buildings and allowed private architects to be commissioned for these buildings. Thus, the major federal government building in Chicago—a replacement for the custom house and post office originally designed by Mullett and refashioned by William Potter—was designed and constructed outside the supervising architect's office by Henry Ives Cobb. This development did not occur without extensive discussion in Congress between 1893 and 1896 over whether this practice should be instituted, for it effectively bypassed the administrative agency charged with supervising the expenditure of funds, and it opened the door to the lobbying of congressmen by every city or state that wanted a federal building. When Lyman J. Gage, the former president of the Columbian Exposition, became secretary of the treasury (1897), he immediately activated the provisions of the Tarsney Act. They were put into effect in 1898 with the selection through competition of three firms to build post offices at Norfolk, Virginia, and Camden, New Jersey, and the new immigration facility on Ellis Island.

Over the next fifteen years the Tarsney Act was used only thirty-five times, primarily because of the problems caused by the government's lack of control over the execution of the designs. Suggestions by the supervising architect that the act be so altered that only the designs of the buildings would be chosen through competition but the execution would remain under central control were not accepted by Congress, which had in any case become increasingly suspicious that the Tarsney Act was only a vehicle for providing exorbitant fees to members of the American Institute of Architects. Despite an intensive lobbying campaign by that professional group, in 1912 Congress repealed the act after examining a report that detailed the amount of architectural fees paid out when it was enforced. Despite the brief existence of the act and the few times it was employed, some of the largest government buildings were erected according to its terms: vast new post offices and custom houses for New York City, by McKim, Mead and White, and Cass Gilbert; in Cleveland, by Arnold W. Brunner (figure 79); in Washington, D. C., by Daniel H. Burnham and Co.; in Indianapolis, by Rankin & Kellog; and in Baltimore, by Hornblower & Marshall. All were designed in the new Beaux-Arts style that was now considered to be representative of the national purpose they were both to serve and signify.

Shortly after the provisions of the Tarsney Act were first utilized in 1898, the Office of the Supervising Architect was filled by a staunch supporter of the classical style, James Knox Taylor, who had previously worked in Minneapolis as a partner of Cass Gilbert and was himself an architect unreservedly on the side of the use of the classical style for the nation's buildings. Thus, only four years after the vision of a classical America had been unveiled at the Columbian Exposition, its proponents were in a position to realize this ideal for buildings representing the national government. Taylor was given an immediate opportunity to demonstrate

*Figure 79*  Arnold W. Brunner.
*U. S. Post Office, Custom House, and Courthouse, Cleveland.*
Design published in the *S. A. T. Report*, 1901.

what his occupancy of the Office of the Supervising Architect foretold by his design for the government building at the Trans-Mississippi Exposition held at Omaha in 1898. Unlike the shunned government pavilion at Chicago, now the building representing the United States was a proper classical building that dominated the Grand Court and was the focal point for the parade of Beaux-Arts buildings leading up to it along the central waterway (figure 80). Taylor more than made up for the poor showing of the United States at Chicago five years earlier, and both his building and his government received plaudits rather than disdain. Clearly, the direction of the Office of the Supervising Architect of the Treasury had undergone a substantial change.

An equally rapid and stunning declaration of Taylor's intended direction was proclaimed by his drastic alteration of the 1896 Spanish Colonial design made by his predecessor, William Martin Aiken, for the San Francisco post office and courthouse (figures 81 and 82). Taylor transformed it from an example of regionalism into a vigorously classical building with a high heavily rusticated lower level and a strongly accented upper story with sharply marked bays and window decorations, crowned by a straight balustrade. This was, in essence, a type that would reign supreme in the design of all federal buildings during Taylor's fifteen-year-long stewardship (1898–1912) in the supervising architect's office.

During his tenure, Taylor was able to alter the image of America's federal buildings not only because his occupancy of the office was so long, but also because the number of new federal buildings authorized by Congress during that time exceeded the total number of buildings erected since the beginning of the Republic. When Taylor took over, the number of federal buildings commenced, constructed, or authorized stood at 313. When he left office, the total was a staggering 1,126 buildings. Thus Taylor alone was responsible for bringing into being more than 800 federal buildings. Over the years 1898–1912 the work of the office showed a ninefold increase in the number of buildings begun each year (15 in 1898; 134 in 1912) and a fivefold increase in the number of buildings completed each year (15 in 1898; 77 in 1912). In his final year in office, Taylor was presiding over an operation that initiated ten new buildings each month and completed six. With such a wealth of projects Taylor was able completely to transform the federal image not only across the nation, but also in the new territories beyond the continental boundaries of the expanding nation, in the Philippine Islands, Hawaii, and Puerto Rico.

Within the fifteen-year span during which classical buildings emerged from Taylor's office, certain stylistic characteristics tended to be emphasized at different periods. The earliest works, such as the 1900 Altoona post office (plate 89), feature rusticated ground floors with arched openings and plain upper-wall surfaces with heavy window surrounds. Designs for buildings of similar size but from a slightly later period, such as the 1903 post office in Laramie, Wyoming, (figure 83), tend to rely upon more elaborate stone fronts with sharply recessed openings that accent the patterning of the masonry and provide a smooth planar surface against which

*Figure 80    View of Grand Court, Trans-Mississippi Exposition, Omaha, 1898.* Photograph by F. A. Rinehart, 1898.

the intricate wrought-iron lamp standards and sculptured ornament of the center section are seen in sharp relief. Other buildings of the same size and the same period, as in the 1904 post office at Oil City, Pennsylvania (figure 84), are given a more articulated structure by wall surfaces that are treated as if they were columnar elements separated by the void of the windows and an entry portico provided with engaged columns in a triumphal-arch motif. This combination of classical elements was particularly favored by Taylor, and even though such a composition frequently recurred, it always retained an individuality that makes each building seem especially designed for its community. The whole spectrum of these eight hundred buildings is amazing testimony to the variety and richness that can be produced by a sensitive handling of a classical vocabulary following its own integral grammatical rules.

Another aspect of the Beaux-Arts style favored by Taylor is seen in the post office of 1904 for Muskegon, Michigan (plate 90), which features a colorful array of brick and white stonework knit together in a playful but strong rhythmical series of contrasting window frames, pilasters, and wall surfaces. A more sober architectural composition employed by Taylor throughout his tenure is demonstrated in the post office of 1901 at Oakland, California (plate 92). In this early building and in subsequent examples, Taylor followed the principle of setting a colonnade of colossal columns, either one and one-half or three stories high, into a clearly defined rectangular building block surmounted by a pronounced cornice and capped by an openwork or solid balustrade. Occasionally his designs would take on a very particular character, when, for example, he was inspired by a fresh model, such as his design of the 1910 post office in Wichita Falls, Texas (plate 95), which was based on the just completed Pan American Union building in Washington, D. C., designed by Paul Cret and Albert Kelsey.

*Figure 81*  William Martin Aiken.
*U. S. Post Office and Courthouse, San Francisco.*
Design published in the *S. A. T. Report,* 1896.

*Figure 82*  James Knox Taylor.
*U. S. Post Office and Courthouse, San Francisco.*
Design published in the *S. A. T. Report,* 1898.

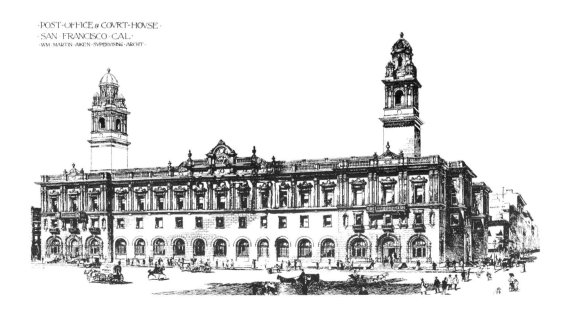

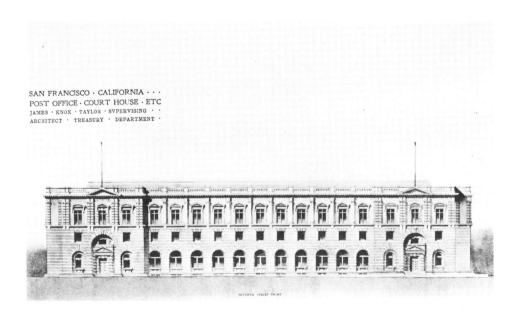

*Figure 83*   James Knox Taylor.
*U. S. Post Office, Laramie, Wyoming, 1903–6.*

*Figure 84*   James Knox Taylor.
*U. S. Post Office, Oil City, Pennsylvania, 1904–6.*

2583   United States Government Building, Laramie, Wyoming.

That Taylor could provide such a diversity of high-quality buildings all within the same general stylistic idiom, and at the breakneck speed demanded by the largess of Congress, is a tribute to his talents both as architect and administrator. And although today his name almost never appears in any history of architecture, he was truly the sole creator of the architectural image of the central government that prevailed before 1940 in the minds of most citizens. To put this phenomenon in context one must again consider what took place during his administration. The overall increase in the number of federal buildings provided by Congress during this period was in the order of 260 percent, while during the same period the population had increased by only some 30 percent and the annual national budget by about 56 percent. As the number of Congressmen increased during this same time by only thirty-three and the number of Senators by four, the potential amount of building funds each member of Congress could bring home to his constituents had risen by an astonishing sum—far beyond the population growth and, therefore, beyond what was actually needed for providing federal services.

The obvious result of rapidly increasing appropriations for public buildings for a slow-growth population and relatively stable number of Congressmen was the erection of federal buildings in ever smaller towns and communities. This led to a continuous stream of accusations from the press about pork-barreling and constant attacks on the supervising architect chastising him for a practice for which Congress, not he, was responsible. Indeed, Congress had opened the floodgates to this torrent of construction by inventing and, in 1902, passing what came to be called the "omnibus" public building bill, which replaced for the most part the previous practice of enacting individual bills for each building with one that authorized over one hundred fifty new buildings at a time. The same practice took place in 1908 and 1910, and again in 1913, the year after Taylor's term in office ended. This wholesale authorization for buildings gave every Congressman the possibility of providing his district with a federal building, regardless of need. The practice became so flagrant that in the 1913 omnibus bill, Congress itself applied the criteria that where there was no federal activity other than the post office, no buildings could be authorized unless the postal receipts amounted to at least $10,000 annually—thus finally adopting a policy that the first head of the Construction Branch, Alexander Bowman, had unsuccessfully tried to have instituted some sixty years before.

The dilemma produced for Congressmen by attempting to restrict the character of a federal building in a small town is dramatically demonstrated in an unusually revealing speech by the chairman of the House Committee on Public Buildings and Grounds, Frank Clark of Florida, delivered on the floor of the House on January 17, 1916. First he attempts to exonerate Congress from being at fault if too many magnificent buildings have been erected in small towns by explaining that Congress only allocated the money to be spent on buildings, it did not decide what should be spent where (a disclaimer unsupported by all other actions of Congress), and he points to the limit Congress already had imposed in 1913 on what could be spent for buildings related to postal revenue. He then goes on to say:

Notwithstanding the facts as disclosed by the record, a certain element of the metropolitan press and a certain class of magazines denounce us as "pork-barrel devotees" or "looters of the Treasury" every time we propose to construct a modest public building in a live, progressive, wide-awake town in the rural districts, but when we propose to expend millions for the erection of a marble palace in one of the great cities of the country we are pictured as broad-minded, progressive, and patriotic statesmen. [Laughter and applause.]

The chairman proposes ways in which the performance of the Office of the Supervising Architect might be improved, one of which is to institute "standardization of buildings wherever possible." He continues,

I am fully aware that both climate and the topography of the country are to be considered, but from the first floor up a standard type can be used no matter what "the lay of the land" or climatic conditions may be. . . . My plan of standardization would be to divide the States of the Union into groups with particular reference to climate and topography, and then divide the cities and towns of each group into classes. For instance, I would form one group of the New England States, which for my present purposes I shall call "Group A." I would then take all the towns or cities in group A where the annual postal receipts were from ten to twenty-five thousand dollars and I would designate this as "class 1." I would then have the Supervising Architect draft plans and specifications for a post-office building for a town in class 1 of group A, and these plans and specifications would answer for every town of this class and group. It is absolutely nonsensical to tell me that a post-office building suitable for a certain-sized town in New Hampshire would not be equally suitable for the same-sized town in Rhode Island, or that a post-office building for a certain-sized town in Mississippi would not be equally suitable for a town of like size in Louisiana.

Having made the case for improved efficiency in the conduct of the Office of the Supervising Architect, Congressman Clark then addresses the other side of the coin: what factors should dictate the appearance of a public building? He ends his oration by describing the symbolic role played by the nation's public buildings in a manner that clearly reveals his thoughts to be directly descended from those of Washington and Jefferson on the importance of the architectural imagery of the new Republic.

The great rural population of this country constitutes the very "bone and sinew" of the land—the backbone of the Republic. If I had the time, I believe I could show that they pay the great bulk of the taxes necessary to support the Government in times of peace, and God knows that in times of war the American country boy follows Old Glory where "thickest falls the red rain of human slaughter." He sees very little of the blessings of government beyond the post office and the rural carrier, and if I had the power I would erect for every presidential post office throughout the broad domain of the Republic a Government building representative of the sovereignty and the glory of this great country. From Maine to California and from the Great Lakes to the Gulf, in every town of sufficient importance to have the President name the post-master, I would erect a suitable but not extravagant building, and from its apex the Stars and Stripes, proud emblem of the glory of the

Republic, should forever wave an inspiration to the youth of the land. Suppose here and there it should be a little more expensive in dollars and cents to own a building than it is to rent. Is it worth nothing to inspire patriotism and love of country in the hearts and minds of the youth of the country? No youth or citizen ever looked upon a Federal building in which the business of his country was being conducted but that he became a better American.

The struggle to establish an efficient system which could produce similar building types without, however, sacrificing their symbolic aspect as representatives of the central government would continue long after Congressman Clark's peroration. A portent of the eventual solution began to appear in the 1920s with the design of buildings identified simply as "Federal Office Buildings" (figure 85). Anonymity began to replace symbolism. Briefly in the 1930s, under the WPA and the PWA, programs were begun to establish standardized types of buildings that would serve the different functions of the federal government, but no single system was adopted. Until the late 1930s the classical vision inspired by the 1893 Columbian Exposition and introduced by Taylor in hamlets, villages, towns, and cities across the nation established the national image of the United States. It was uniform, widespread, and embraced and enjoyed by its citizens. By their set of rules that controlled the height and appearance of the buildings along the Court of Honor, Burnham and the board of advisors of the 1893 Exposition became responsible for changing the appearance of buildings in all parts of America. The design principles that governed the Chicago Exposition had a greater impact than any other similar occurrence in the development of an artistic movement. What seemed at the time to be a naive and boastful remark by Augustus Saint-Gaudens,

Post Office, Oil City, Pa.

that the assembly of architects and artists on the board of the fair was the "greatest meeting of artists since the fifteenth century" (Hines, p. 90) proved to be not only prescient, but also modest.

Montgomery Schuyler, in his last report on the Columbian Exposition (1894A), warned of the potential danger the fair's success posed, namely, that it would lead to the copying of individual buildings or their style, in the hope of recapturing in a different environment the quality such buildings had possessed within the context of other buildings at the fair. Schuyler emphasized that the magic allure of the buildings at the fair was derived from three elements, "unity, magnitude and illusion," and that without all three, a copy of a single building would be empty of life. Certainly this turned out to be true of many of the classical buildings set down in small towns across the country during Taylor's tenure; but as singular as they seemed at first, they also were responsible for fulfilling the role that early aestheticians had prophesied would occur when a building of high quality was placed within a community. The structure became an object that raised the aesthetic—if not the moral and intellectual—level of the town's inhabitants and was soon joined by other civic structures—schools, libraries, city halls—designed in a similar style.

The great potential Schuyler saw for the influence of the fair which lay in the combination of "unity, magnitude and illusion" was nowhere more possible than in Washington, D. C. For his first annual report as supervising architect (1898), Taylor commissioned an illustrated cover (figure 86), the first and only time the report of the supervising architect was so adorned. In so doing Taylor appears to have deliberately and consciously wanted it made known that a new era was about to be born in the conduct of the federal government's building program. He chose for the cover a depiction of the Washington Monument from which bands representing the thirteen original states radiate, much like the spokes of the banquet pavilion designed by L'Enfant (figure 1). This image is set within a row of trees that frames the view in a manner reminiscent of L'Enfant's original description of what he intended in his creation of the Mall. This cover announced, then, a new direction in federal architecture and, even more importantly, foreshadowed what would occur in the capital city—a return to the original plan of Washington and L'Enfant for the federal city.

Already in 1896 the supervising architect, William Martin Aiken, had noted that it would be possible and advisable to begin concentrating the major federal buildings along Pennsylvania Avenue (S. A. T. Report, 1896, p. 7). Consideration of a renewed overall plan for the city was then sparked in 1900 by the one hundredth anniversary of the first meeting of Congress in the Capitol. The annual convention of the American Institute of Architects was held in Washington, and a number of plans were presented by which the capital city could be completed. The enthusiasm engendered by these plans led to the decision of Senator James McMillan to find a way to bring together a board of advisors similar to the group

that had planned the Chicago fair to formulate an overall plan for the development of a park system for the city of Washington. Once again, headed by Daniel H. Burnham, the advisors, Frederick Law Olmsted, Jr., and Charles F. McKim, worked together during 1901 and by January 1902 drew up what became known as the McMillan Commission Plan.

The report concentrated on planning the monumental core of Washington and called for a vigorous effort to resurrect the principal design elements of L'Enfant's original scheme. Key to the board's proposal was the reopening of the great axial view from the Capitol to the White House called for in L'Enfant's plan. This goal required the removal of buildings and landscaping that had been established on the Mall during the previous century. At the same time as the Norman style had been adopted for the Smithsonian Institution Building, a new design for the Mall by Andrew Jackson Downing had been adopted, and the portion immediately in front of the Smithsonian Building had been planted according to this plan (see notes to plate 28). The "castle" was provided with a woodsy setting through which passed meandering paths leading to informal groups of trees arranged to produce Picturesque views and arboreal groves (detail of plate 28). The return to the classical style of architecture and the concurrent interest in city planning demanded that these intrusions on L'Enfant's axial design be removed and the

soul-stirring vision that he had intended the viewer to experience when confronted by the stretch of open greensward from the Capitol to the monument to George Washington be reclaimed.

The McMillan Commission report was presented in January 1902 to the legislative and executive members of the government and the public in an exhibition of enormous renderings of the proposed embellishments to the capital city and two gigantic models showing how the city would be altered by the new plan. Although not as compelling as the full-scale buildings at the Chicago fair, the exhibit was nevertheless architectural showmanship at its best and was enthusiastically received by the public, the press, and the architectural community. What was proposed, essentially, was the re-creation in Washington of the White City of Chicago, but in permanent materials and adapted to accord with the formal city plan of L'Enfant. Unfortunately, the mechanism by which these plans could quickly be translated into reality was missing, and the entire proposal was threatened by the hostility of some members of Congress. Not until almost eight years later, when President Theodore Roosevelt established the Commission of Fine Arts with Daniel H. Burnham as its head, was an official way found to ensure that the planning and building of federal structures, monuments, or parks would conform to the standards set in 1902.

One of the key elements in the 1902 plan was not only the re-establishment of the L'Enfant Mall, but also its prolongation beyond the Washington Monument to a point that in L'Enfant's time had been a marshland (figure 87). In 1902 this reclaimed land raised in the eyes of the planners the possibility of establishing a new national monument there which would be equal in both architectural significance and national importance to the one dedicated to Washington. A monument to Abraham Lincoln was the obvious choice. A memorial to Lincoln had been discussed, proposed, but never resolved by Congress ever since his assassination in 1865. In its report the Commission gave several illustrations of how such a memorial might be designed and how it would function within its overall concept of this area of the capital city. As a part of its plan the 1902 Commission also proposed a bridge across the Potomac leading from the projected memorial to Arlington Cemetery, thus binding together the two most powerful symbols of the War Between the States by bridging the geographical boundary between North and South.

Like other parts of the far-sighted McMillan Plan, these two elements were not realized until some years later, but it is a testimony to the members of that group, and to the persistent vigilance of the Commission on Fine Arts under the direction first of Daniel H. Burnham and subsequently of Charles Moore, that these two major extensions and embellishments of the L'Enfant plan were in time carried out as planned. The most fierce battle raged over the location of the Lincoln Memorial, which was pivotal for establishing the entire 1902 plan. The site chosen by the McMillan Commission was dismissed with scorn by some influential members of Congress, whose spokesman was no less than the domineering Speaker of the

*Figure 85* James A. Wetmore.
*Design for a federal office building, Saint Louis, Missouri.*
Ink and wash, 1920. National Archives.

*Figure 86 Cover of the* Annual Report of the Supervising Architect of the Treasury. *1898.*

House, Congressman Joseph Cannon of Illinois, who is reported to have said, "So long as I live I'll never let a memorial to Abraham Lincoln be erected in that God damned swamp" (Craig, p. 262).

The battle not only pitted the architects against members of Congress, but also against each other when opportunities too enticing to be ignored came between their belief in the proper site for the Lincoln Memorial and a possible commission to build one elsewhere. Such, in fact, was the case with Burnham, whose temporary defection from the supporters of the Mall site came about because of the opportunity he was given by a bill introduced into the House in 1908 to locate the Lincoln Memorial within the Union Station–Capitol Hill area. The relocation of the Pennsylvania Railroad Station from the Mall to the area north of the Capitol had been the first major breakthrough in making the 1902 plan possible. Burnham's Union Station, erected between 1903 and 1907, provided an appropriately grand and monumental gateway to the capital city (figure 88). The chance to link the station to the Capitol itself by creating a semicircular colonnaded plaza in front of Union Station, which would also serve as a monument to Lincoln, was irresistible, and over the next year Burnham and his office created hundreds of sketches showing the many possible ways such an idea might be formulated.

The principal problem in any of these schemes rested in the fact that Delaware Avenue, the main axial street between the station and the Capitol, approached it at an oblique angle on the eastern edge of the north wing. Although the dome of the Capitol could serve as a visually dominating terminal point, the actual experience of traversing the avenue to the Capitol would have fallen short of a sense of ceremonial arrival. Burnham swept this fact aside by envisioning the entire area covered with symmetrically arranged classical buildings and by proposing freestanding monuments at either end of the avenue to serve as the focal points (plate 96). As if the entire Capitol Hill area were another Chicago Fair, Burnham's vision surrounded the Capitol itself with uniform, columnar buildings, even, in his imagination, doing away with the recently completed Library of Congress building.

Another scheme (plate 97) shows Delaware Avenue flanked at its Union Station end by two gigantic half-domed monuments that echo the vast barrel-vaulted center section of the station. Placed before them on columns are statues similar to those already in place on the triumphal archway of the station. Both these monumental structures were intended to make up the Lincoln Memorial, as is attested to in many other drawings in this group (see note to plate 97). On the sides of the monuments facing the station are panels intended to bear quotations from Lincoln's writings, similar to what eventually would be included by Henry Bacon in his winning design for the Memorial. In this proposal Burnham worked to disguise the awkward connecting point to the Capitol by blocking it with a gigantic flagstaff and swirling pennant. In another concept (plate 98) Burnham solved the problem by making Delaware Avenue a curving thoroughfare that would sweep into the eastern plaza of the Capitol. He also called for the removal of the surrounding buildings to the west, thereby exposing the full depth of the Capitol.

*Figure 87    The McMillan Commission Plan, 1901–2.*

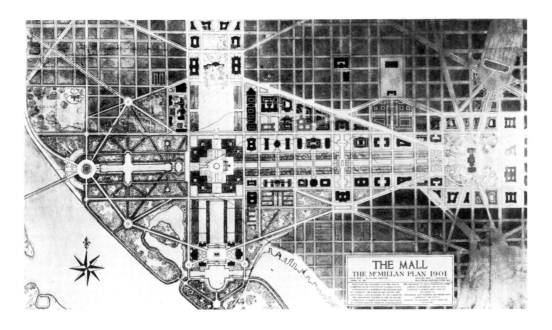

THE MALL
THE McMILLAN PLAN 1901

Along this new approach Burnham proposed to erect an isolated, circular monument to Lincoln, an idea for the interior of which is given in a watercolor rendering (plate 99).

Burnham's fellow members of the original McMillan Commission were aghast at this development, and Burnham finally backed away from the idea, saying that his designs were made only in response to the House bill. Had this legislation passed, however, it probably would have been the end of the grand idea of expanding the Mall westward with a Lincoln Memorial as the new terminal point. Later, when the Commission of Fine Arts was asked to comment on the different sites proposed for the Lincoln Memorial, Burnham's report on the unsuitability of the Capitol Hill area mentions that the Commission reached this conclusion only "after having the opportunity to consider a set of more than one hundred architectural studies representing work carried on over a series of years" (*Lincoln M. C. Report* 1911, p. 21), obviously a reference to his own attempts to locate the monument there.

A Senate bill favoring the Potomac site had been introduced in 1909 and finally, on February 9, 1911, Congress appropriated the funds for the memorial and provided for a commission appointed by Congress to choose the site and the architect. The commission asked Henry Bacon for a design for the Potomac site and subsequently solicited John Russell Pope for proposals for two other sites in the capital city, one, on Meridian Hill due north of the White House (plate 100), the other, due north of the Capitol on the grounds of the Soldiers' Home (plate 101). Despite the compellingly beautiful watercolor renderings prepared for Pope by Otto R. Eggers, the Commission fixed on the Potomac site. On February 3, 1912, both Pope and Bacon were asked to submit plans for that location.

Their subsequent entries pitted the incredible rendering skills of Eggers against the awesome abilities of the delineator Jules Guérin, both of whom performed at peak form. For Pope, Eggers created a 9′ × 4′ rendering (plate 102) showing a design for the memorial similar to the one proposed for the Soldiers' Home site and, more pertinently perhaps, similar to the type initially proposed by the McMillan Commission itself (figure 89). In fact, the rendering by Eggers is almost entirely derived from the McMillan version, complete with splashing fountain in the reflecting pool.

Bacon submitted three different proposals for the Potomac site, all accompanied by 4′ × 6′ renderings executed by Guérin in pencil and wash on canvas which gives a shimmering, ethereal quality to the monument and makes the most of its location on the reflecting pool. Particularly benefiting from Guérin's technique and his use of bare canvas is the variant design featuring a statue of Lincoln isolated on a high pedestal set before an open screen of columns (plate 103). Like Eggers, Guérin chose to set his architect's proposal in a format similar to the rendering of the same scene done for the McMillan Commission (figure 89), for whose 1902 exhibition he had also provided many of the major renderings.

Henry Bacon's design was the choice of the commissioners, probably a foregone conclusion since they had originally chosen him to design the monument for the

*Figure 88*  Daniel H. Burnham.
*Union Station, Washington, D. C., 1903–7.*
Photograph, ca. 1915–20.

*Figure 89*
*Design for a Lincoln Memorial proposed by the McMillan Commission, 1901–2.*
Rendering by Robert Blum. Whereabouts unknown.

Potomac site. How Pope managed to insinuate himself into the proceedings in the first place is masked by the polite and discreet report of the commissioners, but Pope must have had some inkling of what the result would be for he also submitted seven other large ($4' \times 2'6''$) proposals for different types of memorials, all executed in bold and dramatic graphite renderings (plates 104–106) probably the work of Rockwell Kent. The entire group, from relatively conservative classical designs to the more radical ones illustrated here, seems to be an act of bravura on Pope's part, as if knowing he would not win, he set out to shock and astound the Ccommission with the breadth and power of his vision. The official reaction was muted, Burnham simply commenting that as none of them are "as good as the one he has presented in his larger rendered drawing . . . we do not feel it necessary to comment upon them" (*Lincoln M. C. Report* 1912, p. 37).

The Lincoln Memorial was not completed until 1922, when it was dedicated, on May 30, in a ceremony in which Chief Justice William Howard Taft presented the building to President Harding on behalf of the people of the United States. Lincoln's son Robert Todd Lincoln was in attendance, as was a Confederate Guard of Honor. Their presence symbolized that the bonds of the Union which Lincoln had held together by force were slowly being replaced by peaceful bonds of a truly national spirit. From its inception, the memorial to Lincoln took on a meaning beyond its architectural setting, which would become even more poignant in the years of strife over civil rights culminating in the speech given there by Dr. Martin Luther King, Jr., during the 1963 March on Washington.

*Figure 90*
*Plan of Washington, D. C., showing progress made as of 1931 on the McMillan Commission proposals of 1901–2.*

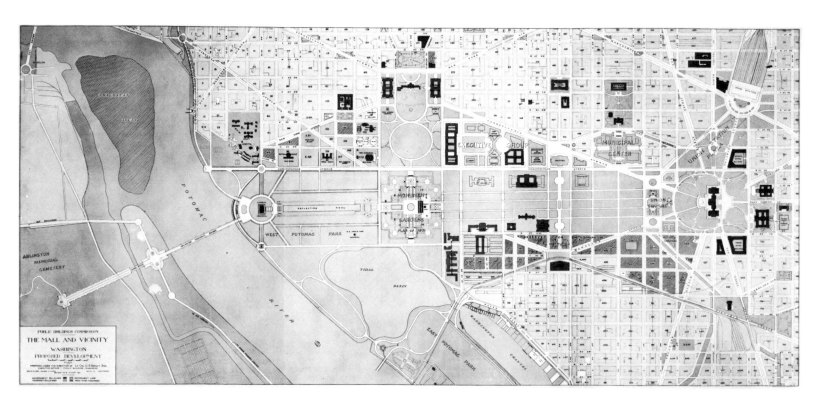

During the same year that saw the completion of the Lincoln Memorial, funds were finally authorized to carry out the second of the two projects so key to the 1902 plan: the construction of a memorial bridge to cross the Potomac. Once a commission had been appointed by the president it moved quickly at its first meeting to fix the broad outlines of the bridge's design, all of which met with the active opposition of the Commission of Fine Arts, which insisted on following the 1902 plan that recommended that the bridge be located on a line from the Lincoln Memorial to the Custis–Lee Mansion in Arlington Cemetery. In December 1922, the Commission of Fine Arts and the Bridge Commission, including President Harding, visited all the sites by automobile and even crossed the Potomac on foot over the new Key Bridge in order to understand the possibilities. At the end of the meeting it was unanimously decided to erect a low-level bridge, with a draw, at the site recommended in the 1902 plan. And believing that a competition for its design would be too time-consuming, the Commission of Fine Arts was asked to recommend names of architects to work with the engineers. McKim, Mead and White of New York, Charles A. Platt of New York, and Paul Cret of Philadelphia were suggested; in April 1923 the executive officers chose the firm of McKim, Mead and White.

The subsequent design included not only the bridge, but also a formalized plan for the roadway and waterfront in front of the Lincoln Memorial, for Columbia Island, which lay between the southern end of the bridge and the mainland, and for a parkway extending from that point to an entranceway to Arlington Cemetery (figure 90). All these elements were represented by McKim, Mead and White in an extraordinary rendering of the entire project which showed in a single view the axial relationship between the Lincoln Memorial and the Custis–Lee Mansion (plate 107). This 3′6″ × 11′ rendering also shows in an insert the majestic treatment intended for Columbia Island, which was to be adorned with a plaza and two stately columns 166 feet high, symbolizing the North and the South, surmounted by statues of Victory and adorned at the base with other sculpture and inscriptions.

The entire bridge project was seen from the start as a highly important symbolic undertaking, the Bridge Commission having declared at its first meeting that "it was to be intended as a memorial to those who have died in the military service of the country" (*Bridge Commission*, p. 32). But in the hands of McKim, Mead and White, and at the urging of the Commission of Fine Arts, the bridge also became a key part of a larger design with regard to both city planning and meaning. The symbolism of the Arlington Memorial Bridge strongly emphasized its role as a link between North and South. Not only was Columbia Island designed with this message in mind, but the bridge itself was also seen as a framework for allegorical sculpture that would convey the image of a united nation. The report described the architecture of the bridge as having been kept

as simple and severe as possible, the structure mainly depending for its beauty upon the perfection of its general proportions and its adornment with significant sculptured pieces of

the highest quality of design. The Washington entrance to the bridge is marked by two pylons, located about 500 feet from the Lincoln Memorial. Similar pylons are placed at the entrance to the shore road and are repeated at the Virginia entrance to the bridge. They are 40 feet high, and are adorned on the sides with sculptured groups and appropriate inscriptions and surmounted by eagles symbolic of the United States of America. These symbols appear also as the only sculptured ornaments on the sides of the bridge, where they are shown in the large disks on both ends of each of the river piers. The sculpture on the sides of the four pylons represent in different ways the recognition of the common bonds and aspirations of the Nation and the final triumph of the idea of a permanent and complete Union.

The pairs of figures on each end of the piers of the bridge represent symbolically the outcome of that harmonious Union, the result of the energies of the entire country in the arts of peace—that is, those inventions and accomplishments in science and art particularly connected with the history of this country. Thus would be symbolized the agricultural, engineering, religious, and educational progress, to mention but a few categories of action. In the opinion of the architect this sculpture vitalizes the entire conception of the design of the bridge, differentiating this memorial from all others and making the reason for its existence intelligible at a glance (*Bridge Commission*, pp. 39–40).

The bridge also became the means by which the axis of the Mall could be carried beyond the Lincoln Memorial to Arlington Cemetery (figure 90) and thereby enlarge the city plan of L'Enfant. The plan called for the Lee Highway, "coming across the entire country from Los Angeles," to enter Washington by a splendid direct approach to the city rather than, as it did then, cross the river at the Key Bridge. The Bridge Commission had set its goals high, for, as the report said, these several features "taken together, will make it the greatest single memorial project undertaken by any Nation in recent times." The members of the Commission were anxious to relate it to the classical past. "Rome," they pointed out, "had its five great avenues of approach: The Flaminia, Praenestina, Aurelia, Ostiensis, and Appian Ways. Washington has none worthy of the name, but in this proposed terminus of the Lee Highway will be created the first and most magnificent of all possible entrances to the National Capital" (*Bridge Commission*, p. 10). The report described the effect: "As the traveler approaches Washington over the brow of Arlington Heights in Fort Myer there will burst on his view a panorama that has few equals in the world; once seen it will never be forgotten, and will live in the memory of the beholder forever as a perpetual inspiration to loyalty, patriotism, and devotion to country" (*Bridge Commision*, p. 5).

Appropriately enough, one of the first men to appreciate the possibilities of such a panorama lay buried in front of the Custis–Lee Mansion only a short distance away—Pierre Charles L'Enfant. His body had been reinterred in a special ceremony in 1909 beneath a slab engraved with his original design of the capital city. Now, as the report indicates, the Arlington Memorial Bridge would carry the work of Washington and L'Enfant across the river and "up to the last resting place of the designer of the original plan of the Capital" (*Bridge Commission*, p. 5).

Although the vast sculptural project of the Memorial Bridge was never completed, the structure itself has become a symbolic avenue between the original city and the national cemetery. The panorama from the gravesite of L'Enfant (figure 91) has taken on today a new national significance. The admiration President John F. Kennedy had for the site led to his burial there and thus created a new national shrine along the axis of the Mall. From there one can see not only the direct relationship between the Capitol and the city before it, as envisioned by the city's planner, but also the series of mute monuments that nevertheless speak so meaningfully of the soul of the country. One cannot help but be aware that next to the Lincoln Memorial lies the newest shrine in the capital city—the Vietnam Veterans Memorial—which offers yet another example of how the country builds its national image.

*Figure 91*
*View of the city of Washington from the grave of Pierre Charles L'Enfant.*
Photograph by Staples & Charles, 1975.

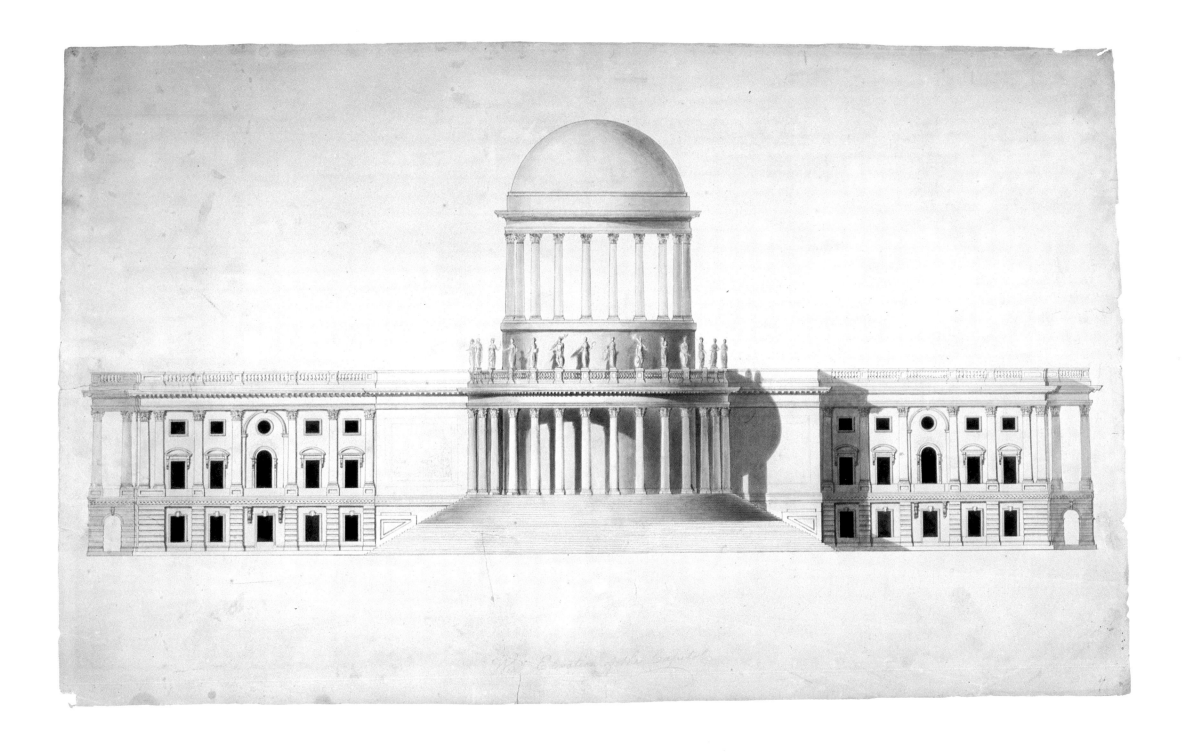

*Plate 1*  William Thornton.  Design for the west front of the U. S. Capitol, ca. 1793–95

*Plate 2*   **Stephen Hallet.  Design for the west front of the U. S. Capitol, 1793**

*Plate 3*  Stephen Hallet.  Cross section of design for the west front of the U. S. Capitol. 1793

*Plate 4* **William Thornton. Design for the east front of the U.S. Capitol, ca. 1793–95**

*Plate 5*    Benjamin H. Latrobe.  Design proposed for the east front of the U. S. Capitol, 1806

GROUND STORY OF THE CAPITOL. U.S.

*Plate 6*   **Benjamin H. Latrobe.  Design proposed for the ground floor of the U. S. Capitol, 1806**

*Plate 7*    Benjamin H. Latrobe. Design proposed for the **U. S. Capitol**, view from the south, 1810–11

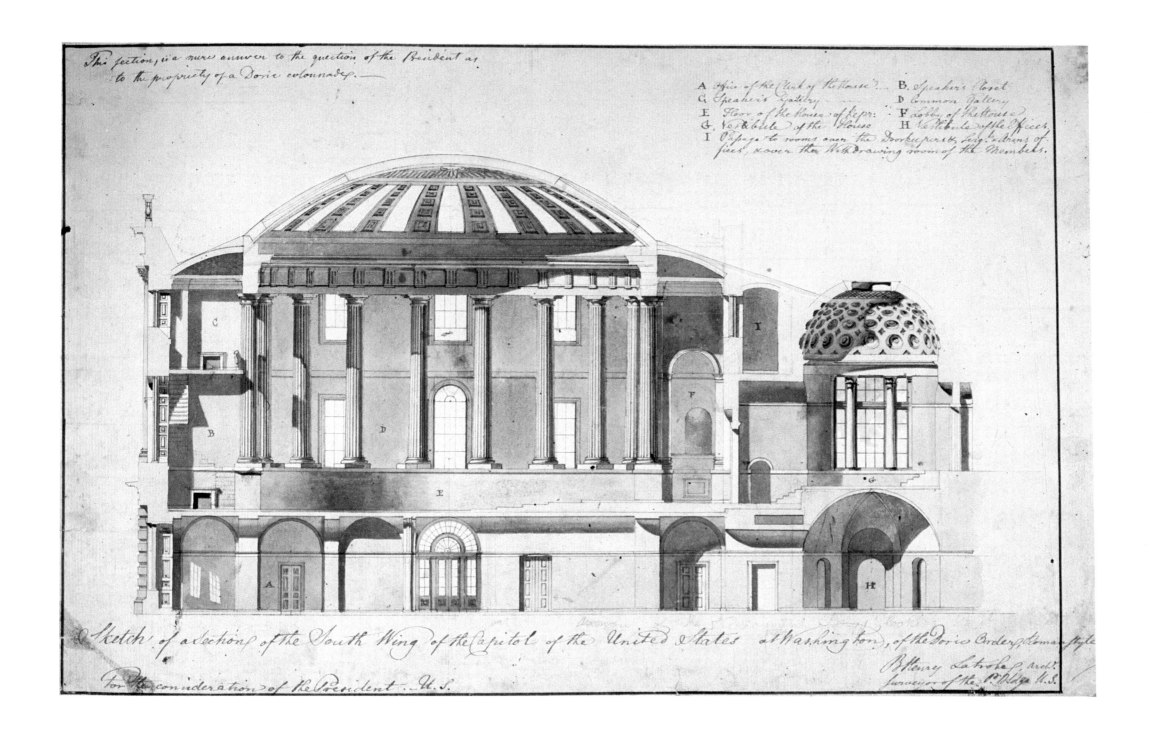

*This section, is a mere answer to the question of the President as to the propriety of a Doric colonnade.*

A  Office of the Clerk of the House.   B  Speaker's Closet
C  Speaker's Gallery             D  Common Gallery
E  Floor of the House of Repr:   F  Lobby of the House
G  Vestibule of the House        H  Vestibule of the Offices
I  Passage to rooms over the Doorkeeper's, Serjeant at Arms of-
   fices, & over the Withdrawing room of the Members.

*Sketch of a section of the South Wing of the Capitol of the United States at Washington, of the Doric Order, Roman style.*

*For the consideration of the President. U.S.*

*B Henry Latrobe, archt.*
*Surveyor of the P. Bldgs. U.S.*

Plate 8    **Benjamin H. Latrobe.   Design proposed for the Hall of Representatives in the U. S. Capitol, 1804**

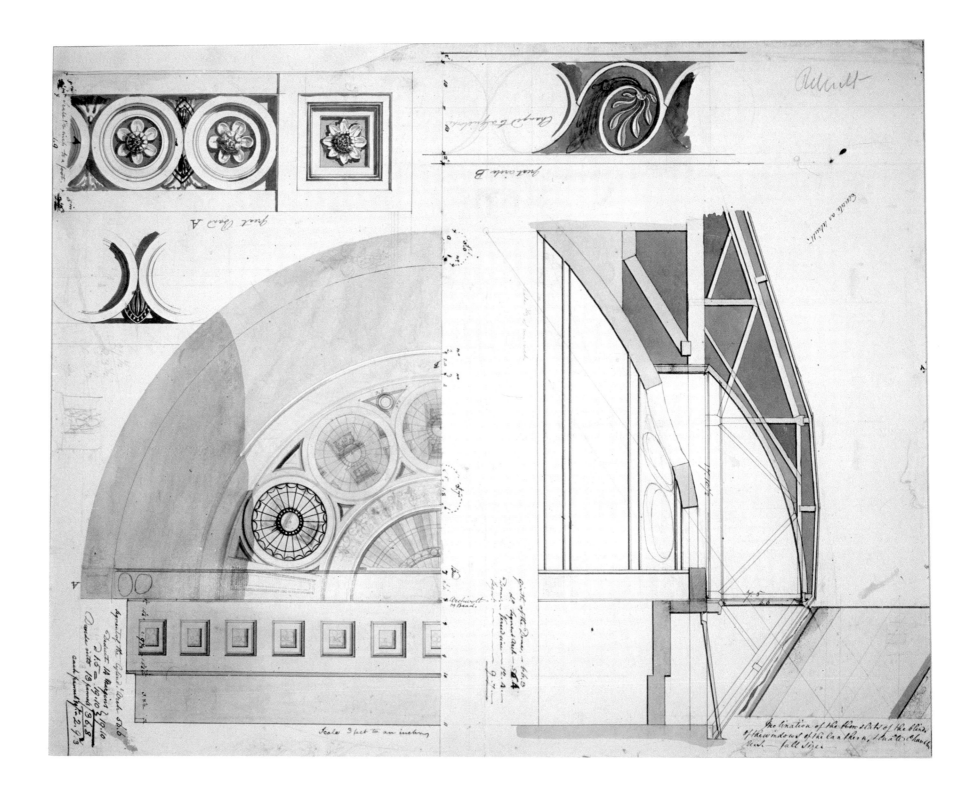

*Plate 9* Benjamin H. Latrobe. Design for the vaulting of the Senate Chamber in the U. S. Capitol, ca. 1816

the East front of the President's House, with the addition of the North external Porticos

*Plate 10* **Benjamin H. Latrobe. Design for the addition of porticoes on the north and south fronts of the President's House, 1807**

*Plate 11*   **Robert Mills.  Design proposed to enlarge the U. S. Capitol, elevation of the west front, 1851**

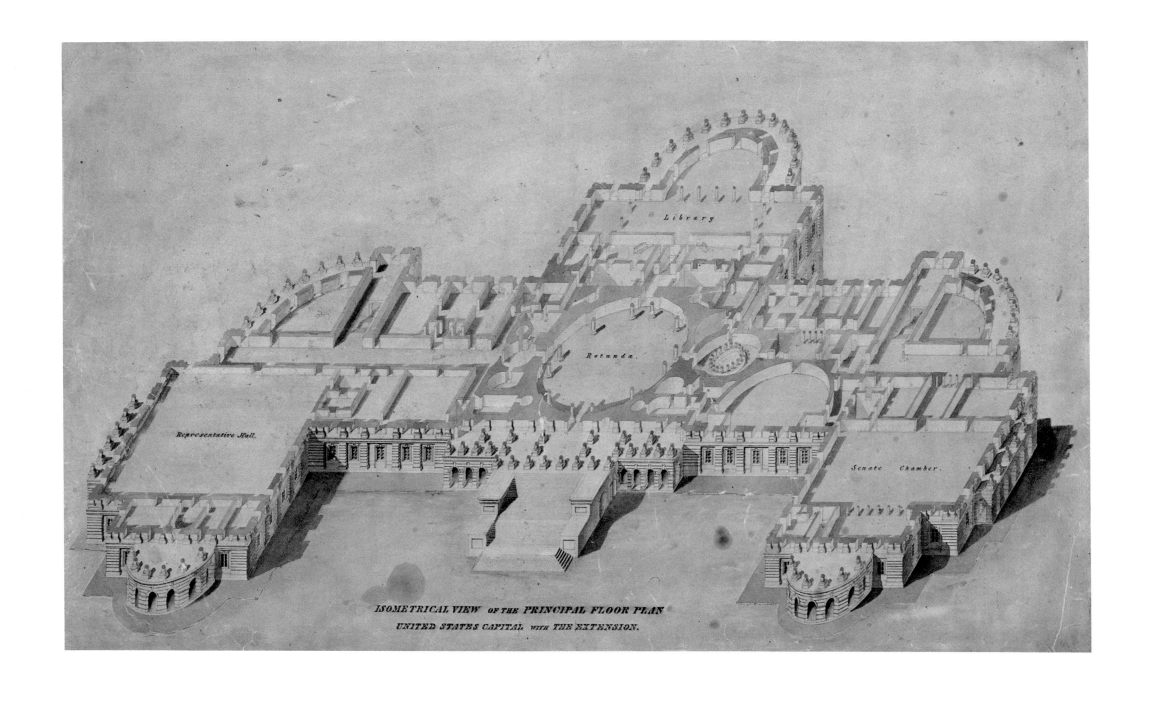

ISOMETRICAL VIEW OF THE PRINCIPAL FLOOR PLAN
UNITED STATES CAPITAL WITH THE EXTENSION.

*Plate 12*    Robert Mills. Design proposed to enlarge the U. S. Capitol, isometric plan of the principal story. 1851

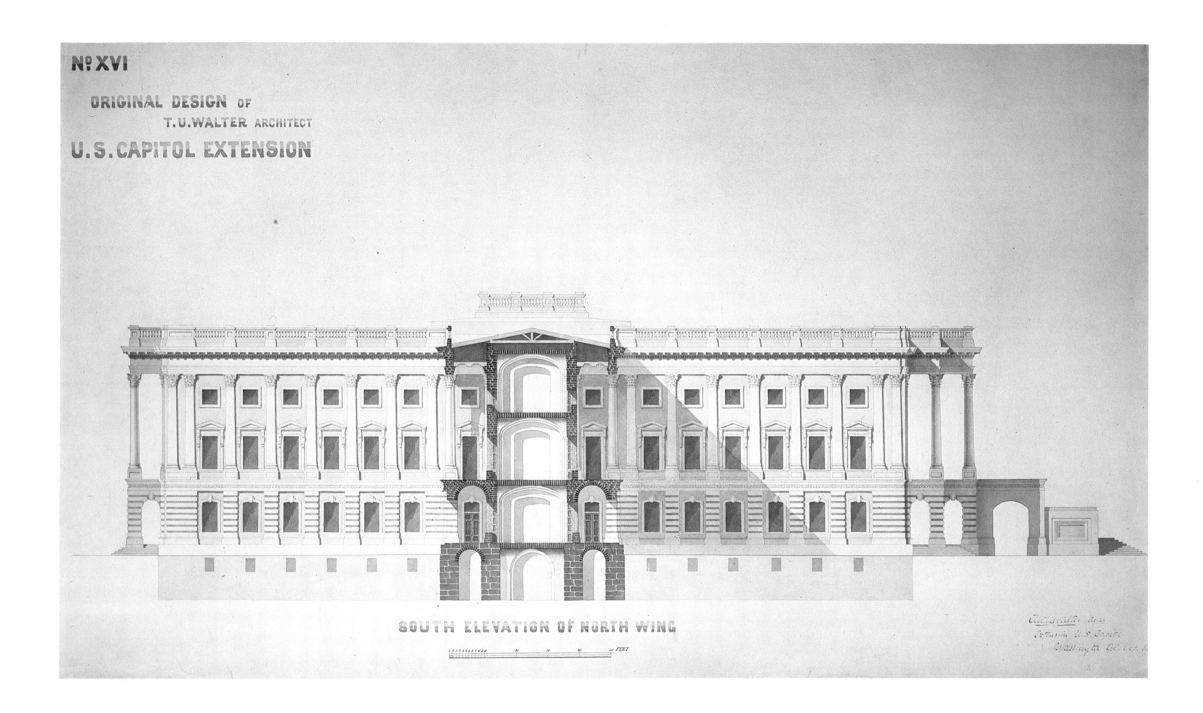

No XVI

ORIGINAL DESIGN OF
T.U.WALTER ARCHITECT
U.S. CAPITOL EXTENSION

SOUTH ELEVATION OF NORTH WING

*Plate 13*   Thomas U. Walter.  Design adopted for the north wing extension of the U. S. Capitol, 1851

*Plate 14*   Thomas U. Walter.  Design for the extension of the U. S. Capitol approved by President Millard Fillmore. 1851

EASTERN ELEVATION OF NORTH WING CAPITOL EXTENSION

*Plate 15*   **Thomas U. Walter and Montgomery C. Meigs.  Revised design for the east front of the north wing extension of the U. S. Capitol, 1853**

*Plate 16*

**Thomas U. Walter.** Design for the entrance doors on the east front of the extension of the U. S. Capitol, ca. 1853

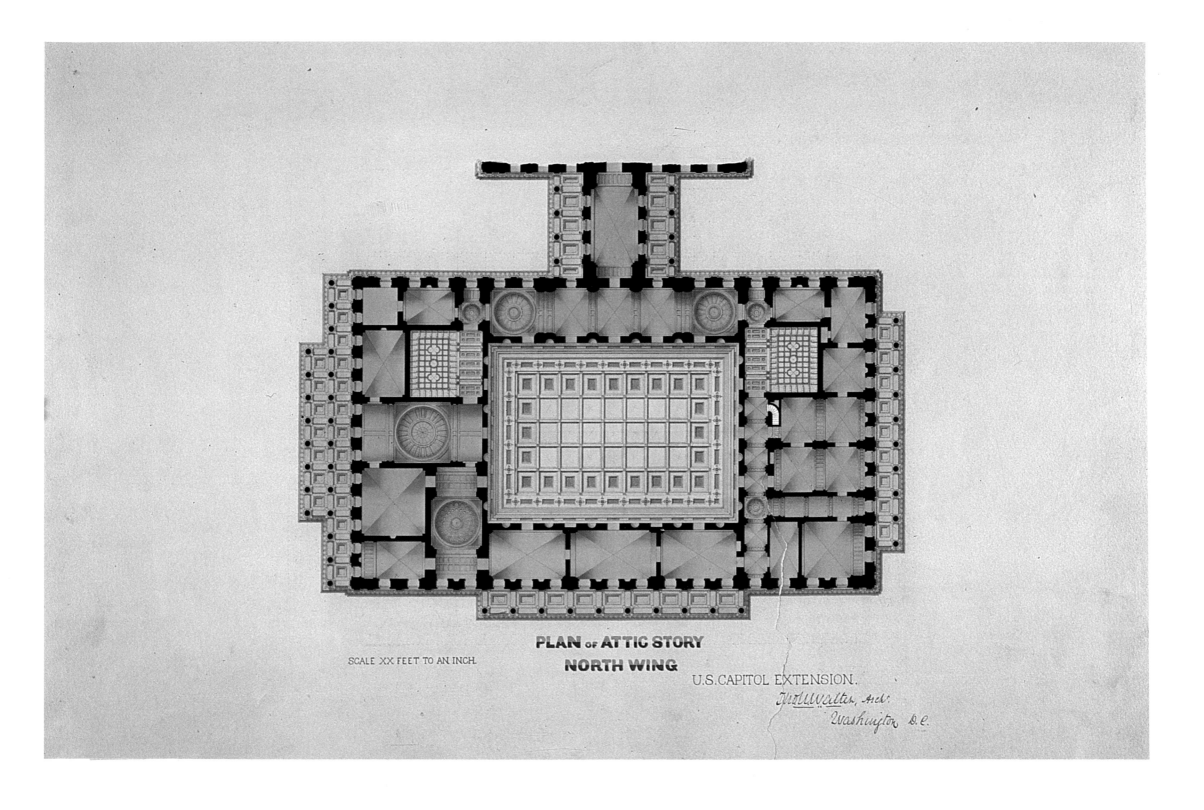

PLAN of ATTIC STORY
NORTH WING

SCALE XX FEET TO AN INCH.

U.S. CAPITOL EXTENSION.

*Plate 17* Thomas U. Walter. Plan of the attic story of the north wing extension of the U.S. Capitol, ca. 1853

*Plate 18* Thomas U. Walter. Design for the interior of the Senate Chamber in the north wing extension of the U. S. Capitol, 1855

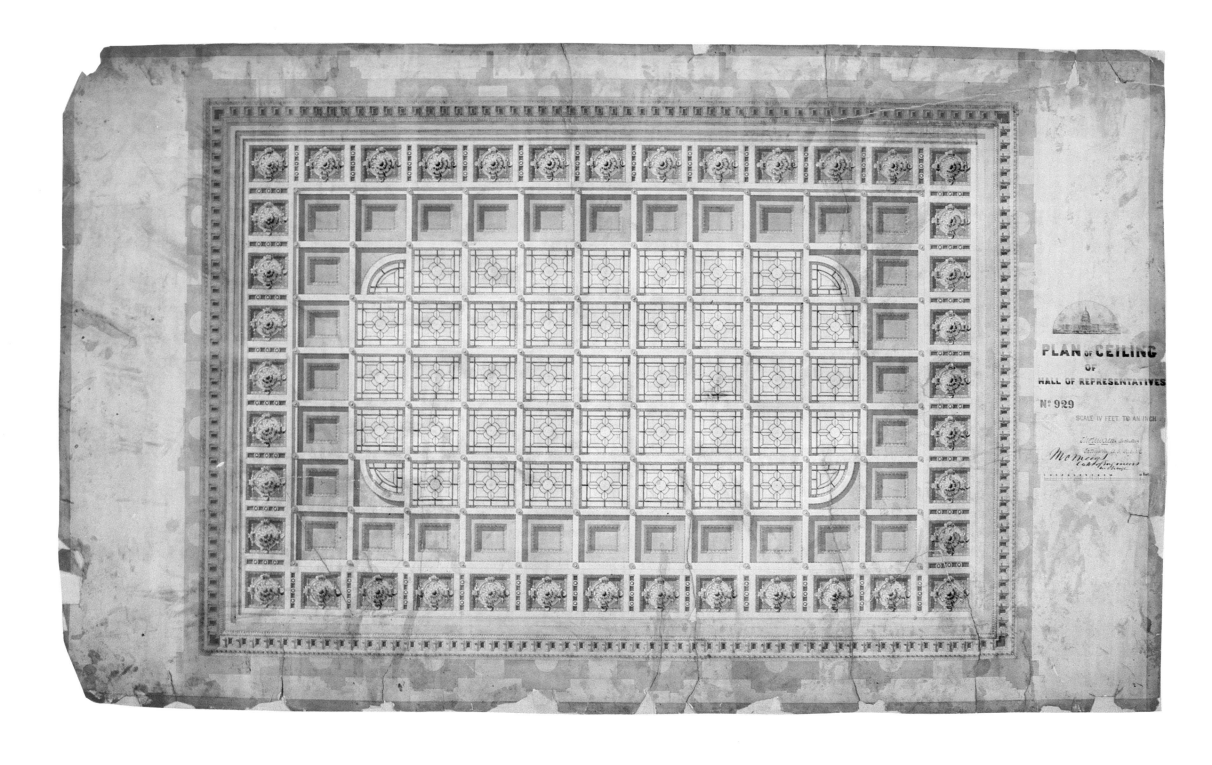

*Plate 19*    Thomas U. Walter.  Design for the stained-glass ceiling over the Hall of Representatives in the south wing extension of the U. S. Capitol, 1855

FAN ROOM, H. OF R.

U.S.C. EXTENSION.

SECTION THRO. C.D. OF PLAN

SCALE

*Plate 20*   **Montgomery C. Meigs.  Design for the fan to ventilate the Hall of Representatives in the south wing extension of the U. S. Capitol, 1860**

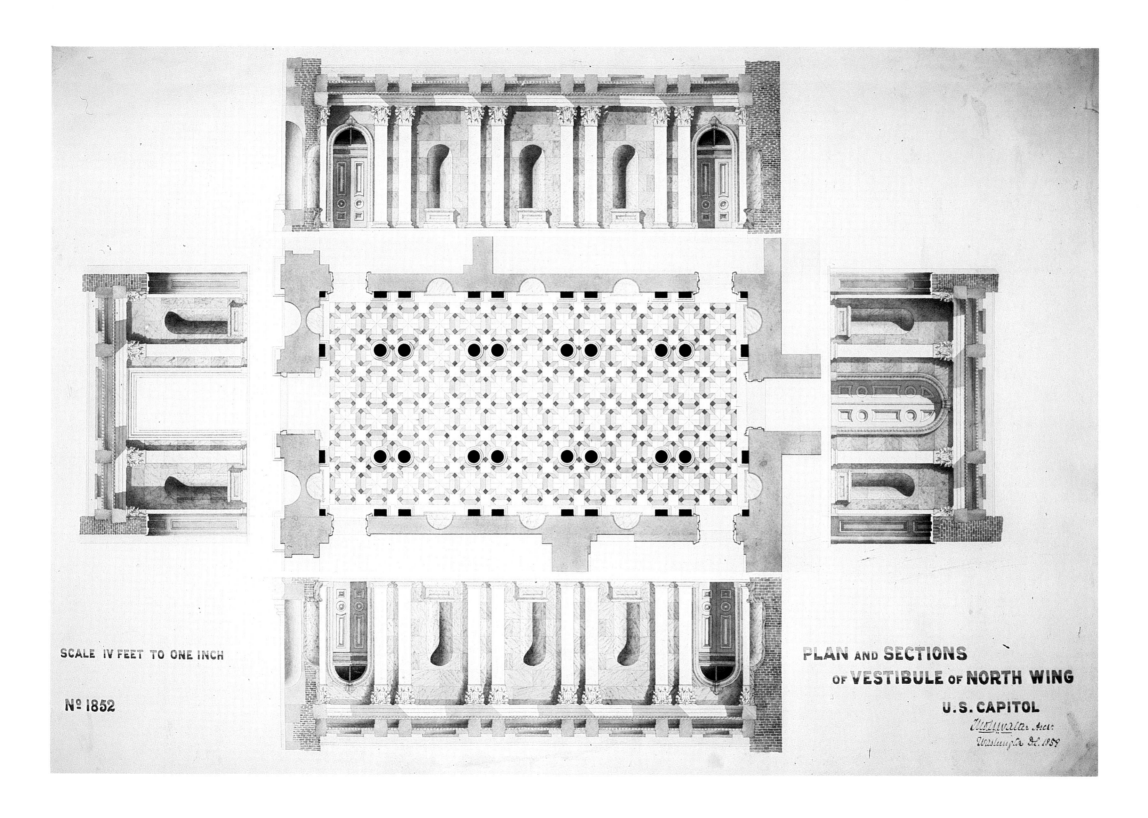

SCALE IV FEET TO ONE INCH

Nº 1852

PLAN AND SECTIONS
OF VESTIBULE OF NORTH WING

U.S. CAPITOL

*Plate 21*  **Thomas U. Walter. Design for the decoration of the vestibule outside the Senate Chamber in the north wing extension of the U. S. Capitol, 1859**

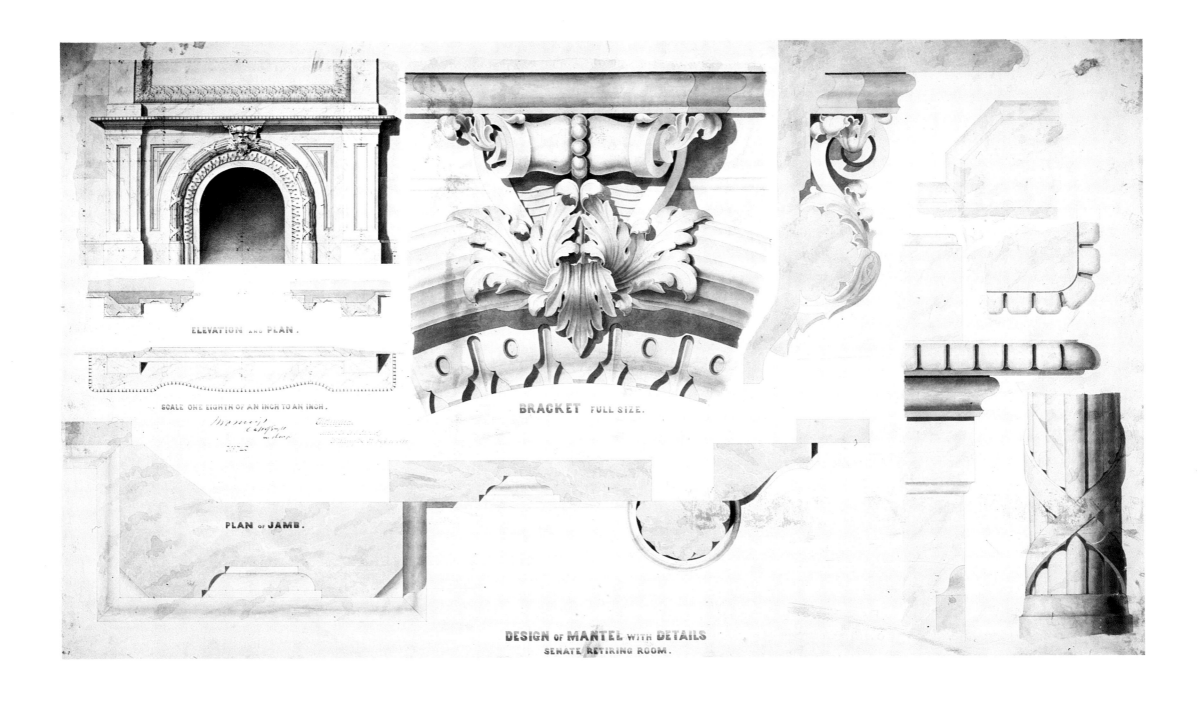

ELEVATION and PLAN.

SCALE ONE EIGHTH OF AN INCH TO AN INCH.

PLAN of JAMB.

BRACKET FULL SIZE.

DESIGN of MANTEL with DETAILS
SENATE RETIRING ROOM.

*Plate 22* **Thomas U. Walter. Design for the mantel installed in the Senate Retiring Room in the north wing extension of the U. S. Capitol, 1855**

*Plate 23*
**Thomas U. Walter. Design for the pedestal of the statue of Freedom on top of the Capitol dome, 1862**

*Plate 24*  **Thomas U. Walter.  Design for the extension and new dome of the U. S. Capitol, 1855**

*Plate 25*
**Thomas U. Walter. Design for the interior of the Capitol dome, 1859**

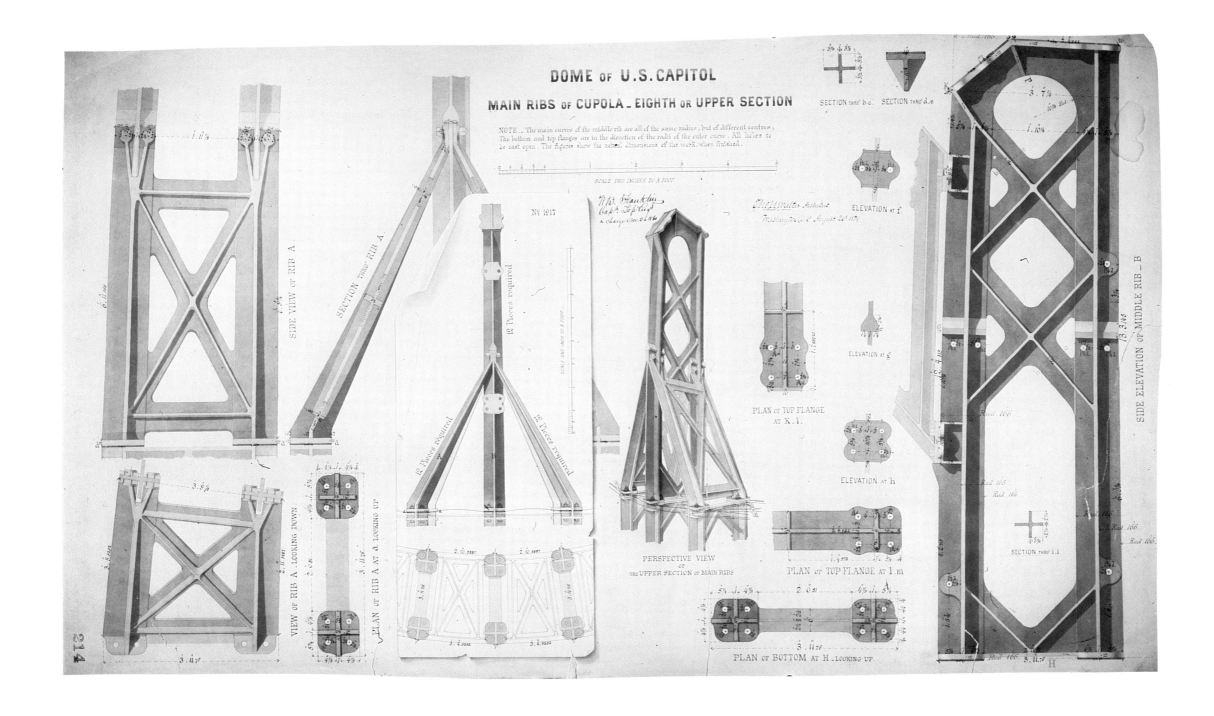

*Plate 26*   **Thomas U. Walter. Design for the structural parts of the ribs of the Capitol dome, 1859**

*Plate 27* Thomas U. Walter. Design for Girard College for Orphans, Philadelphia, 1835

*Plate 28*   **B. F. Smith, Jr.  View of Washington, D. C., with projected improvements, 1852**

*Plate 29*    **Ammi B. Young.  Transverse section of the winning design for the U. S. Custom House, Boston, 1837**

*Plate 30*   Ithiel Town and Alexander Jackson Davis.  Winning design in the competition for the U. S. Custom House, New York, 1800

Architect
A. T. Wood

DESIGN FOR THE
Adopted by the Hon. Rob. J. Walker

Plate 31   Alexander T. Wood.  Design adopted by the secretary of the treasury for the U. S. Custom House, New Orleans, 1847

LEVEE or RIVER FRONT

-ORLEANS CUSTOM-HOUSE,

Commissioners

...tary of the U.S. Treasury. November 22nd A.D. 1847.    Dennis Prieur, Alcée La Branche & W. M. Gwin

*Plate 32* **Alexander T. Wood. Transverse section of the U. S. Custom House, New Orleans, 1851**

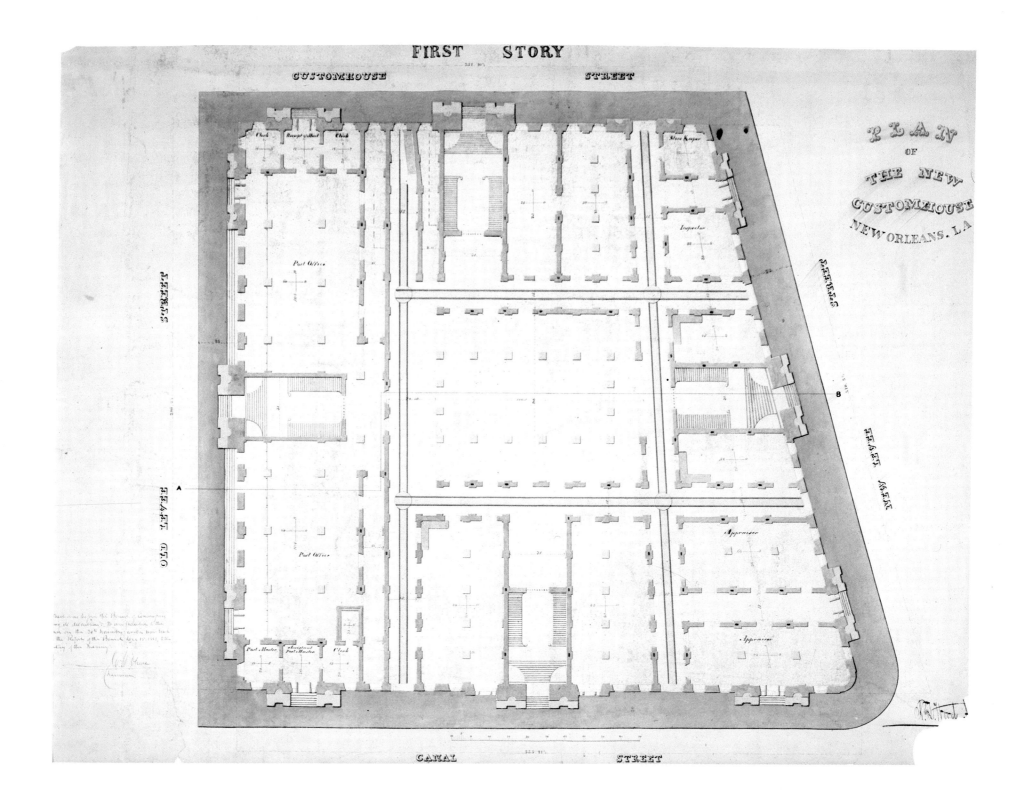

FIRST STORY

CUSTOMHOUSE STREET

PLAN
OF
THE NEW
CUSTOMHOUSE
NEW ORLEANS, LA

CANAL STREET

*Plate 33*   **Alexander T. Wood.  First-story plan of the U. S. Custom House, New Orleans, 1851**

ROOF

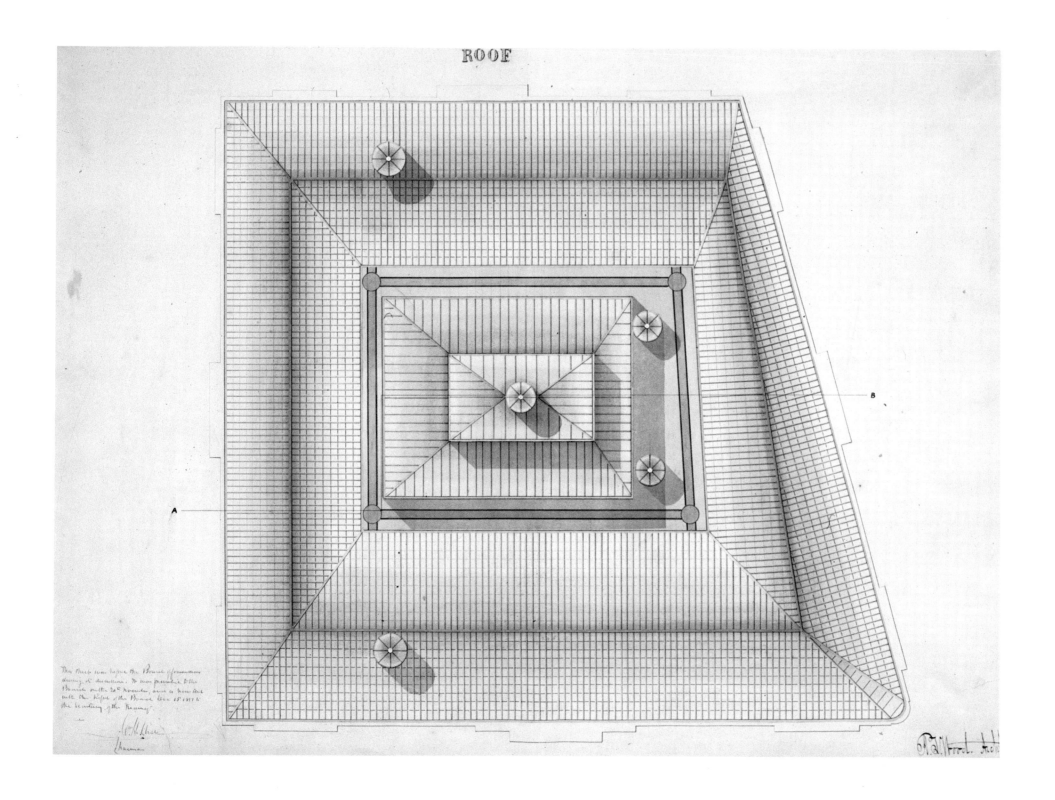

A

B

*Plate 34* **Alexander T. Wood. Roof plan of the U. S. Custom House, New Orleans, 1851**

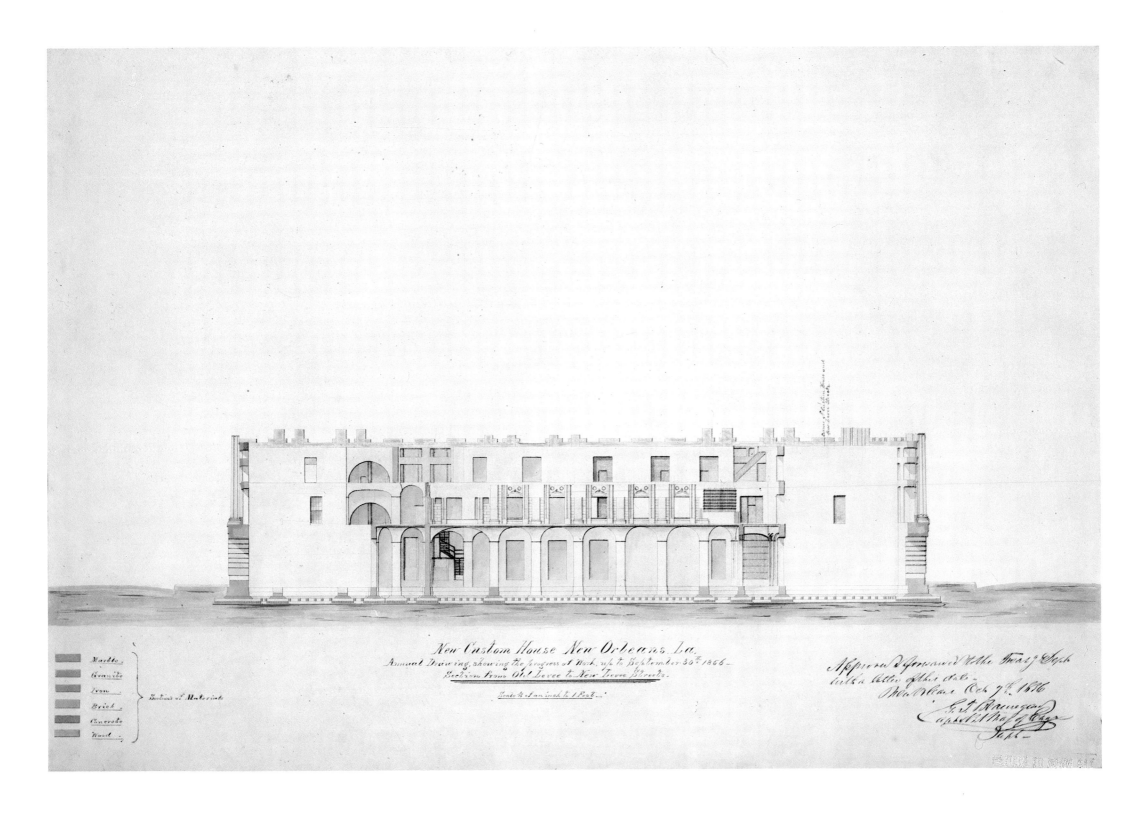

New Custom House New Orleans La.
Annual Drawing, showing the progress of Work, up to September 30th 1856 –
Section from Old Levee to New Levee Streets.

Scale ¼ of an inch to 1 Foot –

Marble.
Granite.
Iron.
Brick.
Concrete.
Wood.

Section of Materials.

Approved & forwarded to the Treasy Dept
with a letter of this date –
New Orleans Oct 7th 1856

P.G.T. Beauregard
Capt U.S. Corps of Engrs
Supt –

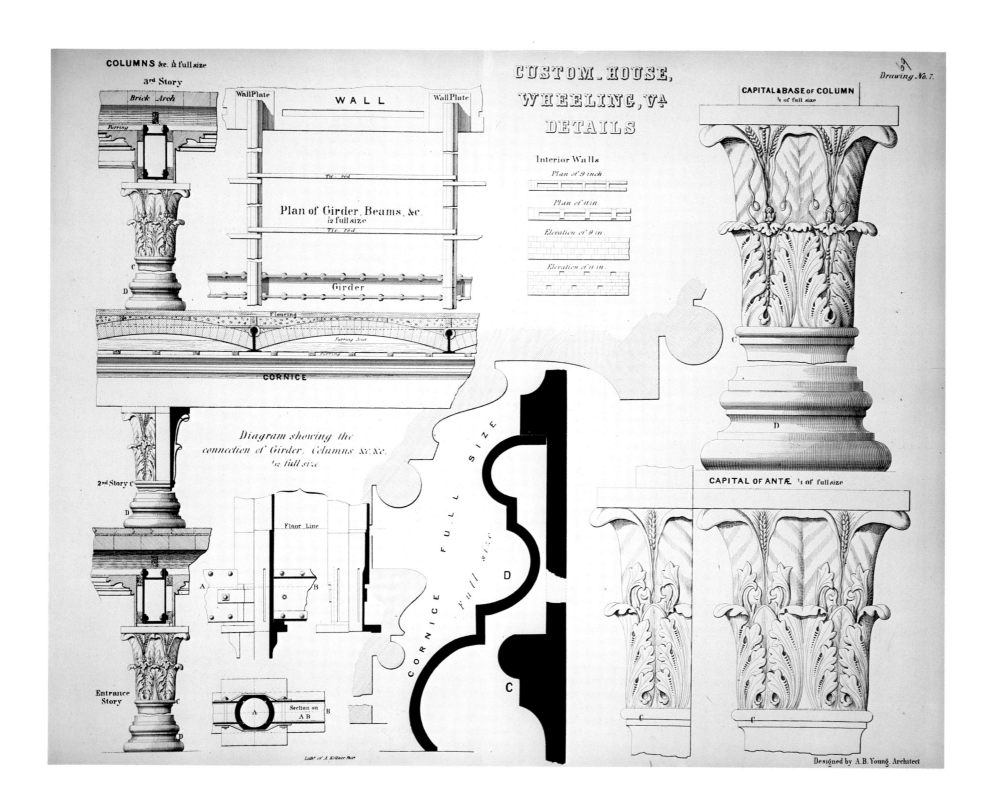

Plate 36    Ammi B. Young.  Details for the U. S. Custom House, Wheeling, West Virginia, 1855

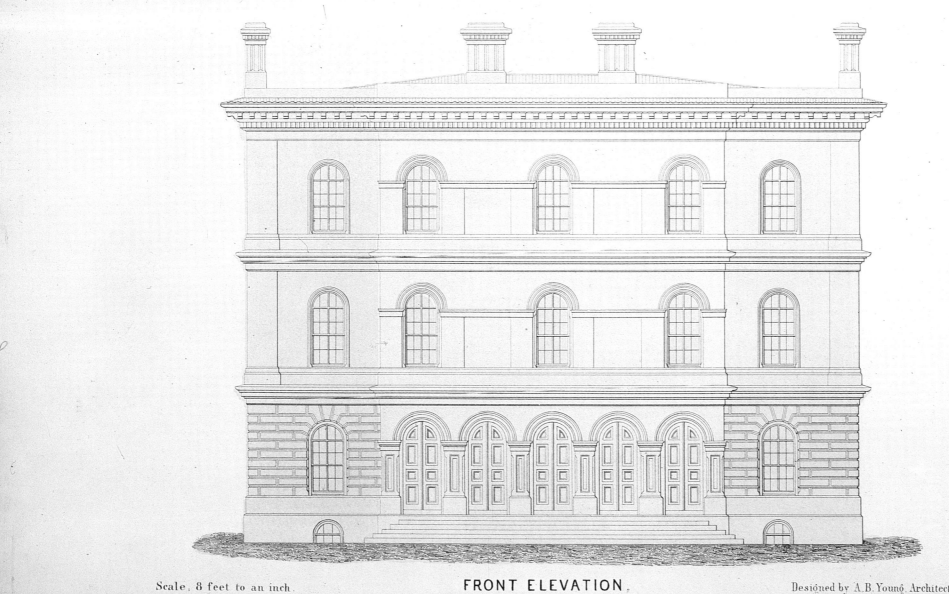

Scale, 8 feet to an inch.          FRONT ELEVATION.                    Designed by A.B. Young, Architect

CUSTOM.HOUSE , CHICAGO, ILL<sup>S</sup>

A Kollner Lith. Philad<sup>a</sup>

Plate 37    Ammi B. Young.  Front elevation of the U. S. Custom House, Chicago, 1855

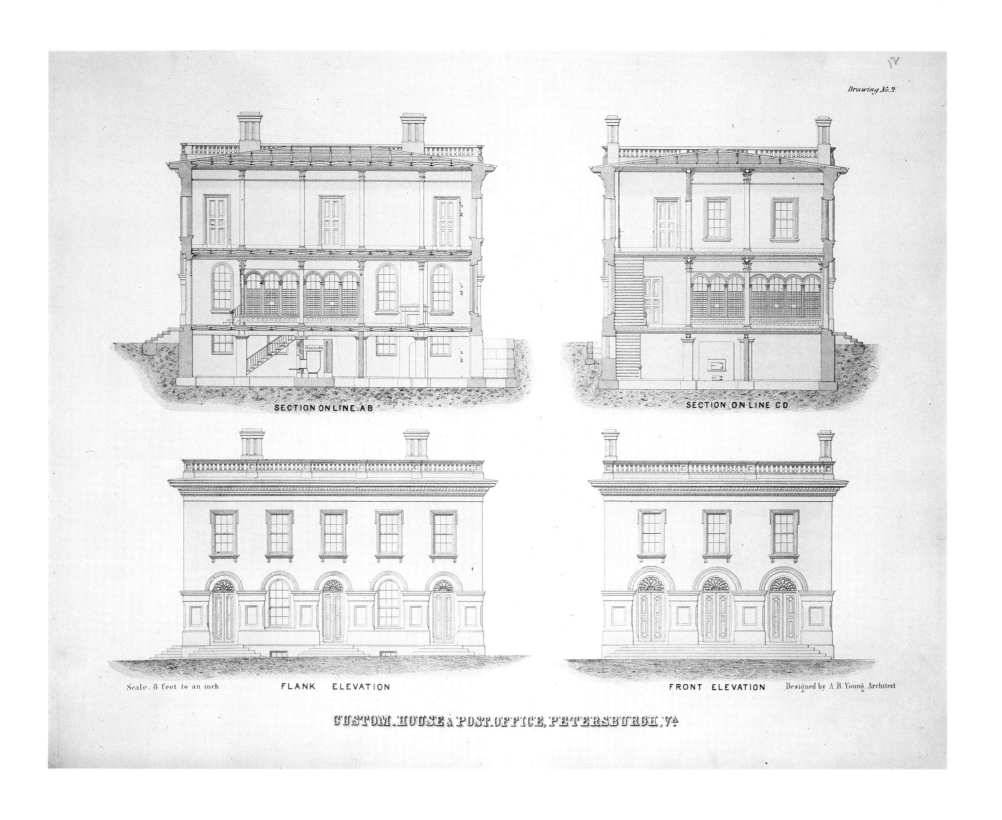

SECTION ON LINE AB

SECTION ON LINE CD

Scale. 8 feet to an inch     FLANK ELEVATION

FRONT ELEVATION    Designed by A.B.Young, Architect

CUSTOM.HOUSE & POST.OFFICE, PETERSBURGH, VA

*Plate 38*    **Ammi B. Young. Elevations and sections of the U. S. Custom House and Post Office, Petersburg, Virginia, 1855**

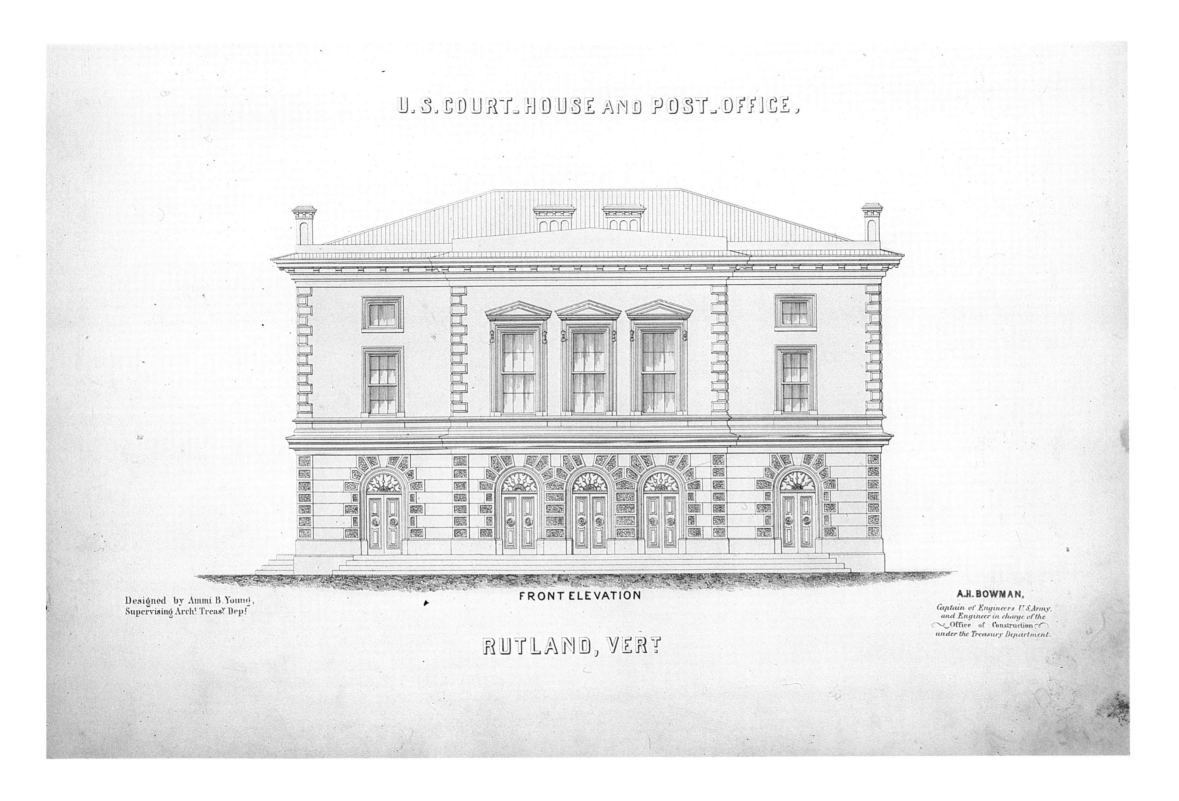

U.S. COURT_HOUSE AND POST_OFFICE,

FRONT ELEVATION

Designed by Ammi B. Young,
Supervising Arch! Treas! Dep!

A.H.BOWMAN,
Captain of Engineers U.S.Army,
and Engineer in charge of the
Office of Construction
under the Treasury Department.

RUTLAND, VERT

*Plate 39*   **Ammi B. Young. Front elevation of the U. S. Courthouse and Post Office, Rutland, Vermont. 1856**

One fourth size

Frieze Ornament 3rd Story Exterior.

One half of the Ornament in Frieze between Pilasters, over Post Office Boxing. one sixth size.

One fourth size

In Belt course under 3rd Story windows.

One sixth of pattern open for Stair riser
One third size.

Half size.

Enrichment of interior Mouldings.  see Drawing No. 12

J

A

A

Full size

B

B

E

End of Step.

Enrichment of Iron Exterior Door
Mouldings, see Drawing No. 18

Enrichment of Interior Mouldings, see Drawing 12
Full size.

Open String Ornament of Stairs; three fourth size.

Spandrel Ornament of Mantel
¼ full size.

C

Moulding of Iron Detention Door.

S. W. CLARK.
Acting Engineer in charge
Office of Construction
under the Treasury Department

A. B. YOUNG.
Supervising Architect
U.S. Treasury Department

DETAILS
OF ORNAMENTATION FOR
THE
U.S. POST OFFICE AND COURTS,
PHILADA PA

A. Kollner's Lith. Phila.

Plate 40    **Ammi B. Young.  Ornamental details for the U. S. Courthouse and Post Office, Philadelphia, 1860**

FULL-SIZE DETAILS
OF CANDELABRA IN
FRONT OF POST. OFFICE_
DELIVERY,

U.S. POST.OFFICE

PHILADELPHIA, Pa.

Section e f

Section c d

Section

PLAN
OF
TRIPOD FEET
OF
CANDELABRA
½ size

Section a b

BRASS RAIL
2'2" Diam.
encircling Pedestal

THE FASCÆS
(⅓ of full-size)

DRAWING No. 22.

Glass globular shade

BELL 2' Diam.

Diam. 2'7.

Diam. 2' 7.

Diam 7.8.

Diam. 2' 7½.

S. M. CLARK.
Acting Engineer in charge
Office of Construction
under the Treasury Department.

Designed by
A. B. YOUNG.
Supervising Architect
U.S. Treasury Department.

2' 6¼ Diam.

MOULDING DEVELOPED

SECTION OF FASCÆS
AT FOOT
one eighth

Section ½ b

Screw

Diam.

13 of these
Brackets
to each Pedestal

Section
i j

Section

Frieze Cornice &c circular

Plan of Foot of Bracket

Diam.
2' 3.

Diam. at
Angles
2'3½
Polygon
of
13 sides

i

j

g

e

h

c

f

d

ELEVATION OF BASE OF COLUMN

N.B.
The Bell to be
a fac-simile
Copy of the
old 'Indepen-
dence Bell'
half. size.

Diam. 5 inc.

INVERTED PLAN OF CAPITAL &c HALF
4¼ sqr.

Outline Plan of Base

Diam. 4⅜ inc.

PLINTH

LINE OF FLOOR

HEAD OF BELL

ELEVATION OF PART
OF THE
ENTABLATURE
&C.

Diam 2'5.

SHAFT 2 ft.

From centre of
Pedestal to centre
of Column 12'5"
(13 Columns)

Total height from floor to indicator 8'8½"

Elevation of one-half foot of Candelabra and top of Bell.

Elevation of one-half head of Candelabra.

A. Kollner Lith. Phila.

*Plate 41*   **Ammi B. Young.  Decorative details of lighting fixtures for the U. S. Courthouse and Post Office, Philadelphia, 1860**

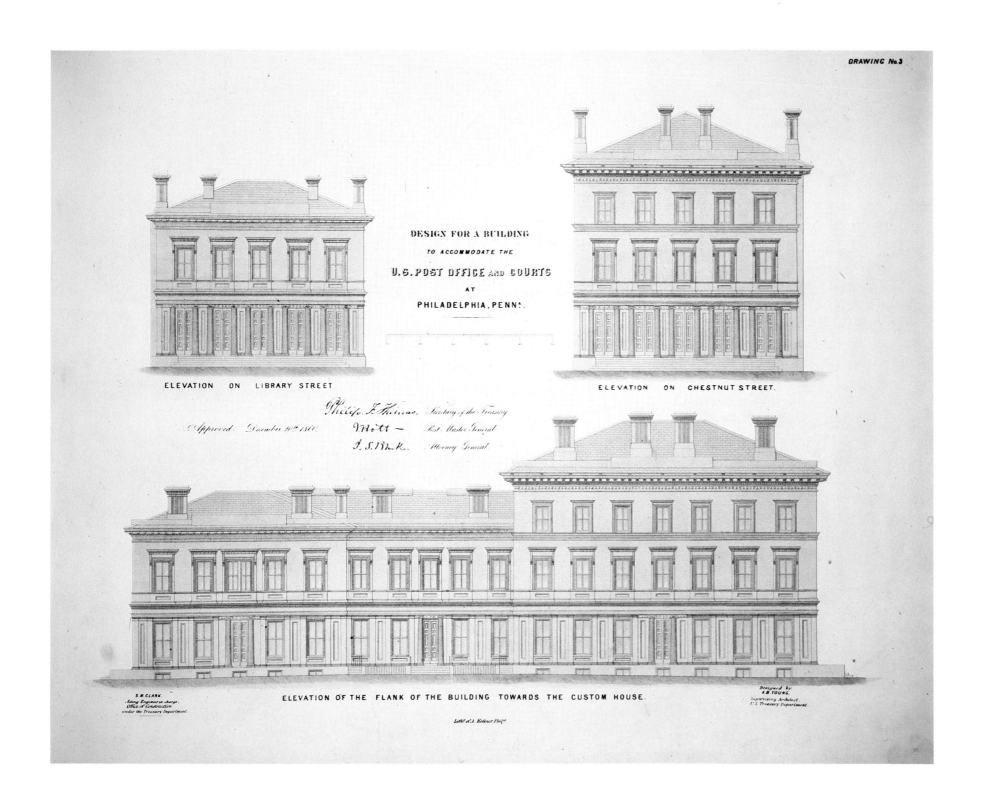

DESIGN FOR A BUILDING

TO ACCOMMODATE THE

U.S. POST OFFICE AND COURTS

AT

PHILADELPHIA, PENN².

ELEVATION ON LIBRARY STREET.

ELEVATION ON CHESTNUT STREET.

Philip F. Thomas, *Secretary of the Treasury*

Approved December 20th 1860.

Mott — *Post Master General*

J. S. Black. *Attorney General*

ELEVATION OF THE FLANK OF THE BUILDING TOWARDS THE CUSTOM HOUSE.

S.M.CLARK
*Acting Engineer in charge.*
*Office of Construction*
*under the Treasury Department.*

Designed by
A.B.YOUNG.
*Supervising Architect*
*U.S Treasury Department.*

Lith. of A. Kollner, Phil.

Plate 42    Ammi B. Young.  Elevations of the U. S. Courthouse and Post Office, Philadelphia, 1860

FRONT ELEVATION.

Scale 4 feet to one inch.

№ 4.

*Plate 43*    **Alfred B. Mullett.  Front elevation of the U. S. Branch Mint, Carson City, Nevada, 1866**

*Plate 44*

**Alfred B. Mullett. Cross section of the customs room in the U. S. Custom House,** Portland, Maine, ca. 1868

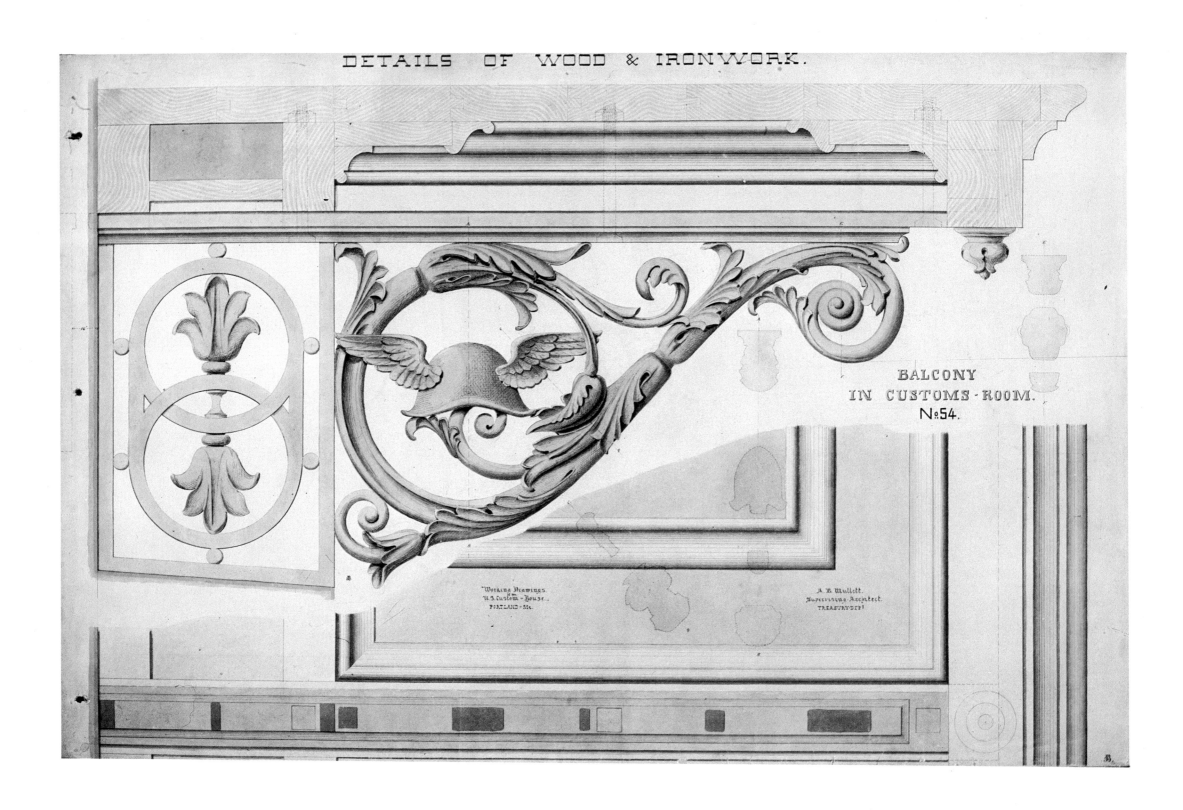

BALCONY
IN CUSTOMS-ROOM.
N.º 54.

*Plate 45* **Alfred B. Mullett. Details of the wood- and ironwork for the balcony in the customs room of the U. S. Custom House, Portland, Maine, ca. 1868**

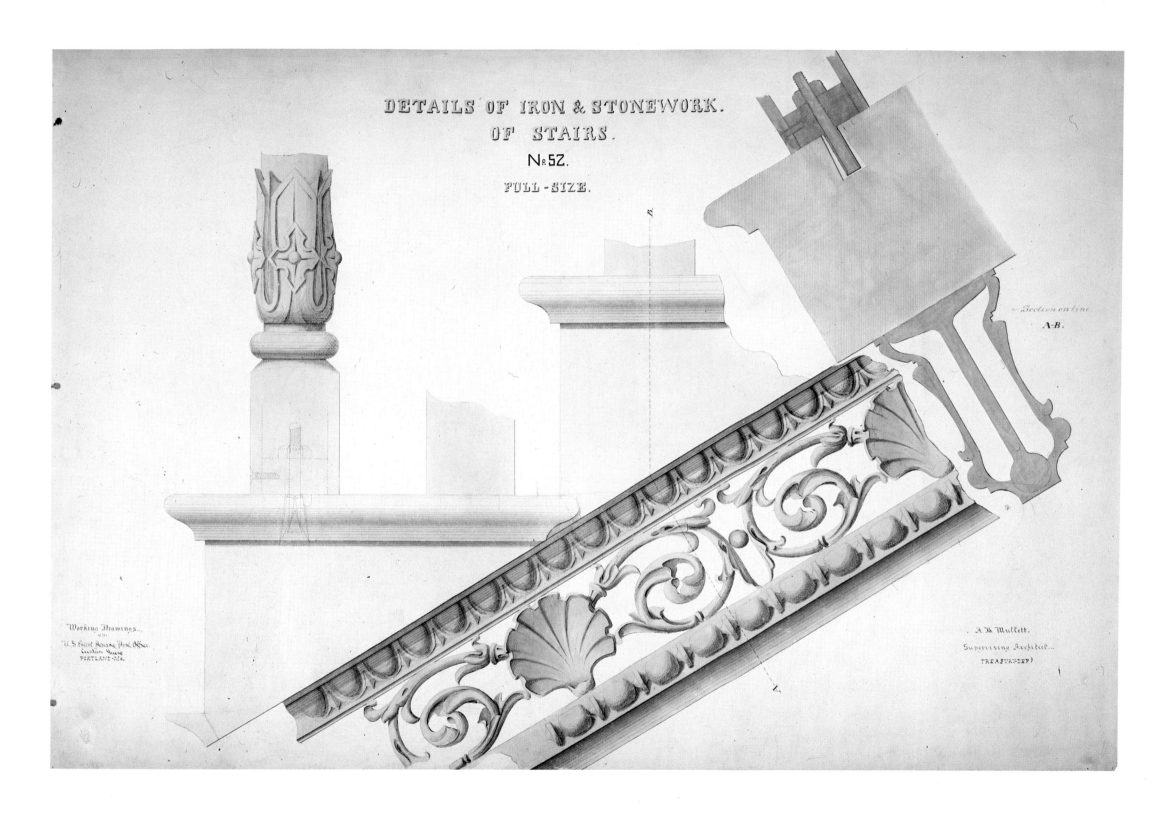

Plate 46    Alfred B. Mullett.  Full-size details for the iron- and stonework of the stairs in the U. S. Custom House, Portland, Maine, ca. 1868

# DETAILS OF PLASTERWORK.
## FULL SIZE.

FRIEZE OF MAIN CORNICE
IN
CUSTOMS ROOM.

Nº 49.

Working Drawings of the
U. S. Custom House.
PORTLAND·Me.

A. B. Mullett.
Supervising Arch.t
TREASURY DEP.t

Plate 47    Alfred B. Mullett.  Full-size details for the plasterwork of the cornice frieze in the customs room of the **U. S. Custom House**, Portland, Maine, ca. **1868**

FULL SIZE DETAILS
OF IRON WORK FOR STAIRS.

ELEVATION OF NEWEL POST.

Nº 50

Working Drawings
for U. S. Custom House at
ST PAUL, MINN.

A. B. Mullett
Supervising Arch't
TREASURY DPT

*Plate 48*
**Alfred B. Mullett.  Full-size details of the ironwork for the stairs in the
U. S. Custom House, Saint Paul, Minnesota, ca. 1868**

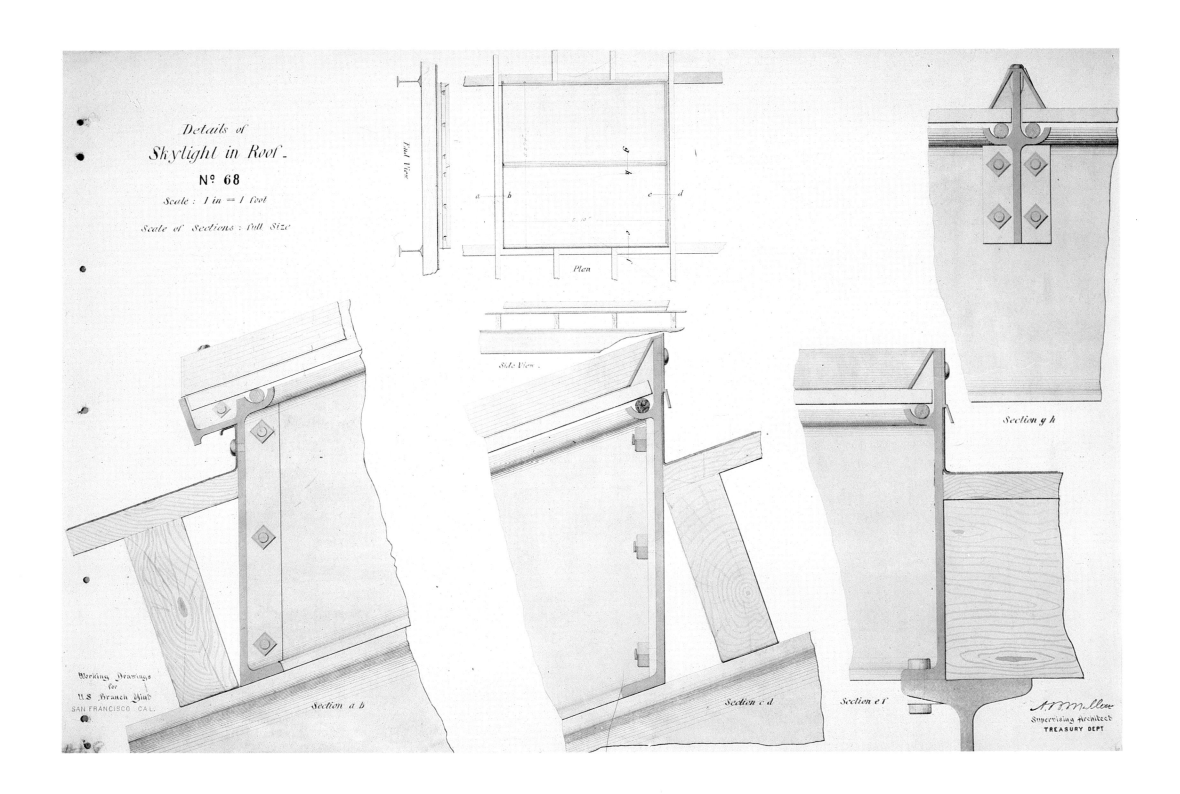

*Details of*
*Skylight in Roof.*

Nº 68

Scale : 1 in = 1 foot

Scale of Sections : full Size

End View

Plan

Side View

Section g h

Section a b

Section c d

Section e f

Working Drawings
for
U.S. Branch Mint
SAN FRANCISCO CAL.

Supervising Architect
TREASURY DEPT

Plate 49    Alfred B. Mullett.  Details of a skylight for the U. S. Branch Mint, San Francisco, ca. 1870

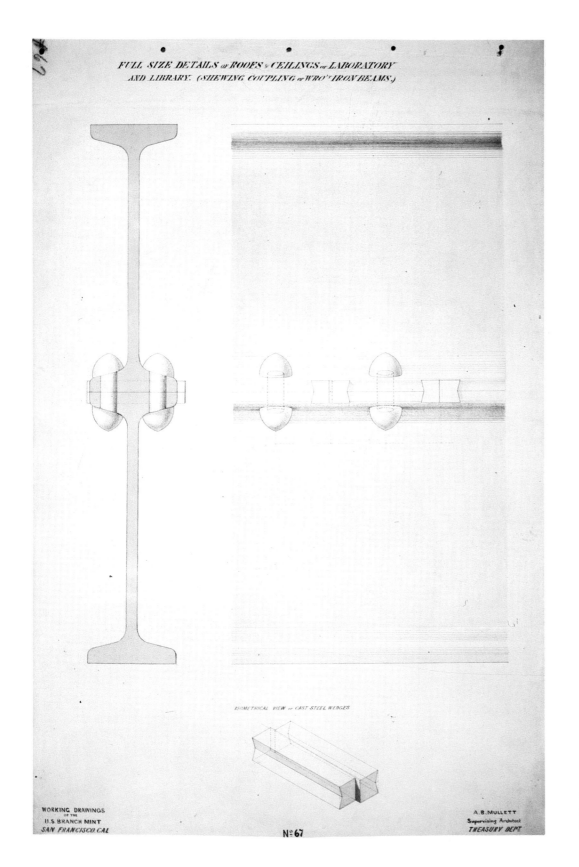

*Plate 50*

**Alfred B. Mullett.  Full-size details of the wrought-iron beams for the roof of the U. S. Branch Mint, San Francisco, ca. 1870**

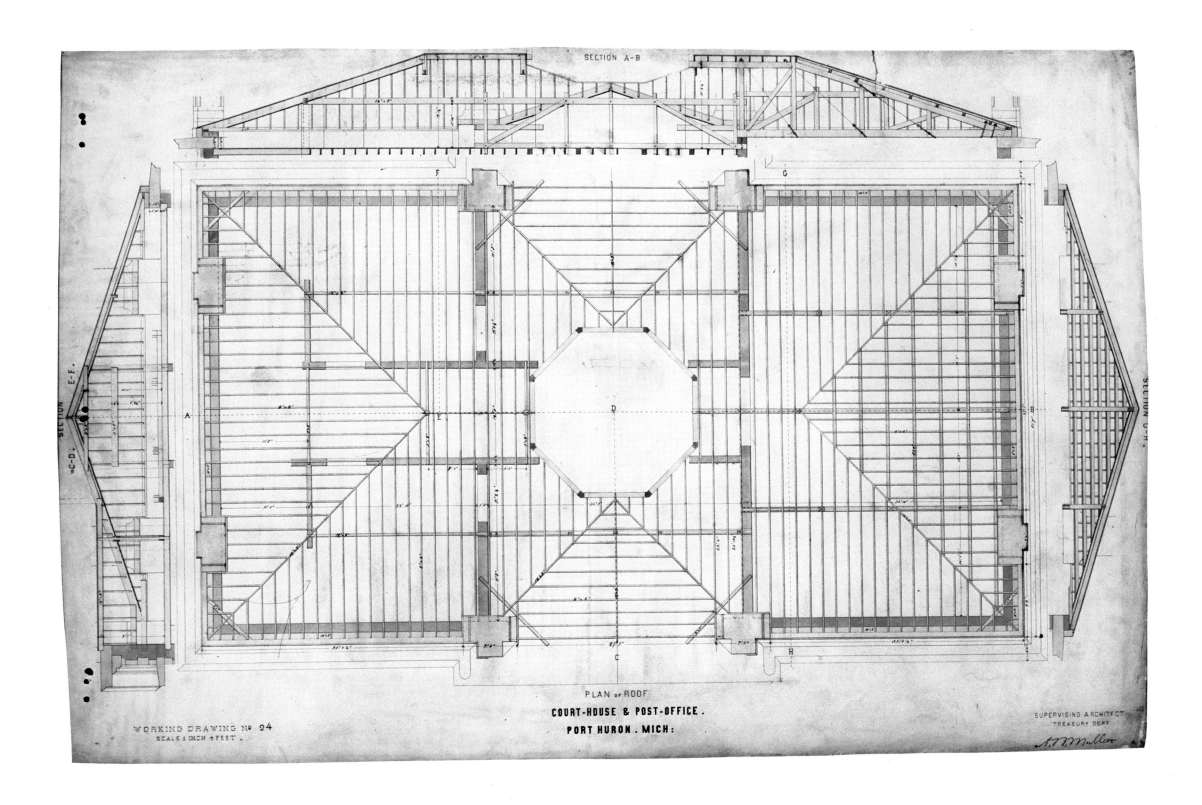

SECTION A-B

PLAN of ROOF

**COURT-HOUSE & POST-OFFICE.**

**PORT HURON. MICH:**

WORKING DRAWING Nº 24
SCALE 1 INCH 4 FEET

SUPERVISING ARCHITECT
TREASURY DEPT

*Plate 51*    Alfred B. Mullett.  Plan and sections of the roof of the U. S. Custom House and Post Office, Port Huron, Michigan, ca. 1874

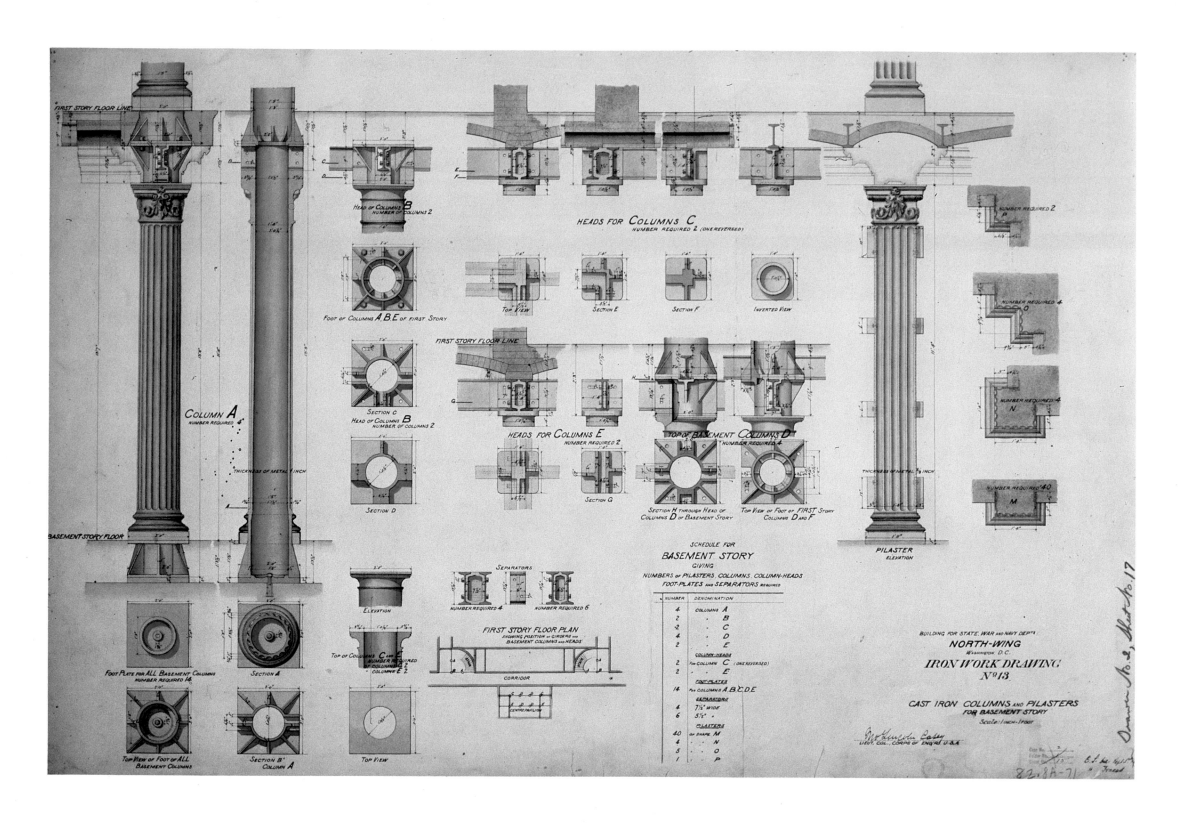

Plate 52    Detail drawing for the ironwork of the north wing of the State, War and Navy Building, Washington, D. C., ca. 1880

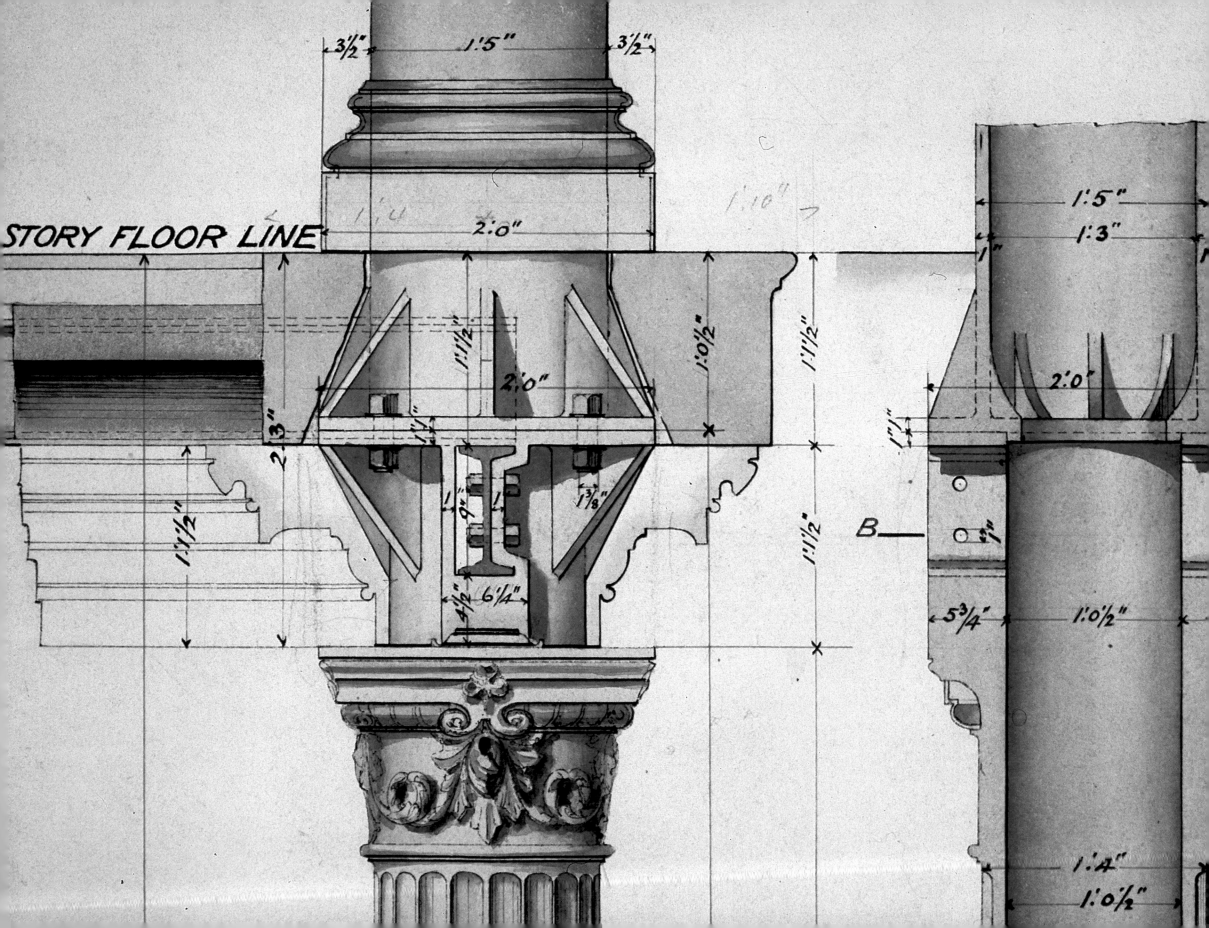

STORY FLOOR LINE

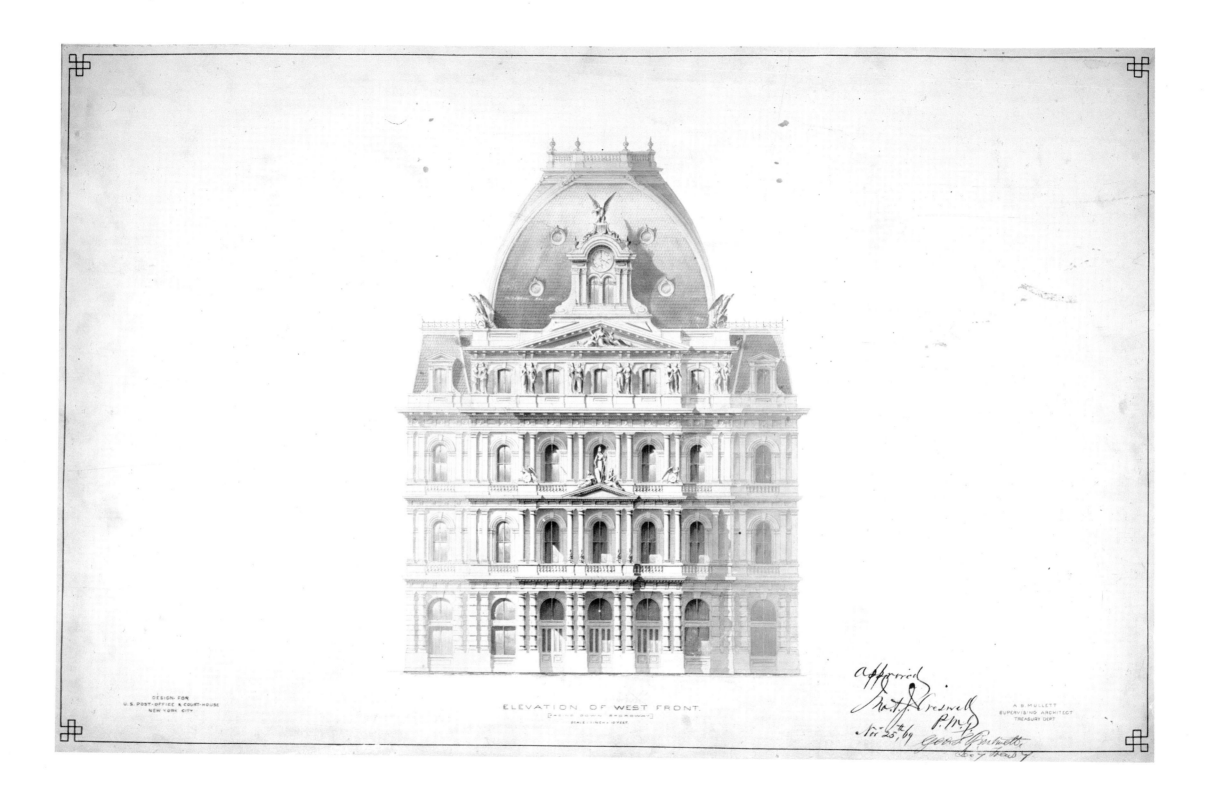

ELEVATION OF WEST FRONT.

DESIGN FOR
U.S. POST-OFFICE & COURT-HOUSE
NEW YORK CITY

A. B. MULLETT
SUPERVISING ARCHITECT
TREASURY DEPT

*Plate 53* **Alfred B. Mullett. Elevation of the west front of the U. S. Post Office and Courthouse, New York, 1869**

ELEVATION OF BROADWAY FRONT

U.S. POST OFFICE & COURT HOUSE

NEW YORK

SCALE_EIGHT FEET_ONE INCH_

*Plate 54*   **Alfred B. Mullett.  Elevation of the Broadway front of the U. S. Post Office and Courthouse, New York, 1868**

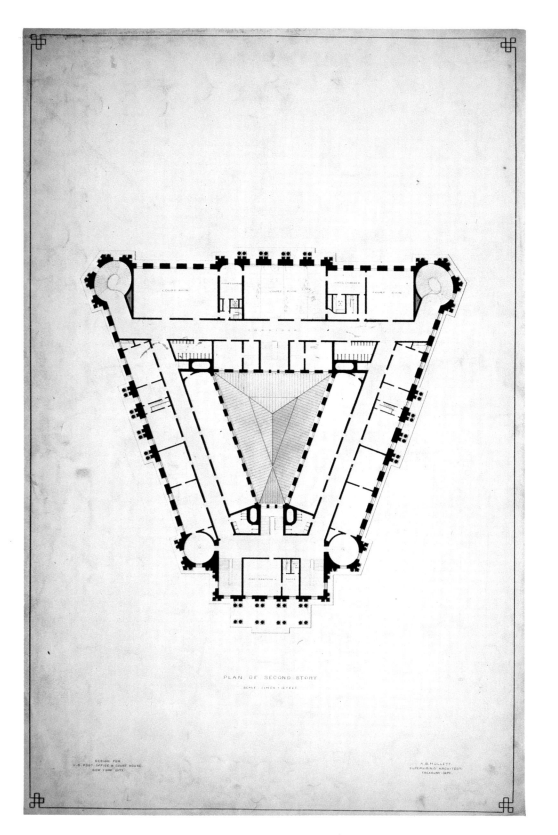

PLAN OF SECOND STORY

*Plate 55*

**Alfred B. Mullett.  Plan of the second story of the U. S. Post Office and Courthouse, New York, 1869**

FRONT ELEVATION
US CUSTOM HOUSE & POST OFFICE FALL RIVER MASS

WORKING DRAWING.
Nº 7

RETURN TO ROOM 411

*Plate 56*  **William A. Potter.  Front elevation of the U. S. Custom House and Post Office, Fall River, Massachusetts, 1876**

*Plate 57*   **James Renwick.  View of the north elevation of the winning design for the Smithsonian Institution Building, 1848**

*Plate 58*   **James Renwick.  View of the south elevation of the winning design for the Smithsonian Institution Building, 1848**

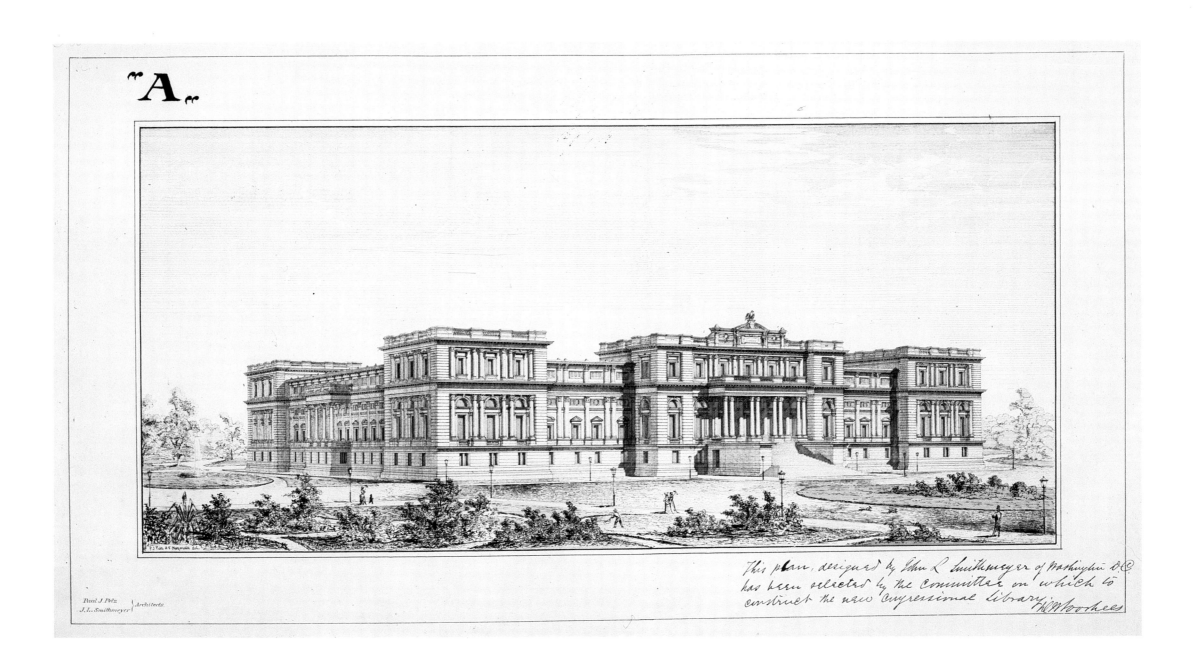

"A"

This plan, designed by John L Smithmeyer of Washington D.C. has been selected by the Committee on which to construct the new Congressional Library. H. W. Voorhees

Paul J. Pelz | Architects.
J. L. Smithmeyer |

*Plate 59*  **Smithmeyer & Pelz.  Winning design in the 1873 competition for the Library of Congress.**

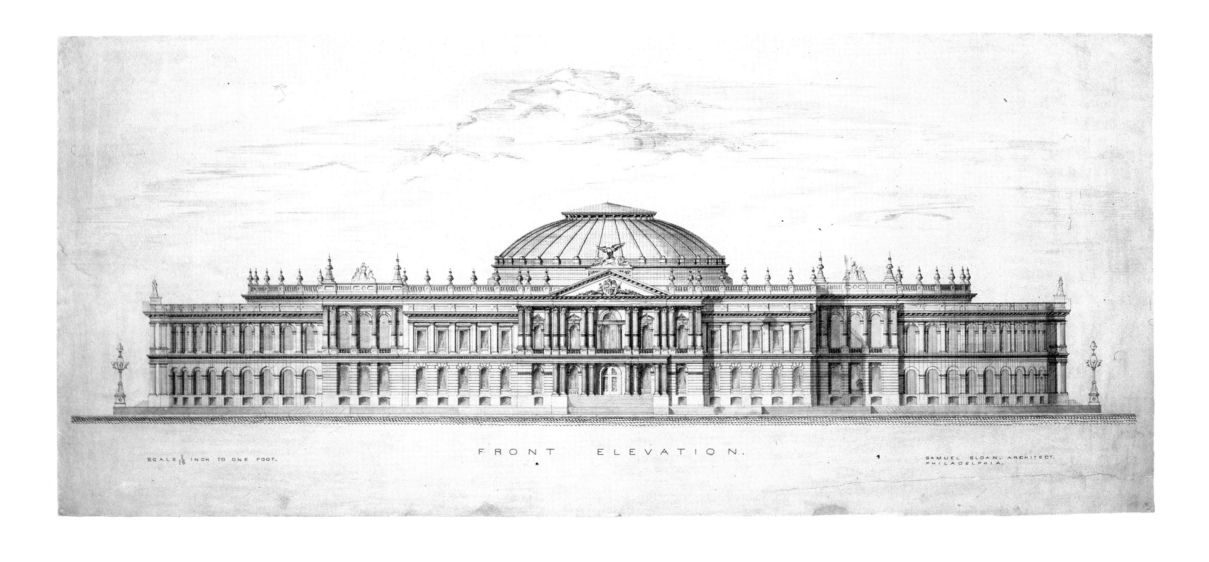

FRONT ELEVATION.

SCALE $\frac{1}{16}$ INCH TO ONE FOOT.

SAMUEL SLOAN, ARCHITECT.
PHILADELPHIA.

*Plate 60*   **Samuel Sloan.  Front elevation of design entered in the 1873 competition for the Library of Congress**

LIBRARY OF CONGRESS
ART GALLERY
ADOLPH. E. MELANDER — ARCHT — BOSTON.

*Plate 61*
**Adolph E. Melander.  View of art gallery featured in design entered in the
1873 competition for the Library of Congress**

*Plate 62*   **Leon Beaver.  Perspective view of design entered in the 1873 competition for the Library of Congress**

PROPOSED CONGRESSIONAL LIBRARY, WASHINGTON, D.C.

*Alex R. Esty*

*Plate 63*   **Alexander R. Esty.  Perspective view of design for the Library of Congress, ca. 1875**

*Plate 64*   **Smithmeyer & Pelz.  Perspective view of "Victorian Gothic" design for the Library of Congress, 1874**

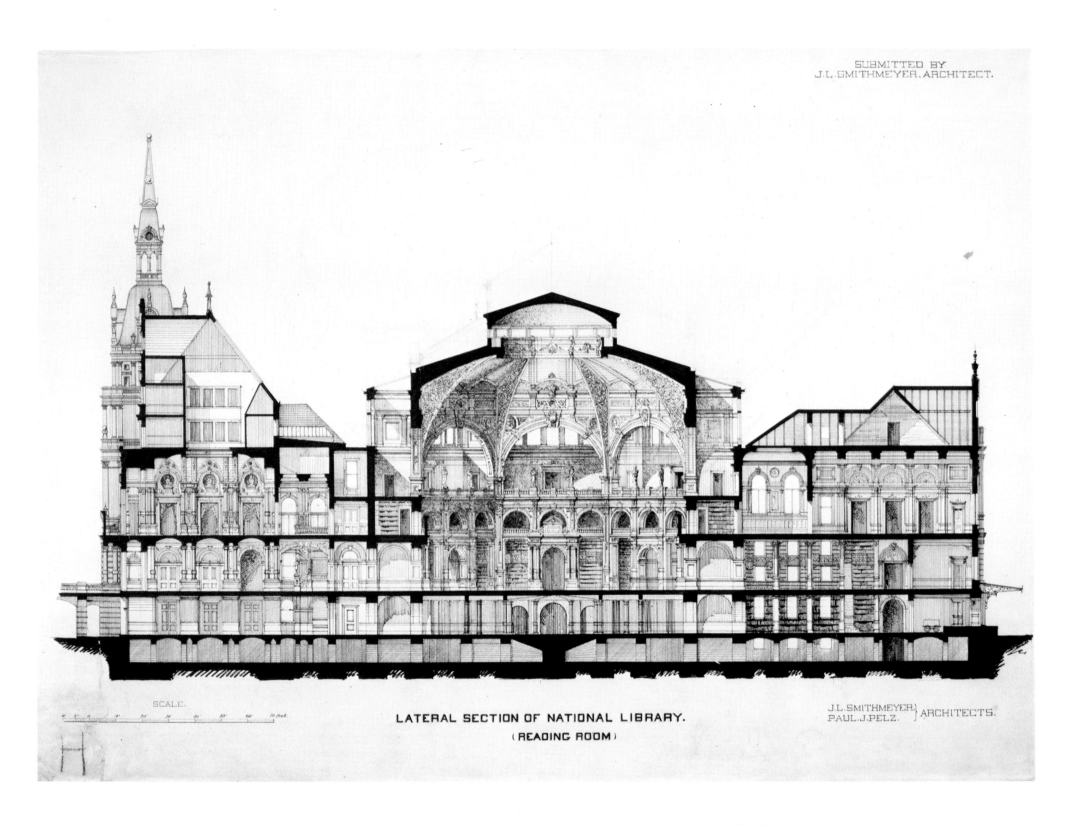

SCALE.

LATERAL SECTION OF NATIONAL LIBRARY.

(READING ROOM)

J.L.SMITHMEYER,
PAUL J.PELZ. } ARCHITECTS.

*Plate 65*   **Smithmeyer & Pelz.  Lateral section of "German Renaissance" design for the Library of Congress, ca. 1875–80**

M.3

*Plate 66* **Smithmeyer & Pelz. Perspective view of 1885 design for the Library of Congress**

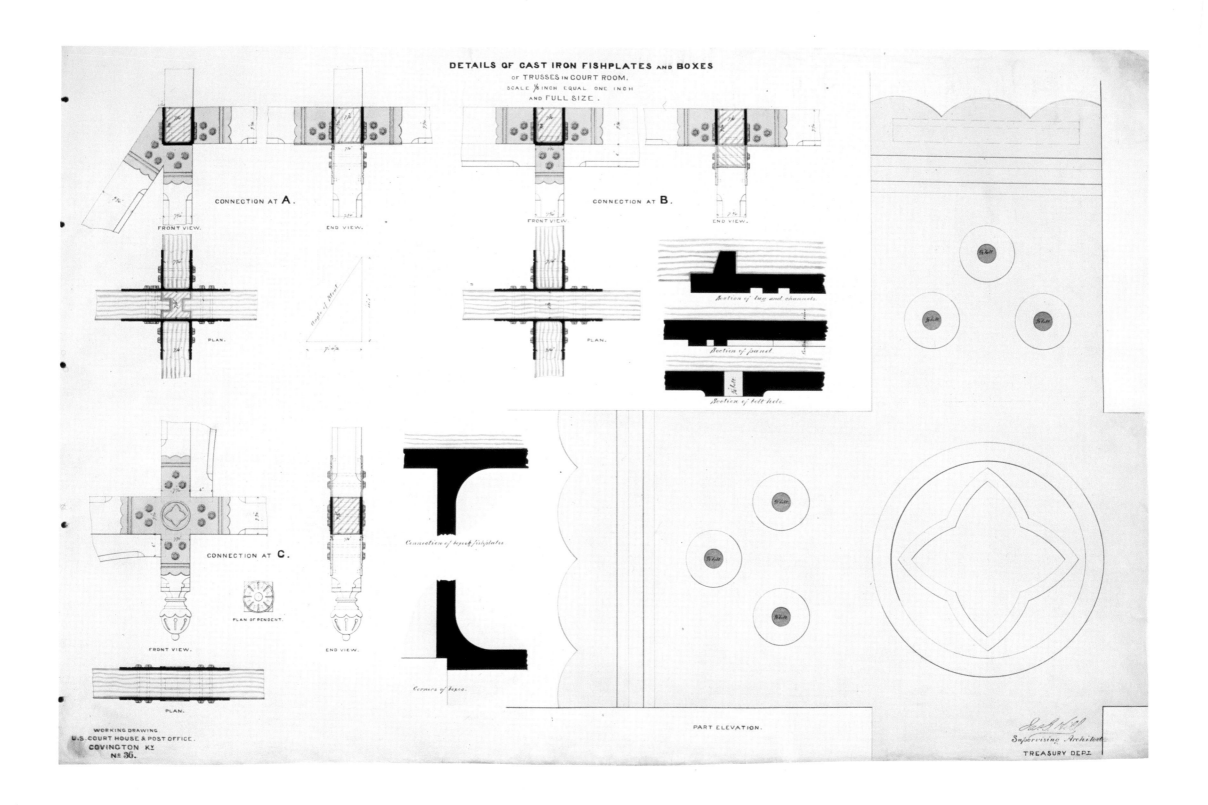

*Plate 67*    **William A. Potter.  Details of hardware for connecting beams of the trusses in the courtroom of the U. S. Courthouse and Post Office, Covington, Kentucky, ca. 1876**

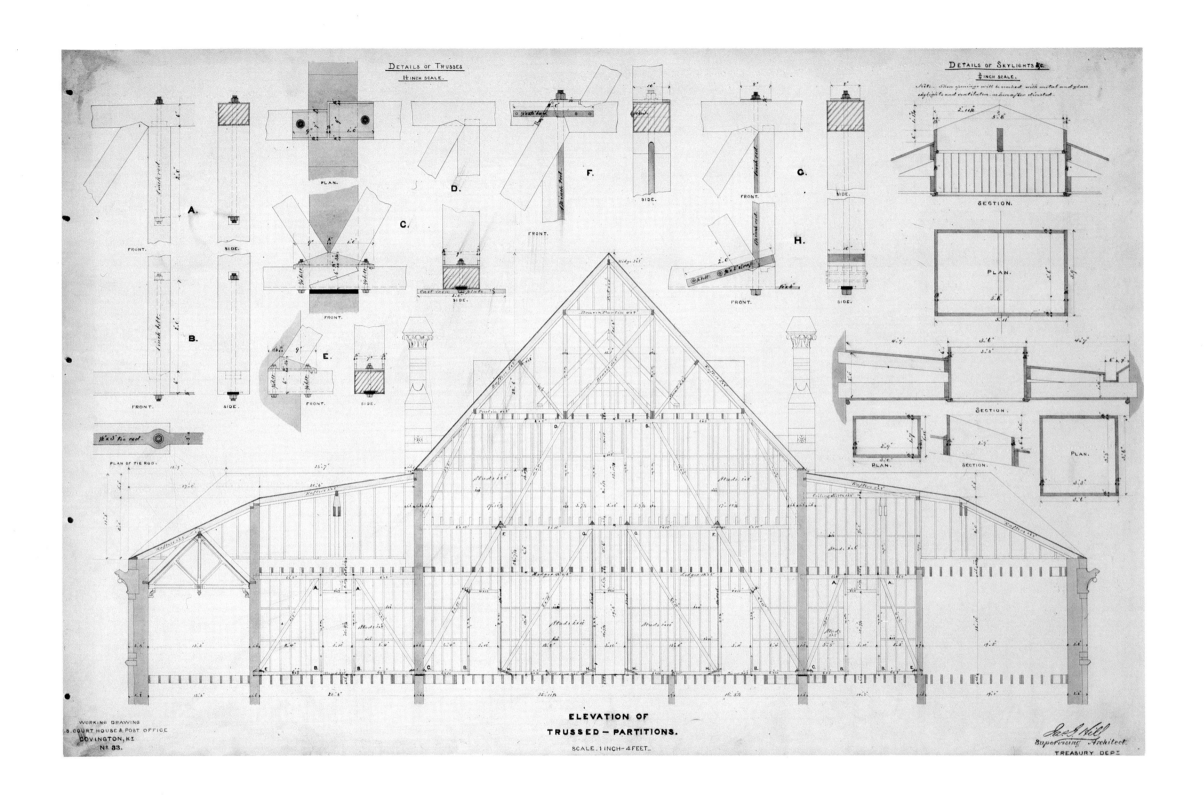

*Plate 68*   **William A. Potter.  Elevation of wooden trusses for the U. S. Courthouse and Post Office, Covington, Kentucky, ca. 1876**

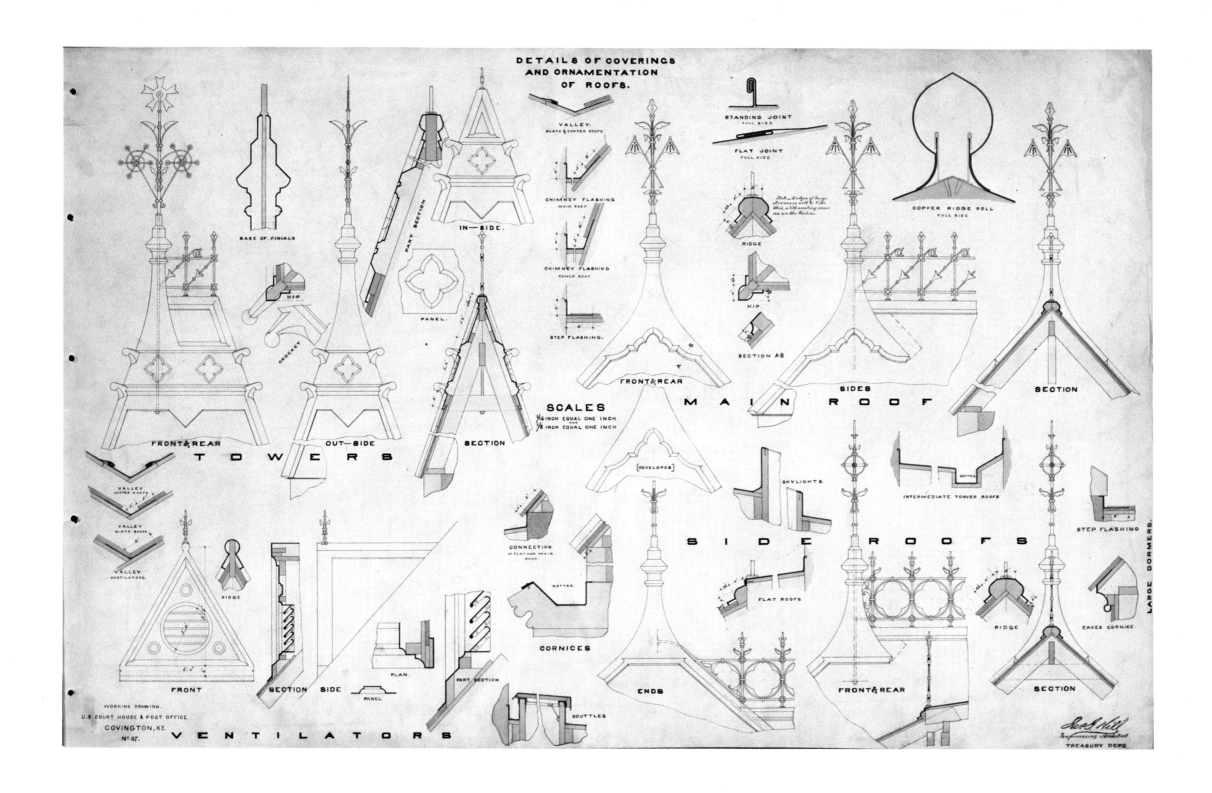

Plate 69   William A. Potter.  Details of roof ornament for the U. S. Courthouse and Post Office, Covington, Kentucky, ca. 1876

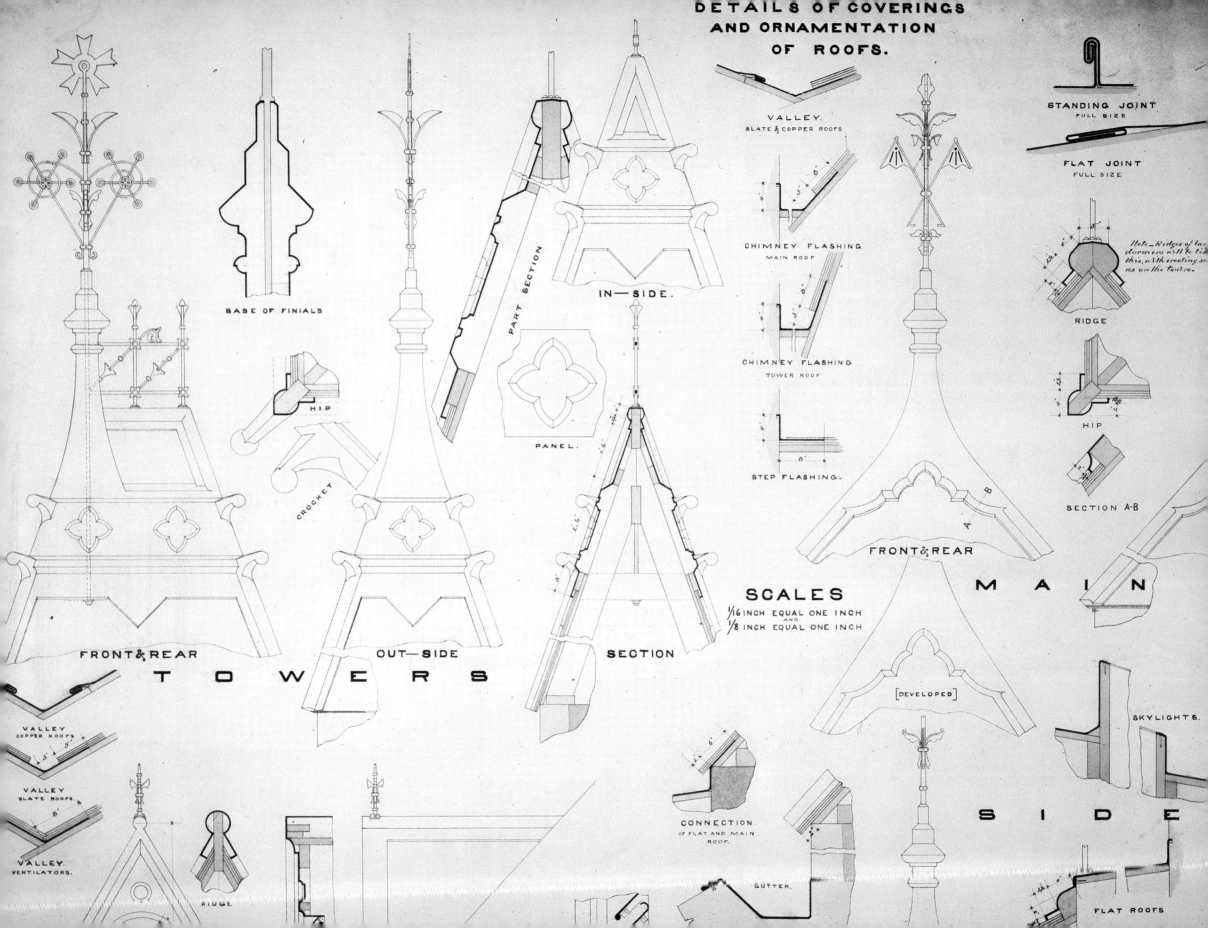

# DETAILS OF COVERINGS
# AND ORNAMENTATION
# OF ROOFS.

STANDING JOINT
FULL SIZE

FLAT JOINT
FULL SIZE

VALLEY.
SLATE & COPPER ROOFS

CHIMNEY FLASHING.
MAIN ROOF

CHIMNEY FLASHING
TOWER ROOF

STEP FLASHING.

Note.— Ridges of large
dormers will be like
this, with cresting so
as on the towers.

RIDGE

HIP

SECTION A-B

BASE OF FINIALS

HIP

CROCKET

PART SECTION

IN—SIDE.

PANEL.

SECTION

SCALES
1/16 INCH EQUAL ONE INCH
AND
1/8 INCH EQUAL ONE INCH

FRONT & REAR

MAIN

FRONT & REAR

OUT—SIDE

[DEVELOPED]

T O W E R S

VALLEY
COPPER ROOFS

VALLEY
SLATE ROOFS

VALLEY.
VENTILATORS.

RIDGE

CONNECTION.
OF FLAT AND MAIN
ROOF.

GUTTER.

SKYLIGHTS.

S I D E

FLAT ROOFS

U.S. COURT HOUSE & POST OFFICE, JACKSON, MISS.
JAMES G. HILL, SUPERVISING ARCHITECT,
TREASRY DEPARTMENT.

R.H. ATKINSON DEL.

*Plate 70*  **James G. Hill. Design for the U. S. Courthouse and Post Office, Jackson, Mississippi, 1882**

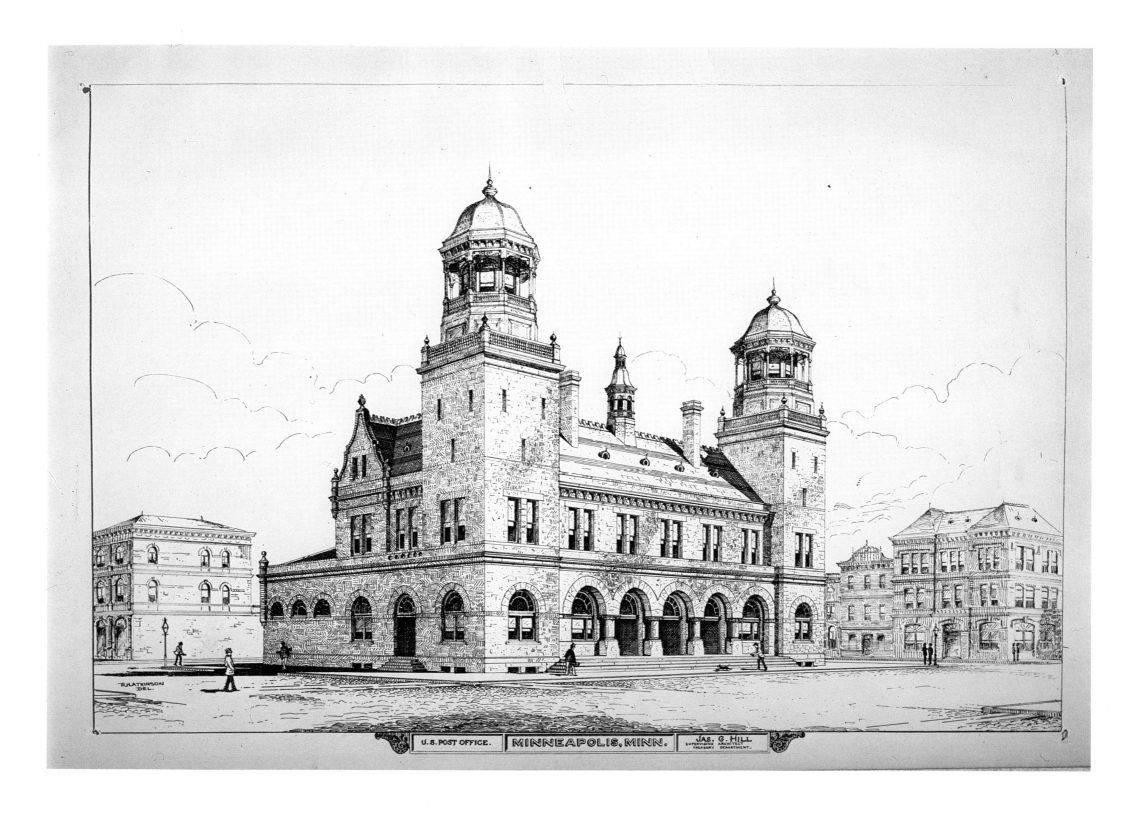

U.S. POST OFFICE. MINNEAPOLIS, MINN. JAS. G. HILL SUPERVISING ARCHITECT TREASURY DEPARTMENT.

R.H.ATKINSON DEL.

*Plate 71*　　**James G. Hill. Design for the U. S. Post Office, Minneapolis, 1883**

*Plate 72*   **Mifflin E. Bell.  Design for the U. S. Post Office, Hannibal, Missouri, 1884**

*Plate 73*    **Mifflin E. Bell.  Design for the U. S. Courthouse and Post Office, Louisville, Kentucky, 1884**

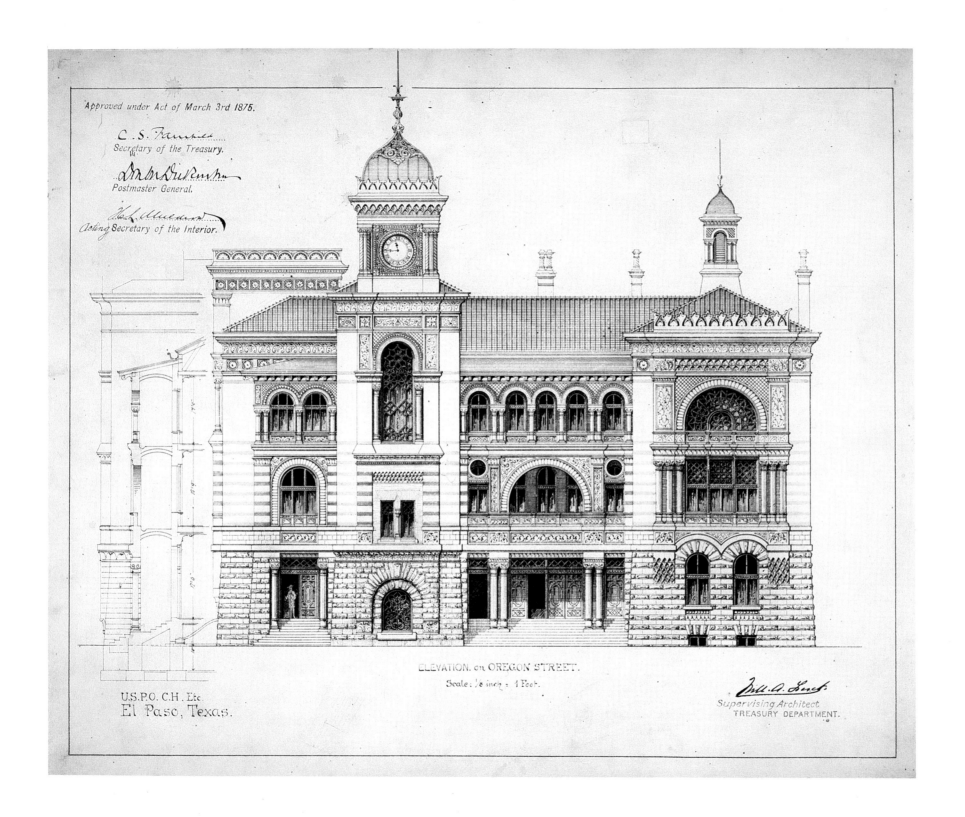

*Plate 75* **William A. Freret. Side elevation of the U. S. Courthouse and Post Office, Houston, Texas, ca. 1888**

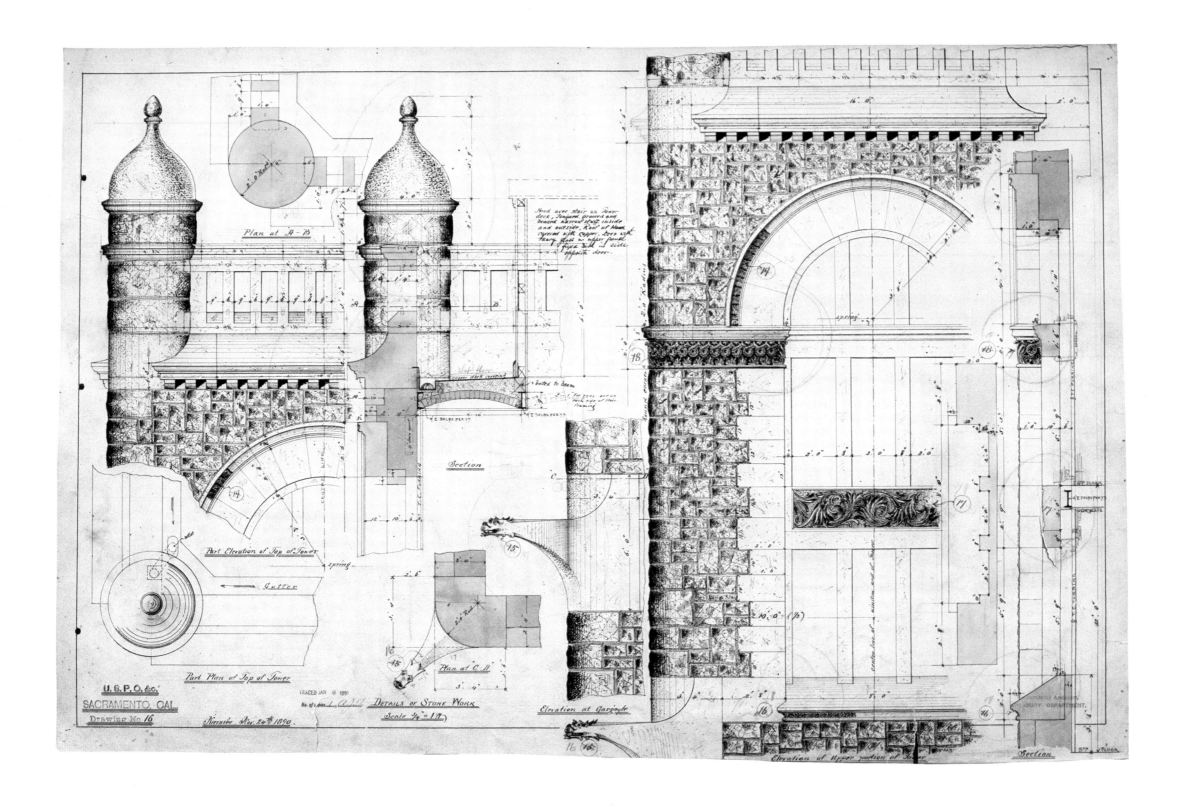

*Plate 76*   **James H. Windrim.   Details of stonework for the U. S. Post Office, Sacramento, California, 1890**

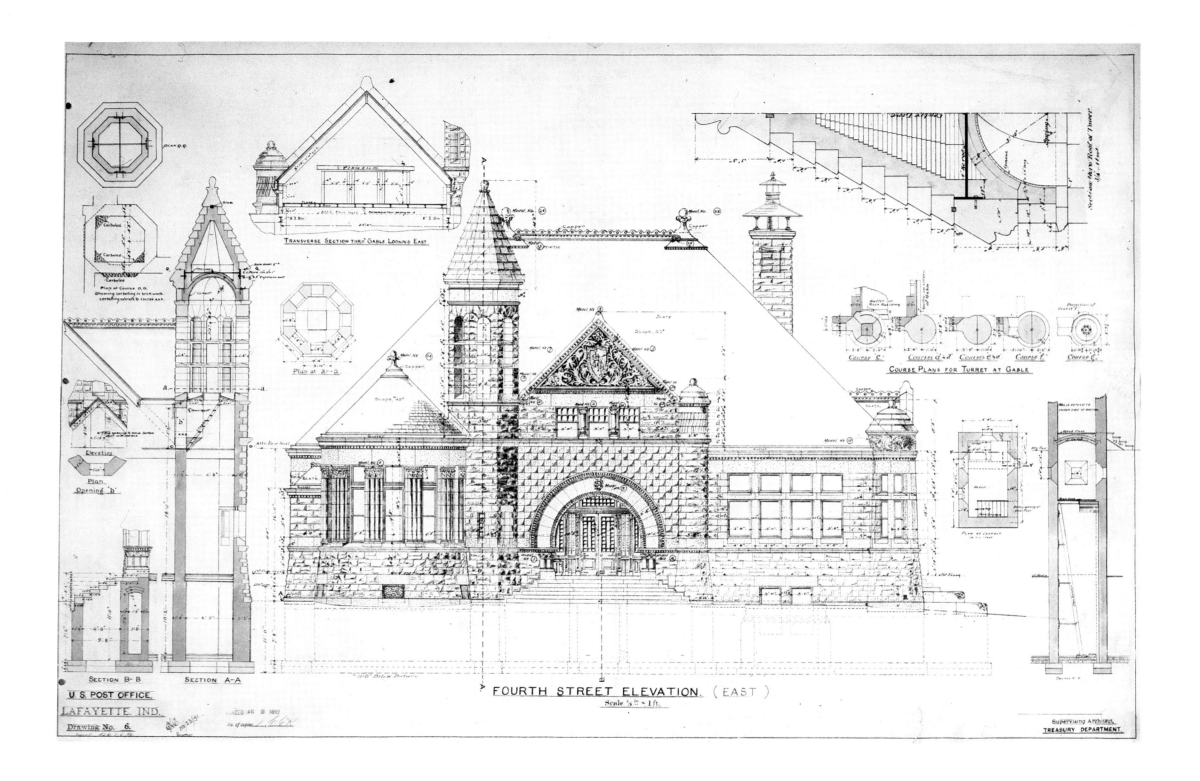

FOURTH STREET ELEVATION. (EAST)

Scale ½ in = 1 ft.

*Plate 77* **Willoughby J. Edbrooke. Front elevation of the U. S. Post Office, Lafayette, Indiana, 1891**

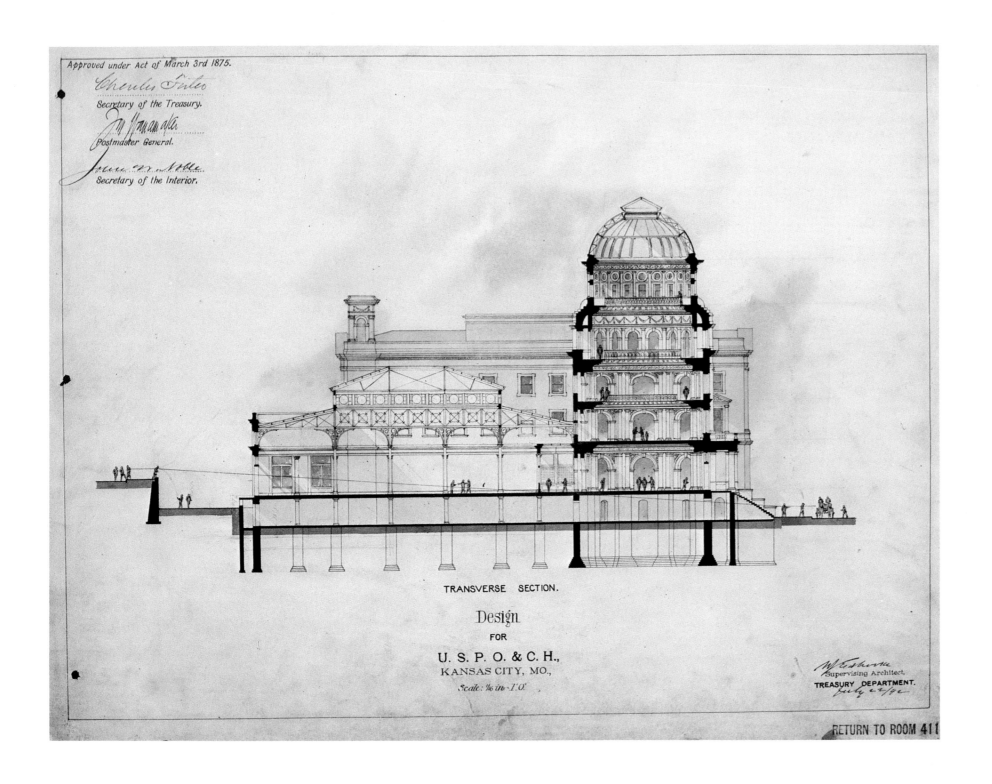

Plate 78    Willoughby J. Edbrooke.    Transverse section of the U. S. Post Office and Courthouse, Kansas City, Missouri, 1892

ELEVATION ON FIRST AVE.

NOTE, THIS BLDG DEMOLISHED IN 1929 AND
A NEW P.O. & CT.HO. BUILT ON SAME SITE.

Design
FOR
U. S. P. O.
FARGO, N. DAK.
Scale ⅛ in = 1 ft.

*J. Windrim*
Supervising Architect
TREASURY DEPARTMENT
April 19/93

Plate 79    Willoughby J. Edbrooke.   Front elevation of the U. S. Post Office, Fargo, North Dakota, 1893

U. S. POST OFFICE.
TAUNTON, MASS.

Jeremiah O'Rourke
Supervising Architect
TREASURY DEPARTMENT.

*Plate 80* **Jeremiah O'Rourke.  Perspective view of design for the U. S. Post Office, Taunton, Massachusetts, 1893**

Approved under Act of March 3rd 1875

*Charles S. Hamlin*
Acting Secretary of the Treasury.

*W S Bissell*
Postmaster General.

*Wm H Sims*
Acting Secretary of the Interior.

Design
FOR
U.S. POST OFFICE
NEWBURGH, N. Y.
Scale ⅛ in.=1 ft.

ELEVATION ON SECOND ST.

OLD BLDG. VACANT 2-22-44
NEW P.O. OCCUPIED IN 1932.

*Jeremiah O'Rourke*
Supervising Architect
TREASURY DEPARTMENT.

Plate 81    Jeremiah O'Rourke.  Side elevation of the U. S. Post Office, Newburgh, New York, ca. 1894

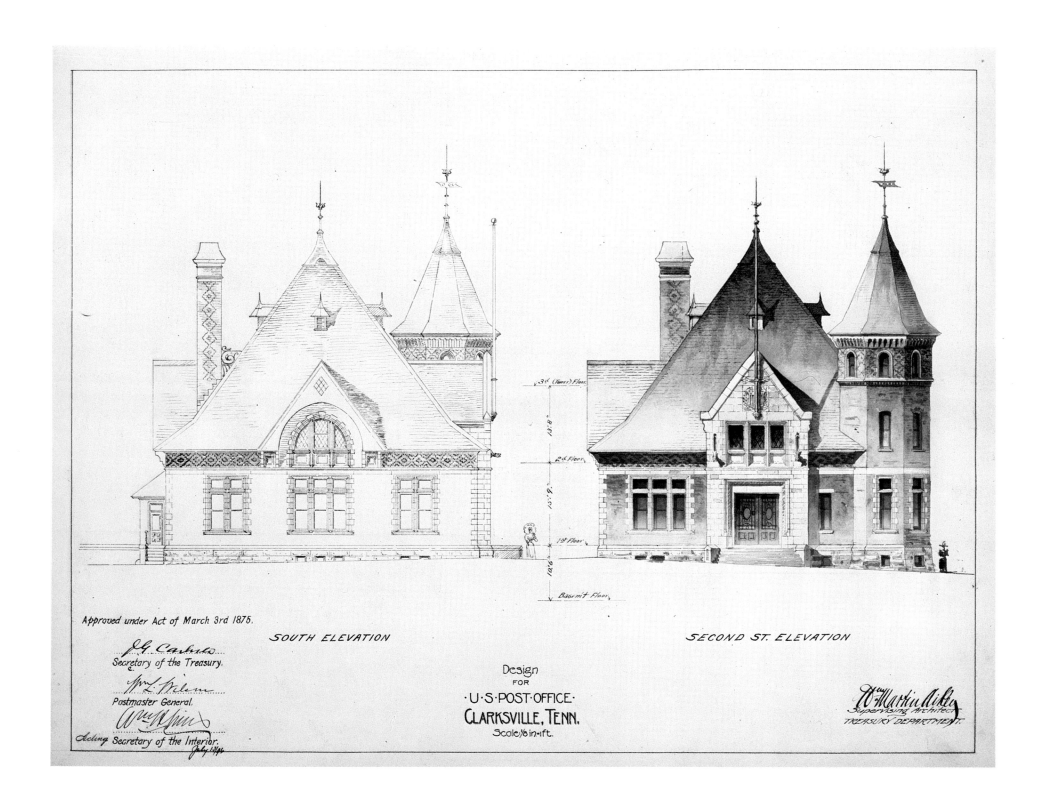

Approved under Act of March 3rd 1875.

*J.G. Carlisle*
Secretary of the Treasury.

*Wm L. Wilson*
Postmaster General.

*Chas N. Spinks*
Acting Secretary of the Interior.
July 1896

SOUTH ELEVATION

3d (Tower) Floor.

2d Floor.

1st Floor.

Basem't Floor.

SECOND ST. ELEVATION

Design
FOR
·U·S·POST·OFFICE·
CLARKSVILLE, TENN.
Scale ⅛ in.=1 ft.

*W. Martin Aiken*
Supervising Architect
TREASURY DEPARTMENT.

*Plate 82*  **William Martin Aiken.  Elevations of the U. S. Post Office, Clarksville, Tennessee, 1896**

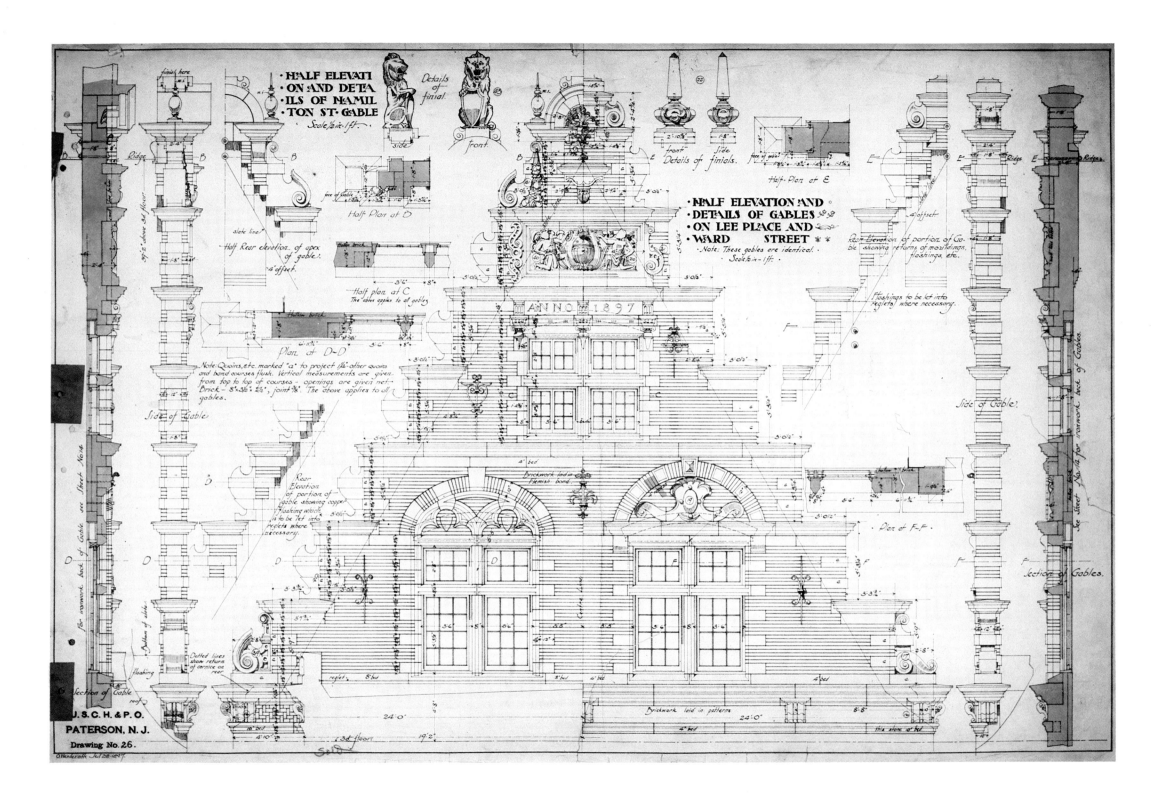

*Plate 83*   William Martin Aiken.   Half-elevation and details of gables for the **U. S. Courthouse** and **Post Office, Paterson, New Jersey, 1897**

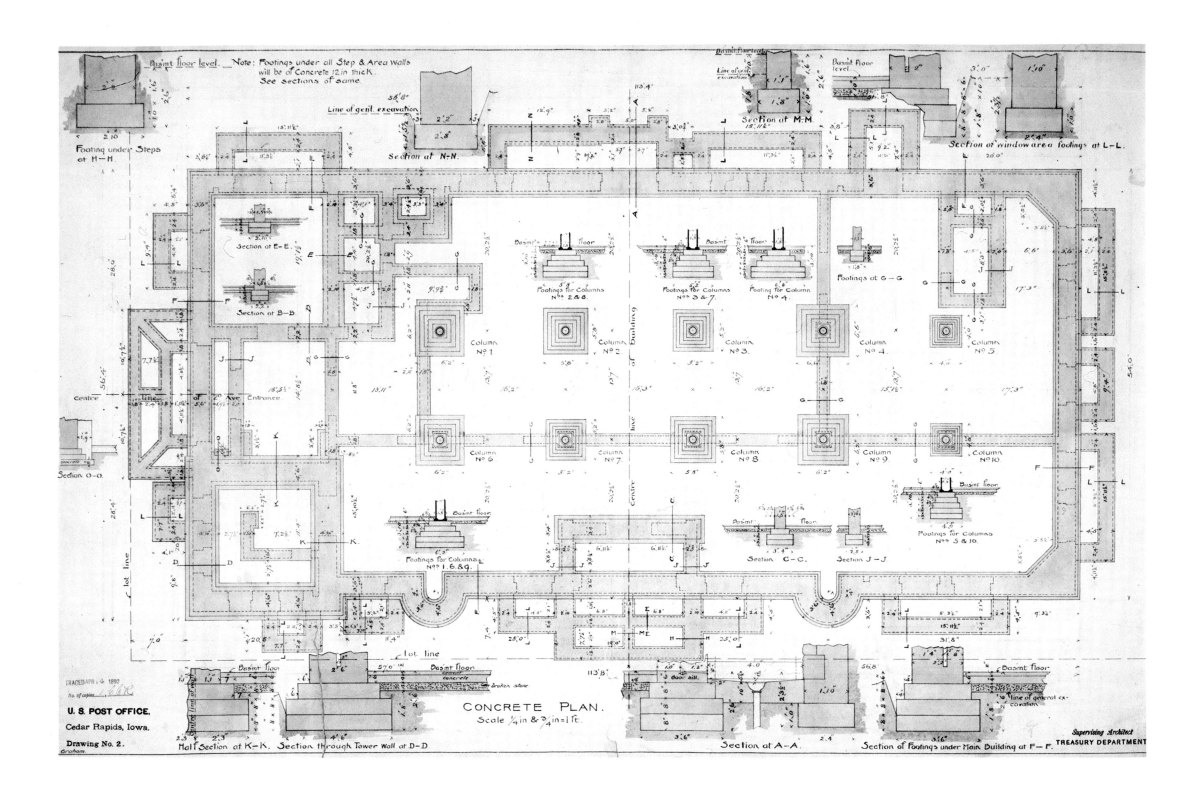

Plate 84   Willoughby J. Edbrooke.   Plan of concrete foundations for the U. S. Post Office, Cedar Rapids, Iowa, 1892

*Plate 85*  **Details of the ironwork for the stairs of the U. S. Courthouse and Post Office, Pittsburgh, 1890**

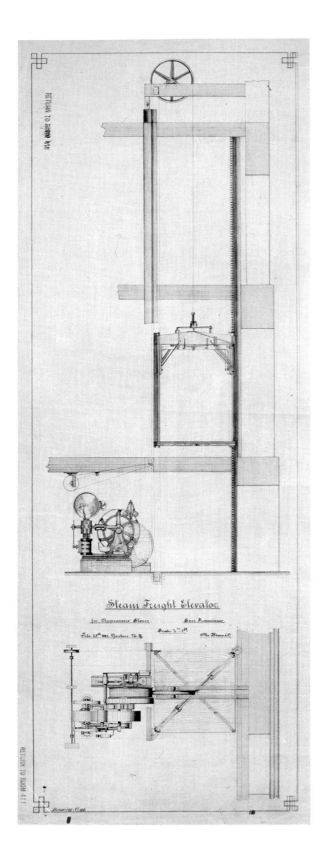

*Plate 86*
**Design of a steam freight-elevator by Otis Bros. & Co., for the U. S. Appraisers' Stores, San Francisco, 1881**

# Steam Freight Elevator

## for Appraisers' Stores.          San Francisco.

Scale: ½ in = 1 ft

Febr. 25th 1881. Yonkers. N.Y.          Otis Bros & Co.

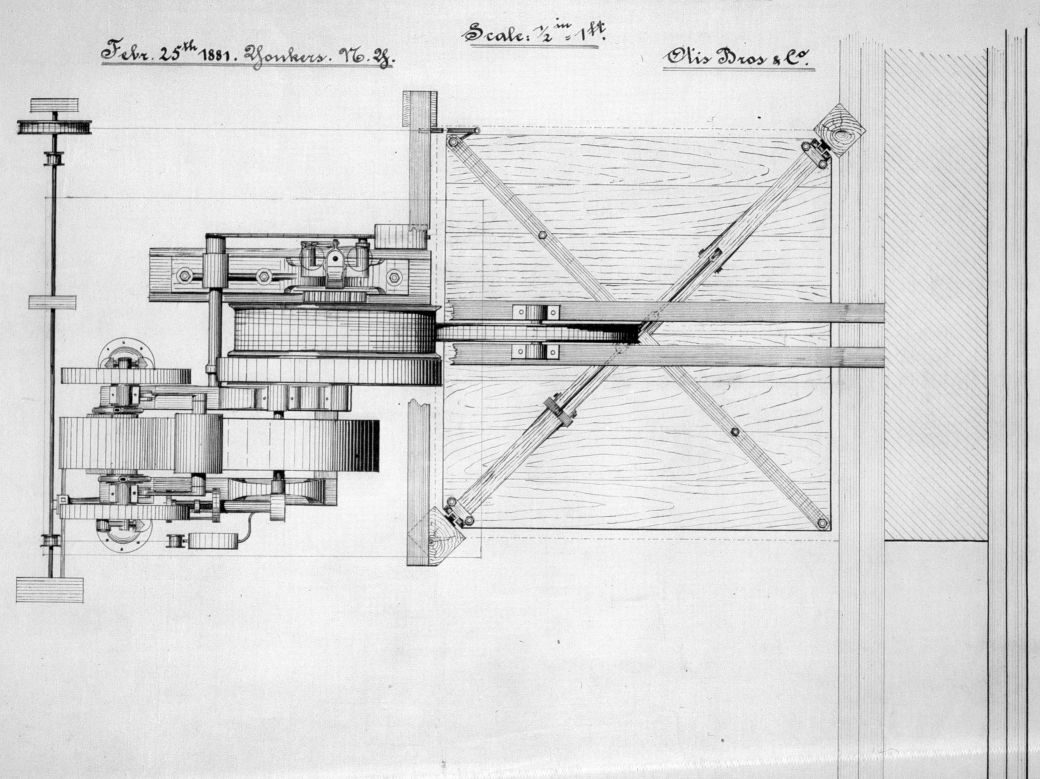

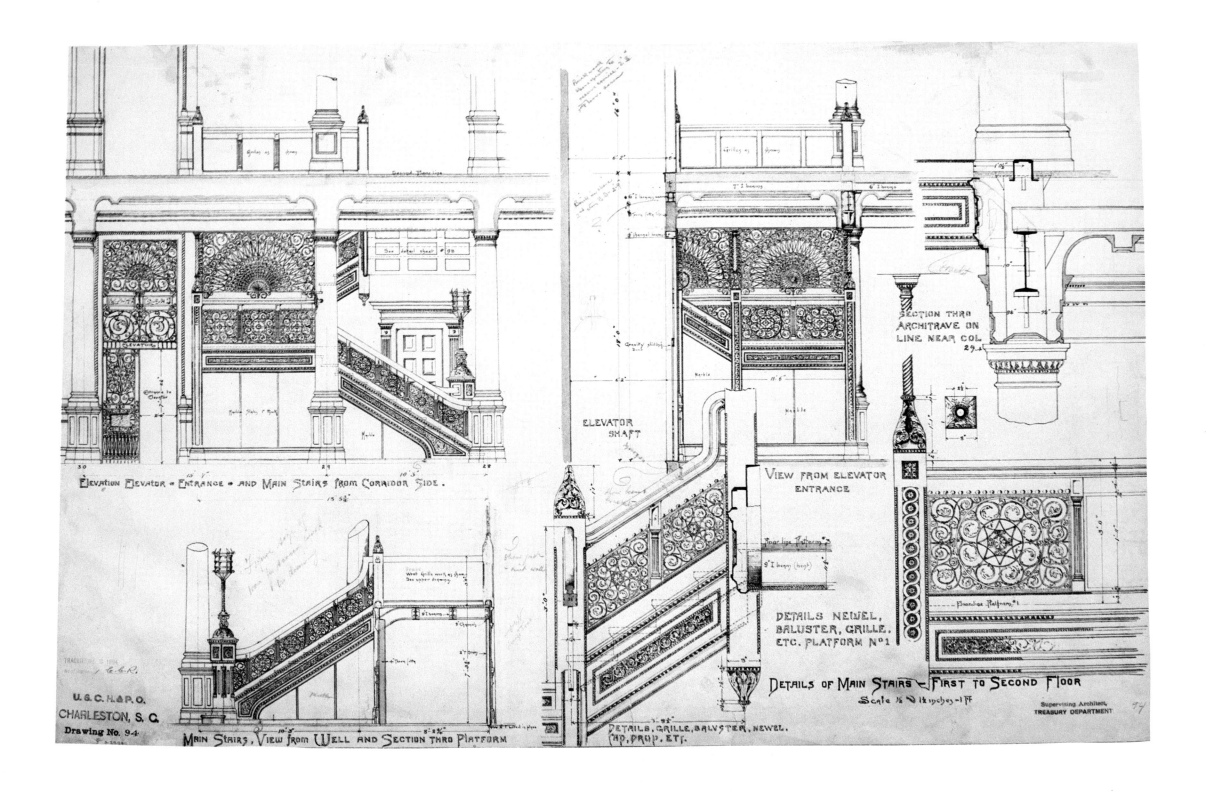

*Plate 87*  Jeremiah O'Rourke.  Detail of elevator grille and main stairway for the **U.S. Courthouse and Post Office, Charleston, South Carolina, 1894**

Car Design 4009, for the U.S. C.H. & P.O. Bldg., Charleston, S.C.

The Graves Elevator Co.
DRAWING No 158

*Plate 88*

**William Martin Aiken. Design of an elevator car for the U. S. Courthouse and Post Office,
Charleston, South Carolina, 1896**

First Floor

MONEY O.
REGISTRY
LOBBY
LOBBY
P. O. WORK ROOM
PUBLIC LOBBY
POST MASTER

· FIRST · FLOOR ·

INTERNAL · REVENUE

· SECOND · FLOOR ·

UNITED STATES MAIL

V · S · COVRT · HOVSE · AND · POST · OFFICE ·
ALTOONA · PENNA.
JAMES · KNOX · TAYLOR ~ SVPERVISING · ARCHITECT ·

THIS BLDG. NO LONGER USED AS A POST OFFICE.
A NEW P.O. BLDG. WAS CONSTRUCTED AND OCCUPIED IN 1933.

Plate 89    James Knox Taylor.   Perspective view and plans of the U. S. Courthouse and Post Office, Altoona, Pennsylvania, 1900

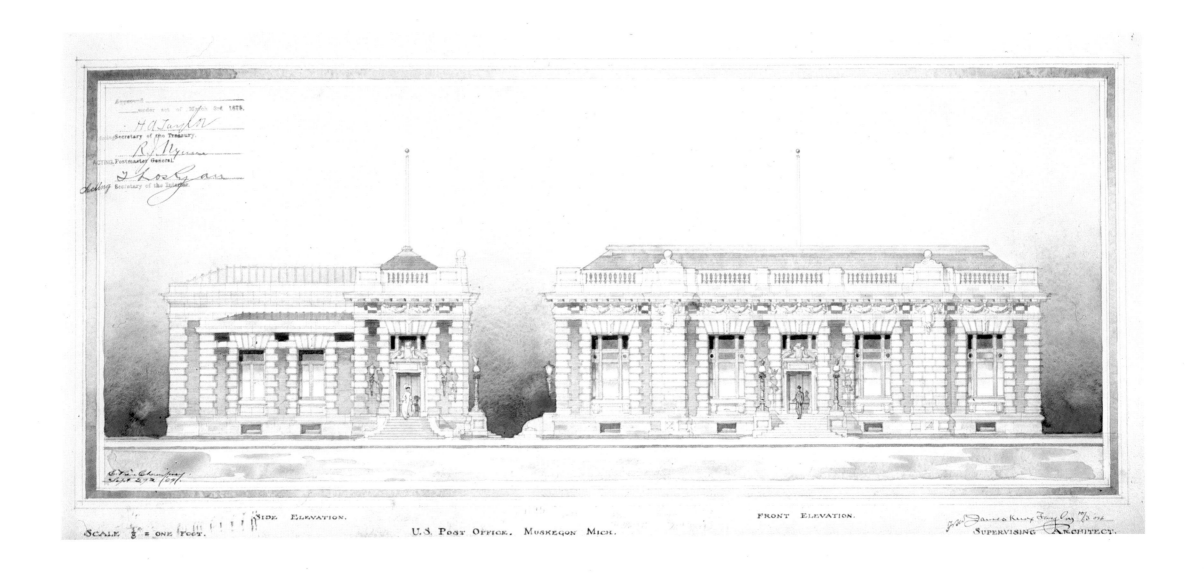

*Plate 90*  **James Knox Taylor.  Front and side elevations of the U. S. Post Office in Muskegon, Michigan, 1904**

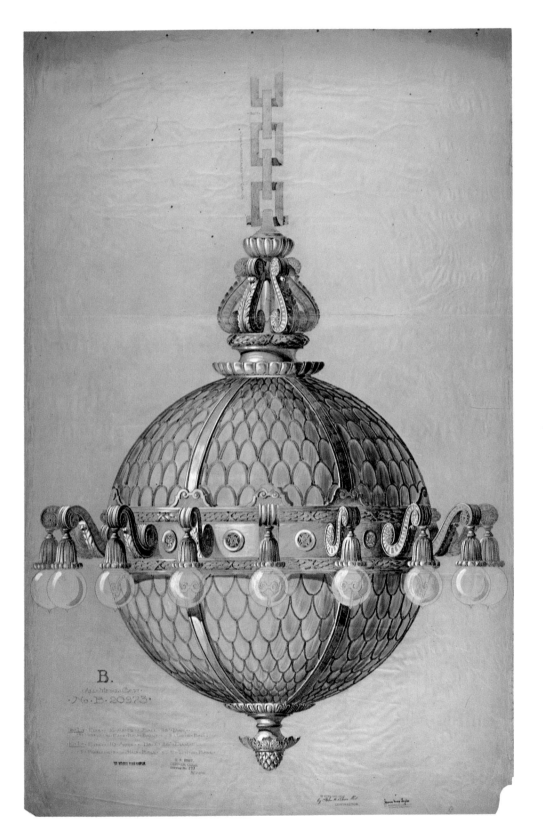

*Plate 91*
**James Knox Taylor. Design for a chandelier in the U. S. Branch Mint, Denver, Colorado, 1904**

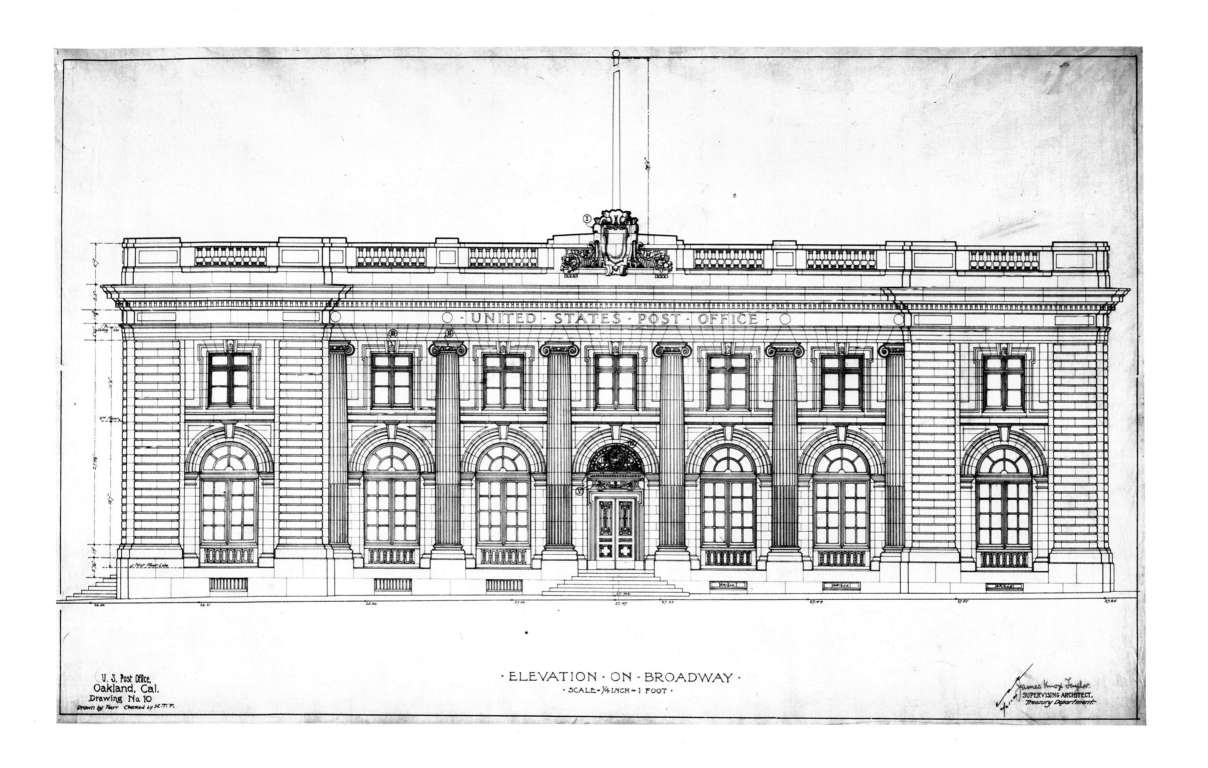

UNITED · STATES · POST · OFFICE

· ELEVATION · ON · BROADWAY ·
· SCALE · ¼ INCH = 1 FOOT ·

James Knox Taylor.
SUPERVISING ARCHITECT.
Treasury Department.

*Plate 92*   James Knox Taylor.  Front elevation of the U. S. Post Office, Oakland, California, 1901

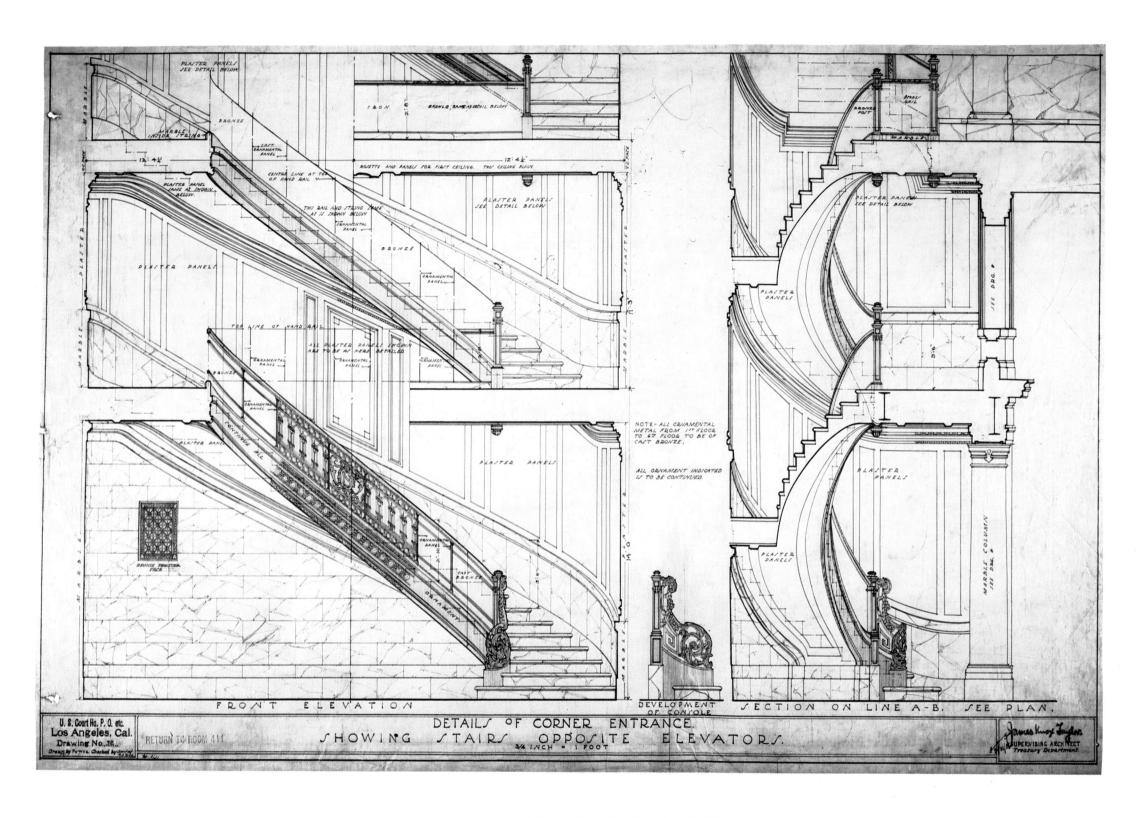

*Plate 93*   **James Knox Taylor.   Design for a staircase in the U. S. Courthouse and Post Office, Los Angeles, 1906**

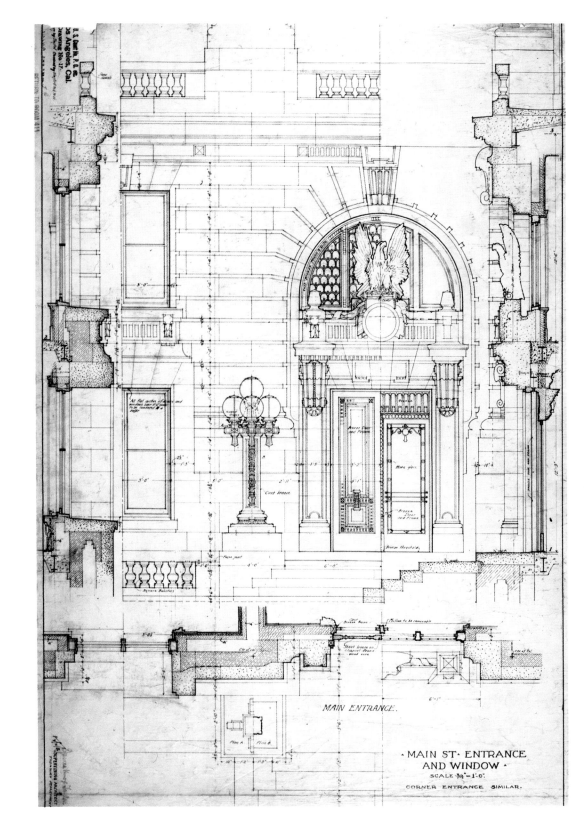

*Plate 94*

**James Knox Taylor. Design for the Main Street entrance of the U. S. Courthouse and Post Office, Los Angeles, 1906**

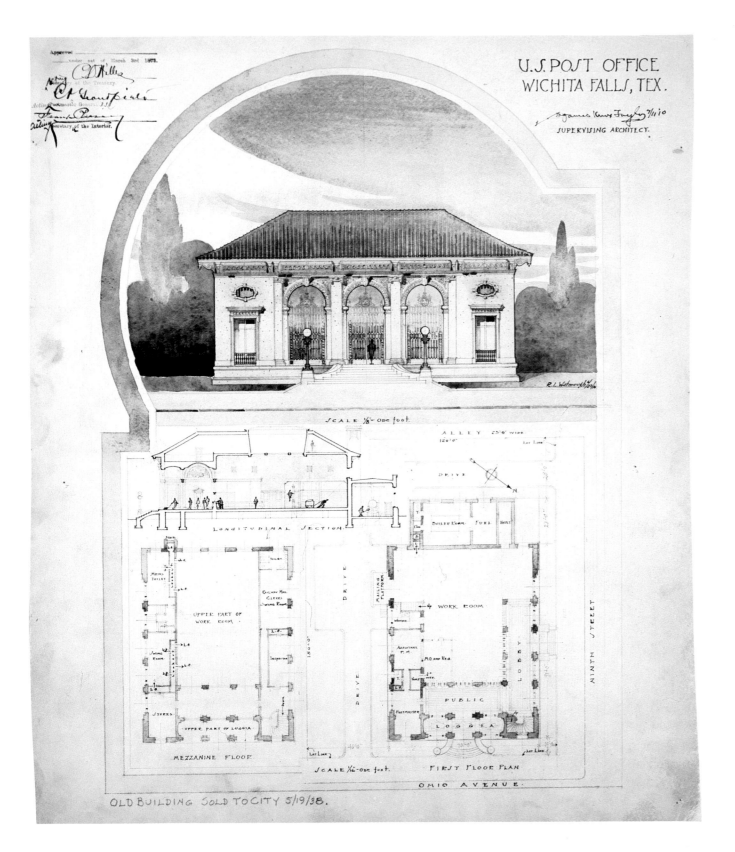

*Plate 95*

**James Knox Taylor. Elevation, section, and plans of the U. S. Post Office, Wichita Falls, Texas, 1910**

SCALE ⅛" = One foot.

LONGITUDINAL SECTION.

STACK·

*Plate 96*
**Daniel H. Burnham. Proposal for locating a monument to
Abraham Lincoln in front of Union Station, Washington, D. C., 1908–9**

*Plate 97*   **Daniel H. Burnham.  View toward the Capitol from a proposed monument to Abraham Lincoln in front of Union Station, Washington, D. C., 1908–9**

*Plate 98*    **Daniel H. Burnham.   Proposal for locating a circular monument to Abraham Lincoln on Delaware Avenue leading to the Capitol, 1908–9**

*Plate 99*

**Daniel H. Burnham.  View of a circular monument to Abraham Lincoln proposed for a site on Delaware Avenue, Washington, D. C., 1908–9**

*Plate 100*
**John Russell Pope. Competition proposal for a monument to Abraham Lincoln located on Meridian Hill, viewed from the White House, 1911**

*Plate 101*

John Russell Pope.  Competition proposal for a monument to Abraham Lincoln
located on the Soldiers' Home grounds, viewed from the Capitol, 1911

*Plate 102*
**John Russell Pope. Competition proposal for a
monument to Abraham Lincoln located at the
western end of the Mall, 1912**

*Plate 103* **Henry Bacon. Competition proposal for a monument to Abraham Lincoln located at the western end of the Mall, 1912**

*Plate 104*   John Russell Pope.  Alternative design in the form of a pyramid for a monument to Abraham Lincoln at the western end of the Mall, 1912

*Plate 105*    John Russell Pope.  Alternative design in the form of a funeral pyre for a monument to Abraham Lincoln at the western end of the Mall, 1912

*Plate 106*    **John Russell Pope.  Alternative design in the form of ziggurat for a monument to Abraham Lincoln at the western end of the Mall, 1912**

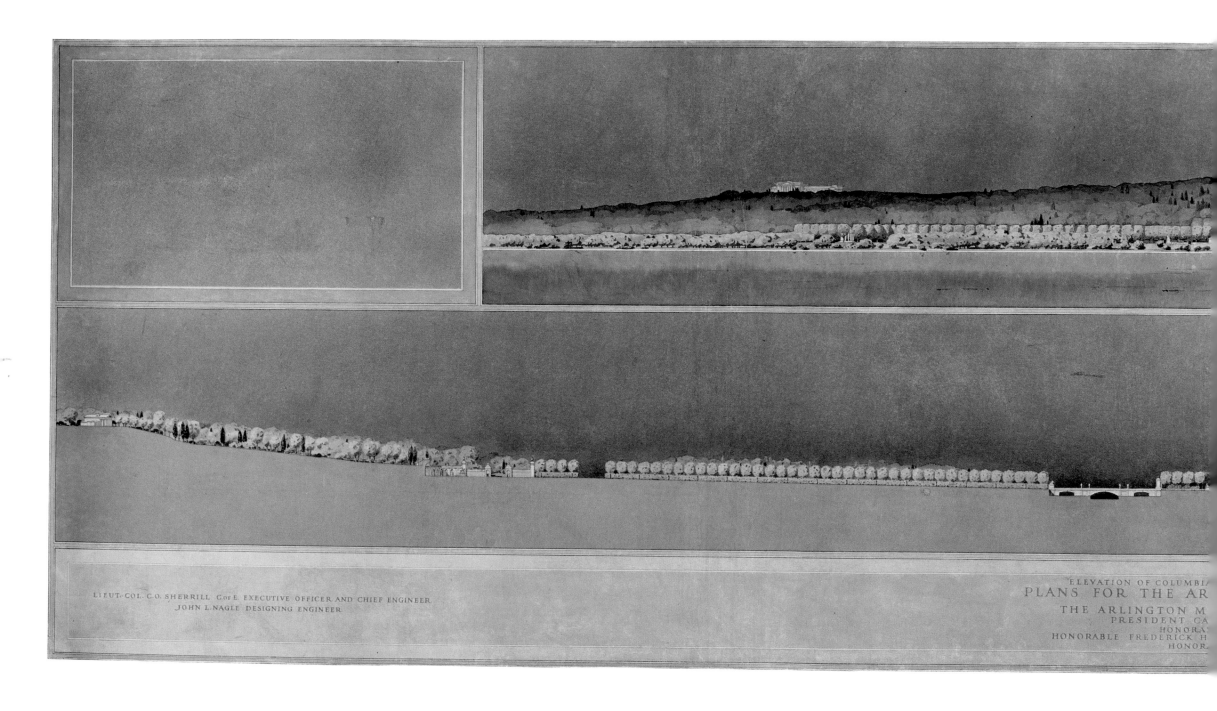

*Plate 107*   **McKim, Mead and White. Design for the Arlington Memorial Bridge, Washington, D. C., connecting the Lincoln Memorial and Arlington Cemetery, 1923**

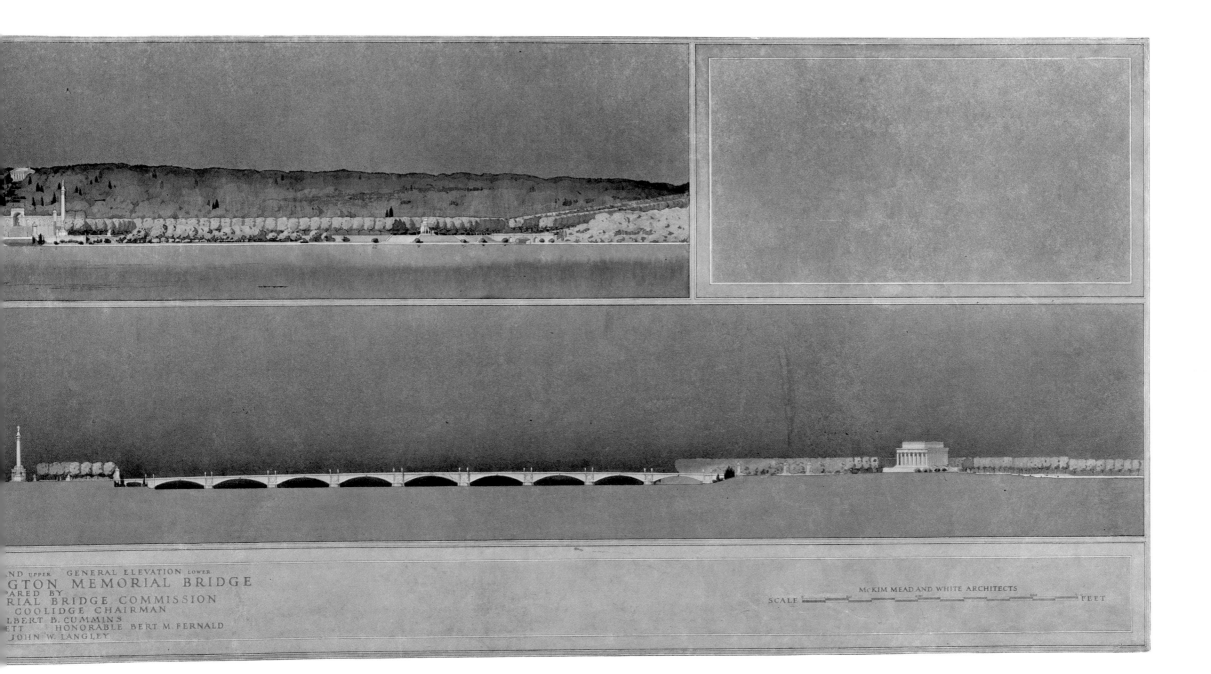

ND UPPER    GENERAL ELEVATION LOWER
GTON MEMORIAL BRIDGE
ARED BY
RIAL BRIDGE COMMISSION                                    McKIM MEAD AND WHITE ARCHITECTS
COOLIDGE CHAIRMAN                                SCALE ▭▭▭▭▭▭▭▭ FEET
LBERT B. CUMMINS
ETT    HONORABLE BERT M. FERNALD
JOHN W. LANGLEY

# NOTES ON THE PLATES

*Plate 1*
U. S. Capitol
**William Thornton**
**Design for the west front, ca. 1793–95**
Pencil, ink, and wash on paper
$15 \times 24\frac{1}{2}$ in. ($38.1 \times 62.2$ cm)
*Library of Congress*

On the design of the west front, the two walls on either side of the semicircular Temple of Fame bear faint pencil sketches of the relief sculpture intended to occupy these surfaces; the one to the north appears to represent the landing of either Christopher Columbus or Sir Walter Raleigh in the New World.

This drawing, along with its companion piece (plate 4), was first published by Glenn Brown in 1900 in his *History of the United States Capitol*, a book that remains the "official" history of the U. S. Capitol. Since Brown describes the two drawings as having been "recently discovered in the Congressional Library" (p. 19), they apparently could not have been part of the large private collection of Thornton papers owned by J. Henley Smith, which did not enter the Library of Congress until 1904. In addition, Brown does not mention these drawings in the earlier articles on the history of the building which he published during 1896 and 1897 in the *American Architect and Building News*, even though he had access to the Smith papers at the time from which he published other Thornton drawings.

Since the initial publication of this elevation by Brown, who identified it as an alternative design for the dome, the drawing has been consistently regarded as an "alternative" design for the Capitol by Thornton, even though all three of Thornton's existing floor plans contain the principal features shown in this elevation. This design was first recognized as a part of Thornton's original scheme for the west front as early as 1923 in an article by Fiske Kimball and Wells Bennett, who observed that "the supposition that [the drawing] is merely an alternative study for crowning the eastern Rotunda is obviously erroneous" (p. 90). Their conclusion has generally been ignored by later historians; however, a more recent investigation of the Thornton documents undertaken by Alexandra Cushing Howard in a Master's thesis at the University of Virginia (1974) has reached the same conclusion.

The article by Kimball and Bennett remains the most thorough and accurate discussion of Thornton's design, although Ms. Howard was the first to analyze the complete description by Thornton of his original design (Thornton Papers), part of which was apparently missing when Kimball and Bennett quoted from it, and not completely reproduced when first presented by Glenn Brown. Ms. Howard's conclusions about the relationship between the Thornton and Hallet design suffer from the circumstance that she was unaware of the 1794 drawings by Hallet which precisely record the foundation work he had begun in 1793. (Both the plan in the Library of Congress and the cross section at the Office of the Architect of the Capitol were first published in Lowry, vol. 2, ch. 1.) In 1983 a brief manuscript description by Hallet, written in 1794, was discovered among the papers of Thomas U. Walter then recently acquired from the Walter family by the Philadelphia Athenaeum. (I am grateful to its director, Roger Moss, for having called this document to my attention and permitting me to use it.) This description establishes without a question that a President's Apartment was included in the original design, even though no existing drawings of the Thornton plan reveal its precise location.

*Plate 2*
U. S. Capitol
**Stephen Hallet**
**Design for the west front, 1793**
Pencil, ink, wash, and watercolor on paper
$19\frac{1}{4} \times 39\frac{1}{4}$ in. ($49 \times 99.7$ cm)
*Library of Congress*
(Photographed before restoration)

*Plate 3*
U. S. Capitol
**Stephen Hallet**
**Cross section of design for the west front, 1793**
Ink and color washes on paper
$18\frac{7}{8} \times 27\frac{3}{4}$ in. ($48 \times 70.5$ cm)
Signed on verso
*Library of Congress*
(Photographed before restoration)

Both of these drawings are part of what is known as Hallet's "Design E," his final proposal for the design of the U. S. Capitol. Design E was submitted after President Washington had already selected Thornton's design for the building.

The fact that the final designs of both Thornton and Hallet contain a circular Conference Room as a principal feature has led to speculation as to whether one or the other architect had copied the plan from his fellow competitor. The existence of the circular form in L'Enfant's design of 1792 puts the relationship between the designs of Thornton and Hallet in a new light (see pages 21–24).

*Plate 4*
U. S. Capitol
**William Thornton**
**Design for the east front, ca. 1793–95**
Pencil, ink, and washes on paper
$14\frac{5}{8} \times 24\frac{1}{2}$ in. ($37.2 \times 62.3$ cm)
*Library of Congress*

The history of this drawing is discussed in the notes to plate 1.

The sculptural decorations of the central pediment are depicted only in faint pencil sketches, but the freestanding sculpture at the apex of the central pediment clearly represents Hercules standing at rest after completing his labors, holding a cornucopia of fruit. In the document accompanying his competition design Thornton explained that he chose this subject because it alluded "to the happiness which America enjoys, as its reward for the labours of past years."

*Plate 5*
U. S. Capitol
**Benjamin H. Latrobe**
**Design proposed for the east front, 1806**
Ink and watercolor on paper
$19\frac{3}{8} \times 27\frac{1}{4}$ in. ($49.3 \times 69.2$ cm)
*Library of Congress*

This design, prepared especially for President Jefferson, shows Latrobe's attempt to alter Thornton's original design by adding a staircase leading to the portico on the principal floor and by extending the colonnade across the entire center front. Both of these departures from Thornton's original design add prominence to the eastern front and, when coupled with Latrobe's plan to eliminate the Conference Room on the west (see plate 6), effectively reverse L'Enfant's original intention, which oriented the Capitol to the west. Jefferson did not formally accept these proposals by Latrobe, although eventually a similar design by Bulfinch would effect these changes in Thornton's design.

*Plate 6*
U. S. Capitol
**Benjamin H. Latrobe**
**Design proposed for the ground floor, 1806**
Pencil, ink, and color washes on paper
$20\frac{1}{8} \times 30\frac{3}{8}$ in. ($51.1 \times 77.2$ cm)
*Library of Congress*

In this plan Latrobe is proposing that the vestibule preceding the circular Conference Room in Thornton's design become the principal feature of the building, thereby eliminating the projecting circular Temple of Fame on the west. Only three years before, in his first report as Surveyor of Public Buildings, Latrobe had referred to the Conference Room as "that beautiful part of the plan" and characterized the approach to the west front as "a magnificent flight of steps."

Latrobe's gift as a draftsman is particularly notable in this plan. By his use of shadow he transforms what would normally be a flat, schematic presentation of the layout of a building into a dramatic and beautiful abstract drawing, which also conveys additional facts about the

character of the building. Note particularly the way Latrobe renders the elliptical stairway—an unusual feature of the Thornton design probably based on the work of the English architect Sir William Chambers—so that the free span over the oval space of the two flights of stairs leading to a central platform is crisply indicated. The various divisions of the Supreme Court Chamber are also clearly set out by the contrasts in light and dark. Finally, Latrobe turns the ground plan into a work of art through his use of watercolor washes; the contrast between the yellow green of the area surrounding the plan on the top of the sheet and the light pink and pink beige of the lower part serve to enhance the three-dimensional appearance of the ground plan.

*Plate 7*
U. S. Capitol
**Benjamin H. Latrobe**
**Proposed design, view from the south, 1810–11**
Pencil, ink, and watercolor on paper
$19\frac{1}{4} \times 30\frac{1}{8}$ in. ($49 \times 76.5$ cm)
*Library of Congress*

It is not known what inspired Latrobe to prepare this design of the Capitol in 1810–11, which is a far more monumental version than the one he had forecast in his 1806 plans. It may reflect a moment in which he realized that his earlier concept (plate 6), which cut off the entire western projection called for by Thornton's design and L'Enfant's chosen location, would result in a building that would not dominate its site. Latrobe's new solution extended the Capitol to the brow of the hill and provided for an architectural conversion of the western slope into a superbly designed sequence of entrances and approaches. Latrobe never succeeded in having this scheme adopted, if indeed it was ever seriously considered, but it led directly to his design for the central portion of the U. S. Capitol which was endorsed by President James Monroe in 1817 and formed the basis of the work by Charles Bulfinch, the architect responsible for completing the central section of the building (figures 21 and 22).

*Plate 8*
U. S. Capitol
**Benjamin H. Latrobe**
**Design proposed for the Hall of Representatives, 1804**
Pencil, ink, and watercolor on paper
$12\frac{1}{2} \times 19\frac{3}{4}$ in. ($31.8 \times 50.2$ cm)
*Library of Congress*

Latrobe's primary task in the first period of his superintendency under President Jefferson was to provide a meeting place for the House of Representatives in the south wing. Thornton fought an intense and continuous battle with Latrobe against his making any changes in the original plan, but Latrobe succeeded in locating the Hall of Representatives on the principal floor rather than the ground level. With regard to the design of the chamber itself, Latrobe engaged in differences of taste with Jefferson, who was adamant that the elliptical shape of the room be retained, and that its ceiling be built along the principles of the Halle au Blé in Paris, with which he had become familiar during his residence there from 1784 to 1789 as United States minister to France. In this market hall glass skylights had been inserted between the ribs of the dome, thereby flooding the interior with light. After many artful attempts to dissuade the president from what he believed to be a proposal that would never prove functional, Latrobe nevertheless produced a strikingly beautiful design following Jefferson's dictates.

The colonnade of the interior was equally admired by contemporaries, but its final design followed the Corinthian rather than the Doric order proposed here as an alternate for the president to consider. Upon its completion this assembly hall was hailed as one of the most beautiful in the world. On July 12, 1812, Jefferson wrote to Latrobe from Monticello praising his work, observing that the "Representative Chamber will remain a durable monument of your taste as an architect." Years later, Latrobe's son would recall that one of his childhood's strongest impressions was "the effect, approaching awe, produced upon me by the old Hall of Representatives . . ." and recalled that the

British officer responsible for putting the torch to the building in 1814 was reported to have expressed regret that "anything so beautiful" should be destroyed (Hamlin, 1955, p. 292).

*Plate 9*
U. S. Capitol
**Benjamin H. Latrobe**
**Design for the vaulting of the Senate Chamber, ca. 1816**
Pencil, ink, and watercolor on paper
$19\frac{1}{2} \times 24\frac{1}{8}$ in. ($49.5 \times 61.3$ cm)
*Library of Congress*

One of Latrobe's keenest talents as a draftsman was his ability to convey in a single drawing a multitude of information about how a particular architectural element would appear and how it should be constructed, while at the same time creating a compositional arrangement of this information which in itself possesses an intrinsic beauty. One characteristic of Latrobe's approach to the sheet on which the drawing was made rests in his treating it as an object to be approached from all sides. For Latrobe there are no tops, bottoms, or sides to a sheet: each discrete piece of information is placed according to his instinct for design within an economy of space. Thus, in this sheet Latrobe shows: in center left, a view of the coffering as it will appear when seen through the glass of the roundels; on the right, how the roundels will be set within the vault; at upper right, the decorative treatment intended for the innermost bank of the vault; and at the upper left, the ornamental details of the outermost band of the vault. All details, as well as the whole, are drawn according to different scales, each identified on the sheet.

Latrobe's ability to convey complicated structures visually was superior to that of most of his contemporaries. The quality of a drawing like this one is such, that it is easy to forget it was made as a working drawing for the builder to follow in constructing the vault.

*Plate 10*
The President's House
**Benjamin H. Latrobe**
**Design for the addition of porticoes on the north and south fronts, 1807**
Ink and watercolor on paper
$15\frac{3}{8} \times 20$ in. ($39.1 \times 50.8$ cm)
*Library of Congress*
(Photographed before restoration)

Working intimately with President Jefferson, Latrobe was able to transform the modest President's House that had resulted from the winning design by James Hoban in the original 1792 competition into an edifice that conformed more with the title usually applied to it during this period—the "President's Palace." The porticoes planned by Latrobe (the foundations for which may have been begun under his direction) were not finally erected until after the burning of the building in 1814; the south portico was finished in 1824, the north one in 1829 under the direction of the original architect James Hoban, who unfortunately did not follow Latrobe's designs.

Latrobe's 1807 design would have produced a far more monumental effect. On the south side he planned an imposing central stairway leading up from the lawn to the portico. When the south portico was actually erected by Hoban he substituted Latrobe's central stairway with two side stairways and introduced a central doorway, which gave a direct but inelegant entry to the basement level. (This link between the south lawn and the President's House has only recently come into its own, providing access from the helicopter pad into the mansion, where the basement area has been renamed the Diplomatic Reception Room.)

Latrobe's design for the north side suffered the most at the hands of Hoban, who rearranged the columns in such a way that the rich and impressive portico intended by Latrobe became a weak and ill-proportioned addition. In Latrobe's plan a broad carriageway is placed in the center of the portico flanked by twin columns. Hoban shifted the carriage drive to the outermost edge of the porch, supporting the entire span of the portico by single

columns at either end and paired columns in the center, which succeed in looking more like temporary props for an excessively long span than objects of dignity and strength. Whatever lay behind Hoban's decision to arrange the portico in this manner, it has resulted not only in a graceless design, but also in a useless amenity, for those arriving at this entrance are left too far from the door to escape totally the wind, rain, or snow that often swirls through the high portico.

*Plate 11*
U. S. Capitol
**Robert Mills**
**Design proposed to enlarge the Capitol, elevation of the west front, 1851**
Ink and wash on paper
$14\frac{1}{4} \times 31\frac{3}{4}$ in. ($36.2 \times 80.7$ cm)
*United States Capitol, Architect of the Capitol*

Although the drawing is unfortunately marred by an erasure or abrasion across the central portion of the elevation, it is still an impressive presentation of Mills's intended design for the west front of the Capitol. The concept resembles the original Thornton design in several respects and, had it been adopted, would have restored the idea of a Temple of Fame as the central element of this front. (Another design by Mills of this period suggests a form for the central dome that is much closer to that finally erected by Walter.) The semicircular side porticoes introduced by Mills at the western corners of the added wings and on the east front would have had the effect of visually providing a continuous columnar base for the dome when viewed from either side, so that even though the dome actually would be farther removed from the two side wings, it would appear more central. In this regard, Mills's design is again reminiscent of Thornton's original plan in which he had called for semicircular porticoes on the north and south side wings because, as he said in his 1793 response to criticism of his design, "every front should exhibit the same or similar elegance of style" (Kimball and Bennett, p. 85).

*Plate 12*
U. S. Capitol
**Robert Mills**
**Design proposed to enlarge the Capitol, isometric plan of the principal story, 1851**
Ink and watercolor on paper
$23 \times 37\frac{5}{8}$ in. ($58.5 \times 95.6$ cm)
*United States Capitol, Architect of the Capitol*

In this exceptional presentation drawing of the floor plan of the Capitol, Mills appears to be following the example set by Latrobe in his ground-plan drawings (plate 6). It is highly unlikely, however, that Mills executed this drawing himself, for its quality is far beyond that of other plans prepared by him (although the identifications on the principal rooms seem to be in his hand). Mills employed draftsmen to make his drawings; two of the drawings of his design for the Capitol are signed "Drawn by W. A. Powell, Arch/."

*Plate 13*
U. S. Capitol
**Thomas U. Walter**
**Design adopted for the north wing extension, 1851**
Ink, wash, and watercolor on paper
$20\frac{1}{8} \times 35\frac{1}{4}$ in. ($51.2 \times 89.2$ cm)
*United States Capitol, Architect of the Capitol*

This drawing shows clearly the connecting passageway Walter designed to link the new wing and the old building, but also visually to separate the two.

*Plate 14*
U. S. Capitol
**Thomas U. Walter**
**Design for the extension of the Capitol approved by President Millard Fillmore, 1851**
Ink and watercolor on paper
$20\frac{1}{8} \times 34\frac{3}{4}$ in. ($51.2 \times 88.3$ cm)
*The Athenaeum of Philadelphia*
(Not included in exhibition)

One of the great recoveries in recent years in the history of American architecture

has been the retrieval of the drawings and papers of Thomas U. Walter through the persistent efforts of the staff of the Athenaeum of Philadelphia. This key drawing, as well as its equally important mate seen in plate 24, were known to historians only through photographs taken at the time they were made, which gave no idea of either their size or their quality. The drawings remained with Walter and his descendants from 1865 when he left Washington, D. C., until 1979, when they were exhibited for the first time at the Athenaeum. In addition to owning these and many other drawings by Walter since acquired from the family, the Athenaeum is now also the repository of an extensive collection of Walter's diaries and letters.

The photograph reproduced here was taken by the Dunlap Society at the time of the Philadelphia exhibition and shows the drawing in its unrestored state. The work is presently undergoing conservation treatment.

*Plate 15*
U. S. Capitol
**Montgomery C. Meigs**
**Revision of design by Thomas U. Walter for the east front of the north wing extension, 1853**
Ink and washes on paper
$25\frac{3}{4} \times 39\frac{3}{4}$ in. ($65.4 \times 101$ cm)
*United States Capitol, Architect of the Capitol*

Work on Walter's design for the north wing began in the summer of 1851, but the architect soon ran into such a storm of criticism concerning both the nature of the foundations he was laying and his method of letting contracts, that in 1853 President Franklin Pierce placed the conduct of the work under the Secretary of the Army, Jefferson Davis, who appointed Montgomery C. Meigs to oversee the construction. Meigs made substantial changes in Walter's design. He was responsible for adding the triangular pediments on the east front, thereby creating an increased opportunity for sculptural decoration, the commissioning of which appears to have been the responsibility of Meigs rather than Walter. Meigs had invited estimates and designs for the east doors and for the sculpture for the east pediment of the north wing in August 1853; on November 30, Thomas Crawford was awarded the commission for the pedimental sculpture. Entitled *The Progress of Civilization*, it is included in this elevation, which must have been made the following month. Crawford modeled the figures for the sixty-foot-long group in Rome and shipped several of them to Washington as early as 1855, where they were carved in marble in shops set up on the Capitol grounds. The composition was completely installed by late 1863. The sculptured figures over the central door, representing Justice and Liberty, were carved by Crawford in Italy and were also installed in 1863.

*Plate 16*
U. S. Capitol
**Thomas U. Walter**
**Design for the entrance doors on the east front of the extension, ca. 1853**
Ink and watercolor on paper
$28 \times 23\frac{1}{2}$ in. ($71.2 \times 59.7$ cm)
*United States Capitol, Architect of the Capitol*

This drawing by Walter apparently antedates the arrival of Meigs in April 1853 and the subsequent changes in Walter's original design for the east fronts of the two wings. The figures depicted here represent Liberty, on the left, pointing to a tablet carrying the inscription WASHINGTON PATER PATRIA and a figure bearing the emblems of Peace and War. Both recline on a half globe inscribed with the name AMERICA.

The bronze doors substituted by Meigs for the ones proposed here are more monumental in scale and provide a stronger central accent to the composition.

*Plate 17*
U. S. Capitol
**Thomas U. Walter**
**Plan of the attic story of the north wing extension, 1853**
Ink and watercolor on paper
$22\frac{3}{4} \times 26$ in. ($57.8 \times 66.1$ cm)
*United States Capitol, Architect of the Capitol*

Renderings such as this were made for every level of each of the wings and include details of all the decorative elements whether, as in this drawing, they concern the ceiling treatments, or deal with the floor decorations, including the type of carpeting. The small size of this kind of drawing makes it unlikely that they were prepared as working drawings, but served rather as presentation pieces for the Congressional committees or the president. Their brilliant watercolor treatment gives them a jewel-like character that could not help but appeal to even the most adamant foe of luxury in government buildings.

*Plate 18*
U. S. Capitol
**Thomas U. Walter**
**Design for the interior of the Senate Chamber in the north wing extension, 1855**
Ink and watercolor on paper
$20\frac{1}{8} \times 26$ in. ($51.2 \times 66.1$ cm)
*United States Capitol, Architect of the Capitol*

Although the niches in the Senate Chamber never received the statuary proposed in this drawing, the overall effect of the room was as luxurious as suggested here. The Chamber was completed in time for the January 4, 1859, meeting of the Senate. Walter also designed the desks and chairs for both legislative halls which complemented the ornate design of the entire room. Nearly all the decorative elements designed by Walter for the Senate Chamber were covered over by the remodeling of 1949–50. The great stained-glass ceiling was concealed by a lower plaster shell and a small central skylight.

All the cast-iron ornament that articulated the walls on the floor and gallery levels of the Chamber was replaced with marble and plaster decoration. The vaulted room under the staircase on the left of the drawing is the present, frequently referred to, "cloakroom" of the Senate.

*Plate 19*
U. S. Capitol
**Thomas U. Walter**
**Design for the stained-glass ceiling over the Hall of Representatives in the south wing extension, 1855**
Ink, washes, and watercolor on paper
$27\frac{5}{8} \times 46\frac{1}{2}$ in. ($70.2 \times 118.1$ cm)
*United States Capitol, Architect of the Capitol*
(Not in exhibition)

The major change made by Meigs in the interior arrangement of the new wings moved the assembly halls away from the window walls, where Walter had located them, to the center of the building. Each of the legislative chambers consequently became a completely enclosed room surrounded on all four sides by committee rooms, stairwells, and vestibules. As a consequence, Meigs was responsible for the design and construction of the skylights introduced over each meeting hall.

The vast size of the skylights and the great expanse of the glass ceilings required a special type of bracing beam which Meigs himself designed. When the beams were cast they bore in raised letters on their surface the inscription, *Capt. M. C. Meigs inv. AD 1854*. Meigs also invented an elaborate system of gas lighting above the ceiling to supplement the daylight. The decorated glass panels in the center are surrounded by ventilation grates in the outer row of coffers, and the entire ceiling is ringed by ninety-six cast-iron rosettes.

Seen in the right-hand margin of this drawing is a lunette-shaped heliotype showing the design adopted in 1855 for the Capitol extension. This print is found on most of the working drawings after this date, and it is also the rule that all drawings are signed by both Meigs, as "Engineer in Charge," and Walter, as

"Architect, U. S. Capitol Extension," until Meigs was removed from his post on November 1, 1859, and replaced by Captain W. B. Franklin.

*Plate 20*
U. S. Capitol
**Montgomery C. Meigs**
**Design for the fan to ventilate the Hall of Representatives in the south wing extension, 1858**
Ink and watercolor on paper
$19\frac{3}{8} \times 22\frac{3}{8}$ in. ($49.3 \times 56.9$ cm)
*United States Capitol, Architect of the Capitol*

Meigs was also responsible for creating a ventilating system that would provide each of the interior halls with an adequate supply of fresh air. The relocation of the legislative halls from the perimeter to the interior of the building was later denounced on the floor of the Senate as being un-Christian, as it deprived the legislative halls of natural light and substituted a steam engine for air "supplied by the Almighty."

*Plate 21*
U. S. Capitol
**Thomas U. Walter**
**Design for the decoration of the vestibule outside the Senate Chamber in the north wing extension, 1859**
Ink and watercolor on paper
$23\frac{1}{4} \times 33\frac{1}{8}$ in. ($59.1 \times 84.2$ cm)
*United States Capitol, Architect of the Capitol*

*Plate 22*
U.S. Capitol
**Thomas U. Walter**
**Design for the mantel installed in the Senate Retiring Room in the north wing extension, 1855**
Ink and brown wash on paper
$27\frac{1}{8} \times 47\frac{5}{8}$ in. ($68.9 \times 121$ cm)
*United States Capitol, Architect of the Capitol*

*Plate 23*
U.S. Capitol
**Thomas U. Walter**
**Design for the pedestal of the statue of Freedom on top of the dome, 1862**
Ink and washes on paper
48⅜ × 27⅝ in. (122.9 × 70.2 cm)
*United States Capitol, Architect of the Capitol*

*Plate 24*
U. S. Capitol
**Thomas U. Walter**
**Design for the extension and new dome of the Capitol, 1855**
Watercolor on paper
23 × 43½ in. (58.5 × 110.5 cm)
*The Athenaeum of Philadelphia*
(Not in exhibition)

See note to plate 14.

This rendering shows a dome higher than the one actually constructed.

The photograph reproduced here was taken by the Dunlap Society at the time of the exhibition of Walter's drawings at the Athenaeum in 1979 and shows the drawing in its unrestored state. The work is presently undergoing conservation treatment.

*Plate 25*
U. S. Capitol
**Thomas U. Walter**
**Design for the interior of the dome, 1859**
Ink, wash, and watercolor on paper
42½ × 24¾ in. (108 × 62.9 cm)
*United States Capitol, Architect of the Capitol*

The draftsman probably responsible for most of the unbelievably detailed and artistically sensitive drawings for the work on the Capitol was Auguste Schoenborn, who had been trained in Germany and had come to Washington in 1851 to work for Walter when he accepted the position as Architect of the Capitol Extension. Schoenborn's hand is not easily distinguished from that of Walter, however, whose ability at watercolor ren-

dering is well documented by his earlier designs for works in Philadelphia, particularly the drawings for Girard College (plate 27). Even the half-shaded form of inscription (as seen, for example, in plate 21) is common to Walter's drawings from both periods.

This incredible drawing delivers a wealth of information about the construction of the central area of the Capitol, beginning with the foundations and passing through every level of the building up to the statue of Freedom. Although investigations made prior to the extension of the east front in 1958–62 determined that the foundations are not as deep below the basement floor as shown here, the drawing accurately records the composition of the central crypt beneath the floor of the rotunda and details as well the two Latrobe vestibules on both the left- and right-hand sides of the Bulfinch rotunda. All the decorative details of the rotunda are depicted—the paintings by Trumbull, the panels of relief sculpture above them, and the newly planned continuous trompe l'oeil frieze within the new dome, fifty-eight feet above the floor of the rotunda. The fresco, painted in shades of brown, black, and white to create an illusion of carved relief sculpture is nine feet high and three hundred feet in circumference. Begun by Constantino Brumidi in 1877, the work was carried on after his death in 1880 by Filippo Costaggini following Brumidi's existing designs. Thirty feet of the frieze remained unfinished, however, until 1953, when Congress commissioned Allyn Cox to complete the work.

The subsequent area of the pilasters, window embrasures, and coffered ceiling are made up entirely of cast-iron ornament. The upper section of the dome shows the canopy fresco, also by Brumidi, which he signed in 1865 after eleven months of work. Entitled *The Apotheosis of George Washington*, the fresco depicts Washington seated near the center of the composition, surrounded by thirteen female figures representing the original colonies. The lowest tier consists of a series of allegorical groups, the one depicted here representing Armed Combat.

*Plate 26*
U. S. Capitol
**Thomas U. Walter**
**Design for the structural parts of the ribs of the dome, 1859**
Ink and watercolor on paper
27⅝ × 48 in. (70.2 × 122 cm)
*United States Capitol, Architect of the Capitol*

Despite the mundane subject matter illustrated here, this drawing is a particularly good example of Schoenborn's work. The detailed rendering of one of the specific construction units intended for the cast-iron ribs of the dome is presented by the draftsman as if it were drawn on a separate piece of paper lying on top of the larger drawing. This required the draftsman to begin by laying a colored wash over the entire sheet, excepting the smaller area which retained the original color of the paper.

Such presentation techniques are common among the thousands of drawings prepared for this building program, in sharp contrast to the meager number of drawings produced in the earlier part of the century for the construction of Thornton's design. By the middle of the century the traditional verbal on-the-site instructions between superintendent and craftsmen were being supplanted by detailed drawings that permitted a finished product that better matched the concept of the architect. Not all such drawings, however, exhibit the high quality of this one.

*Plate 27*
Girard College for Orphans, Philadelphia
Constructed 1833–47
**Thomas U. Walter**
**View of the main building with subsidiary dormitory buildings, 1835**
Watercolor on paper
22¾ × 38 in. (57.8 × 96.6 cm)
*The Athenaeum of Philadelphia*
(Not in exhibition)

See note to plate 14.

Walter clearly had the advantage over others of his generation in being able to present his projects to prospective clients in a compelling, handsome manner. The complete series of drawings Walter prepared for the Girard College competition remains one of the highest accomplishments of American draftsmanship at this time. In addition to this fine example, returned to the public sector by the efforts of the Athenaeum, there exist numerous drawings by Walter that controlled every aspect of the school's construction. By exercising this role Walter garnered more than adequate experience qualifying him to be put in charge of the extension of the U. S. Capitol.

The monument Walter created at Girard College was a major landmark in the development of American architecture, and it still awaits the recognition it deserves. As an icon of American architectural philosophy it is far more meaningful than the vaunted campus design by Jefferson and his advisors for the University of Virginia. The latter represents, essentially, the personal predilection of an amateur architect steeped in the distant past; the Philadelphia campus represents the creation in the new Republic of a complex of buildings that instilled a strong sense that America was inexorably linked with the values and images of an ideal classical past.

*Plate 28*
Washington, D.C.
**B. F. Smith, Jr.**
**View of the city "with projected
improvements," 1852**
Color lithograph
*Library of Congress*
(Not in exhibition)

The all-encompassing view of the central area of the capital city could not have been better rendered even by L'Enfant, although he certainly would have rejected several parts of the proposed additions. The Mills monument to President Washington was located at the precise spot L'Enfant had specified for such a monument. Although L'Enfant's choice for a monument had been for a simple equestrian statue of the general (as had already been voted by Congress), he probably would have favored the more grandiose monument proposed by Mills, who was the architect of the much-admired monument to Washington erected in Baltimore between 1815 and 1829.

The prototype for the monument designed by Mills for the capital city had an impressive circular colonnade that served as the base of an obelisk. It was derived from a project proposed in 1791 by Jacques Molinos and Jacques-Guillaume Legrand to be erected in Paris on the site of the Bastille, that "den of despotism," and was intended to represent a temple of liberty, celebrating significant moments in the life of the French revolutionary assemblies. In this instance the colonnade surrounding the obelisk was to have rested on the debris of a tower of the Bastille, in which one would still be able to see the remains of a dungeon. The design and its description was published in 1792 in a book by Armand de Kersaint, a copy of which was in Jefferson's library and thus readily accessible to Mills when he worked there. (The discovery of this source of Mills's design was made by my research assistant, Pamela Scott, when she was checking what examples of late-eighteenth-century architectural designs had existed in Jefferson's library.)

The three other major building projects by Mills are prominently featured in the distance; at the left is the new Treasury Building, next to the President's House; and farther to the right, the massive white block of the Patent Office is seen adjacent to the smaller General Post Office. The latter two buildings dominate their surroundings for they are placed on the higher ground running parallel to Pennsylvania Avenue which L'Enfant had chosen to be the site of major public buildings.

L'Enfant would certainly not have approved of the landscaping planned for the Mall, which replaced his intended stretch of greensward and a great axial vista with an informal park with meandering paths and seemingly haphazardly planted trees. This view, however, is an accurate rendering of the plan by Andrew Jackson Downing adopted for the Mall by President Fillmore in 1852. The Picturesque planting would have complemented the medieval "castle" of the Smithsonian (seen at the far right) which L'Enfant clearly would have disdained as unworthy of the capital city. On the other hand, he might well have endorsed the suspension bridge linking the Mall with the grounds of the President's House and welcomed Downing's idea for a triumphal arch to be placed between Pennsylvania Avenue and the President's House (not visible in this view). The enlarged Capitol seen in the far distance on the right still dominates the city, but it is likely that L'Enfant would have continued to find its architecture inadequate.

*Plate 29*
U. S. Custom House, Boston
Constructed 1837–47
**Ammi B. Young**
**Transverse section of the winning design, 1837**
Pencil, watercolor, wash, and gouache on paper
$27\frac{5}{8} \times 37\frac{1}{4}$ in. (70.2 × 94.7 cm)
*National Archives*

This rendering by Young is probably the most outstanding example that remains of the drawings that must have been made for the great classical buildings being erected in America at this time. Although not as brilliantly executed as the drawings of Latrobe and Walter, this rendering is presented in such a dramatic contrast of light and shadow that the somber but majestic quality of the interior space is readily evoked. Although this is apparently the only rendering by Young in existence, it clearly seems to be his own work, given the evidence of his skill as a draftsman in other drawings for this building, particularly in a pencil, isometric view of the custom house also in the National Archives.

Although we can still admire most of the exterior of Young's Custom House, the majestic interior space seen in this rendering no longer exists. In a building project of 1913–15 Young's building was used as the base for a great tower designed by the firm of Peabody and Stearns which destroyed the central banking hall and dome. The unusual and distinctive granite ribs and plates of the dome were disassembled and the laboriously carved blocks of curved granite were discarded into the harbor. The monolithic granite columns were re-used as a lofty gateway in Boston's Franklin Park, where they may still be seen today.

*Plate 30*
U. S. Custom House, New York
Constructed 1834–42
**Ithiel Town and Alexander Jackson Davis**
**Prizewinning entry, 1833**
Pencil, ink, and watercolor
$24\frac{3}{16} \times 30\frac{1}{4}$ in. (61.5 × 76.9 cm)
*Museum of Fine Arts, Boston (M. and M. Karolik Collection of American Watercolors and Drawings, 1800–1875)*

Although travel sketches, drawings, and plans by Alexander Jackson Davis, the more artistic member of Town and Davis, the successful New York architectural firm, exist in great quantity, primarily at the Metropolitan Museum of Art and the Avery Architectural Library at Columbia University, we are not as fortunate in the number of presentation drawings that are preserved. This is a particularly fine example. The Davis renderings are characterized by the presence of minute, almost pure silhouette figures who are depicted as either admiring the buildings or absolutely indifferent to their surroundings.

Later used to house the U. S. Subtreasury, the building is now known as Federal Hall National Memorial, named for L'Enfant's creation (figure 4), which once stood on this spot. The building is now under the jurisdiction of the National Park Service, and plans are currently under way to restore the interior to its 1840s appearance.

*Plate 31*
U. S. Custom House, New Orleans
Constructed 1847–88
**Alexander T. Wood**
**Elevation on New Levee Street facing the river front, 1847**
Pencil, ink, wash, and watercolor on paper
2 ft. 6 in. × 7 ft. $10\frac{1}{2}$ in. (76.9 × 240 cm)
*National Archives*

The recent discovery of this impressive drawing of high quality and its positive identification and date require that the contribution of Alexander T. Wood as an architect be re-evaluated. Up to now the charges by James Gallier in his *Autobiography*—that Wood, "having free access to all the plans and models that had been sent in [for the competition] concocted a design in accordance with the taste and ideas of the Secretary" (Scully, p. 162)—have, in the absence of original documents, led to the belief that Wood was not capable of creating an original design and to suggestions that it was the architect James Dakin who was the source of his plan. This drawing would seem to reverse the case. The final design submitted by James Dakin in August 1847 can now be seen as related to Wood's only in that it is much simpler than any of Dakin's other entries.

Dakin made his design only after consulting with the secretary and after examining the drawings and models submitted by others. In his diary Dakin noted that Wood's design was "a most foolish thing for any man having the least pretension to architectural skill" because it covered the entire site with no means of ventilation or air for the interiors except for a skylight over the Banking Hall placed in the center of "the dense mass of [the] building." Dakin characterizes Wood's plan as one that "would have made a tolerable Mausoleum or Tomb for an Egyptian King" (Scully, p. 170).

Known previously only from a woodcut published in the New Orleans *Daily Delta* on February 13, 1848, Wood's design now emerges in this rendering as an exceptionally powerful one with no obvious precedents whatsoever. Wood's entire approach to the composition of the surfaces and voids of the wall is unique. The deeply cut channeling of the masonry which runs continuously across the ground-level story—breaking only above the niches of the three porticoes—and the broad horizontal band above it provide a strong base for the three-story-high wall that rises above it. The treatment of this wall with respect to the window distribution in the areas between the porticoes is exceptionally bold. By their disposition, the windows appear almost as single vertical strips set into the surface of the wall, which in itself reads as a series of flat vertical elements, almost as if they were pilasters, when in fact they are simply parts of the overall wall plane.

An even more complicated window arrangement occurs in the porticoes and above the two grilled entranceways. In all five cases the broader windows are divided into a central unit and two narrower units by masonry posts that are without any articulation or ornament. These become dominant structural elements in the design because they appear to rise uninterruptedly behind the major wall plane from the first story up into the area immediately below the cornice, where they divide small attic windows into the same three parts. These windows are flanked by projecting brackets which not only terminate the vertical thrusts of the window alignments, but create a strong horizontal cap on the building, without, however, actually being identifiable as part of a classical vocabulary. The low, gently inclined pediments form subdued terminations to the two end porticoes and help

retain the very strong, flat roofline which is broken only by the high, rectangular block set above the central portico whose mass bears down on the lotus-style columns.

Wood's design is so original and innovative—although altered, alas, in execution to be more "classical"—it evokes a sense of having been born with the use of a material other than granite in mind, almost as if the vertical and horizontal play inherent in iron-and-glass construction were at hand. But, in fact, Wood has responded to the nature of the quarried granite blocks shipped from Quincy, Massachusetts, which were already in use in seaport cities all along the eastern and southern coasts, where the warehouse buildings were constructed with granite uprights and brick fill. Wood has used the same supports but had embedded them in a more sophisticated setting that allows the characteristics of the material to dominate, with a minimum of ornamental carving.

*Plate 32*
U. S. Custom House, New Orleans
Constructed 1847–88
**Alexander T. Wood**
**Transverse section, showing the proposed manner of finishing the building, 1851**
Ink, wash, and watercolor on paper
$22\frac{3}{4} \times 28\frac{1}{2}$ in. (57.9 × 72.4 cm)
*National Archives*

In 1853, after a period of controversy and a succession of several local superintending architects, Major P. G. T. Beauregard was chosen as superintendent architect for the New Orleans custom house. He carried out the plans of Wood (who died in 1854) except for the dome, which was never built because of inadequate foundations.

Alfred B. Mullett, who would become supervising architect in 1866, disliked the building intensely, and in his 1868 report suggested that "some decision be made in regard to the immense and unsightly mass of granite, popularly known as the New Orleans custom-house. . . . I called attention in my report of 1866 to this building and stated that it had then sunk upwards

of two feet. An application having been recently received at this department for the position of gauger and recorder of the monthly settlement, from the gentleman who held that position before the war, it is presumed that the building is still going down" (*S. A. T. Report*, 1868, p. 182).

*Plate 33*
U. S. Custom House, New Orleans
Constructed 1847–88
**Alexander T. Wood**
**Plan of first story, 1851**
Pencil, ink, and watercolor on paper
$23\frac{3}{4} \times 30\frac{1}{4}$ in. (60.4 × 76.8 cm)
*National Archives*

The inscription on this drawing identifies it as one presented as evidence to an impartial board of examiners established by the secretary of the treasury in November 1851 to evaluate the changes James Dakin wanted to make in Wood's design (see page 51). The board agreed with Dakin that Wood's placement of the business room in the center of the building would eliminate air and light, but accompanied its report to the secretary of the treasury with two sets of plans, one of which was this original design by Wood; the other, Dakin's revised plan. In the end, Wood's plan prevailed.

*Plate 34*
U. S. Custom House, New Orleans
Constructed 1847–88
**Alexander T. Wood**
**Plan of roof, 1851**
Pencil, ink, and colored washes on paper
$21\frac{1}{2} \times 29$ in. (54.6 × 73.7 cm)
*National Archives*

See note to plate 33.

*Plate 35*
U. S. Custom House, New Orleans
Constructed 1847–88
**Alexander T. Wood**
**Drawing showing progress of construction as of September 30, 1856**
Pencil, ink, wash, and watercolor on paper
$19\frac{7}{8} \times 28\frac{5}{8}$ in. (50.6 × 72.8 cm)
*National Archives*
(Not in exhibition)

Because of both the settling of the ground and the political infighting, progress on the New Orleans custom house was slow. This drawing is probably typical of the kind of reports sent in by the site supervisors to the new Construction Branch of the Treasury Department so that the progress of the work could be gauged. After the end of the Civil War, Congress was undecided about what to do with the building. Alfred B. Mullett, as supervising architect, tried to force a decision by writing in his 1869 report:

I desire to call special attention to the necessity of a decision in regard to the unfinished monstrosity known as the New Orleans custom house, which is a disgrace to the government, as well as its designers and builders. I cannot recommend the completion of the building according to the original design. . . . I feel, on the other hand, reluctant to recommend that the immense mass of material now piled on the foundations be used as a quarry, and a proper building erected on the site, though I believe it would be the best plan. I am therefore inclined to advise the completion of the building as a two story structure, and believe that ample room would be found therein for all legitimate purposes (*S. A. T. Report*, 1869, p. 8).

Congress decided to finish the building and Mullett drew up plans for its completion, observing in his 1871 report that the building "will, when finished, though devoid of beauty, be a permanent and substantial structure" (*S. A. T. Report*, 1871, p. 6). However, another seventeen years would pass before the building was finally completed.

*Plate 36*
U. S. Custom House, Wheeling, West Virginia
Constructed 1856–60
**Ammi B. Young**
**Details of columns, 1855**
Lithograph
*National Archives*
(Not in exhibition)

On a single lithograph plate Young was capable of gathering a dense amount of construction information and visual details ingeniously and often attractively arranged, but not on the same artistic level as such sheets by Latrobe (see note to plate 9).

*Plate 37*
U. S. Custom House, Chicago
Constructed 1856–60
**Ammi B. Young**
**Front elevation, 1855**
Lithograph
*National Archives*
(Not in exhibition)

*Plate 38*
U. S. Custom House and Post Office, Petersburg, Virginia
Constructed 1856–59
**Ammi B. Young**
**Elevations and sections, 1855**
Lithograph
*National Archives*
(Not in exhibition)

*Plate 39*
U. S. Courthouse and Post Office, Rutland, Vermont
Constructed 1857–59
**Ammi B. Young**
**Front elevation, 1856**
Lithograph
*National Archives*
(Not in exhibition)

Plates 36–39 were all included in bound volumes entitled *Plans of Public Buildings in Course of Construction for the United States of America under the Direction of the*

*Secretary of the Treasury,* for which J. Goldsborough Bruff, a draftsman in the Construction Branch, designed frontispieces that were used to introduce each set of lithographic prints pulled to serve as working drawings for a particular building (see pages 52–53). Although these volumes are sometimes described as constituting a five-volume set, there was no uniformity in their binding, nor, indeed, in the contents of each.

An examination of the volumes in five different sets reveals that although the basic contents consists of buildings designed in 1855–56, occasionally buildings as early as 1852 are also included. The designs for the Philadelphia post office (plates 40–42) were found only in a bound copy of the plates that had originally been in the library of the Office of the Supervising Architect.

*Plate 40*
U. S. Courthouse and Post Office, Philadelphia
Not commenced
**Ammi B. Young**
**Ornamental details, 1860**
Lithograph
*National Archives*
(Not in exhibition)

*Plate 41*
U. S. Courthouse and Post Office, Philadelphia
Not commenced
**Ammi B. Young**
**Decorative details of lighting fixtures, 1860**
Lithograph
*National Archives*
(Not in exhibition)

*Plate 42*
U. S. Courthouse and Post Office, Philadelphia
Not commenced
**Ammi B. Young**
**Elevations, 1860**
Lithograph
*National Archives*
(Not in exhibition)

The Civil War intervened before Young's design could be executed. Subsequently Alfred B. Mullett designed the much larger structure that was built 1874–84.

*Plate 43*
U. S. Branch Mint, Carson City, Nevada
Constructed 1866–70
**Alfred B. Mullett**
**Front elevation, 1866**
Ink and wash on paper
$22\frac{7}{8} \times 35\frac{7}{8}$ in. (58.1 × 91.2 cm)
*National Archives*

Now used as the Nevada State Museum, the Mint was the first building designed by Mullett upon becoming the supervising architect, and it follows closely the national style created by his predecessor, Ammi B. Young. Though a Congressional bill had recommended a branch mint in the territory of Nevada to eliminate the cost and risk of transporting bullion to San Francisco, the Civil War intervened and no action was taken. However, in view of the economic drain of the war, the prospect of a new rich state was so tempting, the federal government waived the minimum population required for territories to become states, and on October 31, 1864, Nevada became the thirty-sixth state of the Union. The plans and specifications for the building of the Mint were received in Carson City in 1866.

*Plate 44*
U. S. Custom House, Portland, Maine
Constructed 1868–72
**Alfred B. Mullett**
**Cross section of the customs room, ca. 1868**
Pencil, ink, and color washes on paper
$37\frac{1}{8} \times 24\frac{1}{4}$ in. (94.3 × 61.6 cm)
*National Archives*

Ammi B. Young's custom house designed in 1855 was badly damaged in the fire that swept through Portland in 1866. The catastrophe elicited great sympathy from the federal government, evident in the generous appropriations ($500,000) voted to replace the building, which had to be torn down in 1867. Mullett replaced Young's classical structure—which had boasted a colonnade of colossal Ionic columns set above a rank of heavy Tuscan pillars—with a building clearly Italianate in its derivation. Whereas the three stories of Young's building were evident only on the sides, Mullet clearly delineated the three stories on each side of his building by entablatures that establish and emphasize the horizontality of each level and by the repetition of rows of arched windows framed by engaged columns. Mullett's design clearly displays his familiarity with the Italian Renaissance transformation of the ancient orders. When it was finished, the customs collector regarded the building as one which would stand for ages and "would transmit to future times an idea of the architecture of our time."

*Plate 45*
U. S. Custom House, Portland, Maine
Constructed 1868–72
**Alfred B. Mullett**
**Details of the wood- and ironwork for the balcony in the customs room, ca. 1868**
J. Goldsborough Bruff, delineator
Pencil, ink, wash, and watercolor on paper
$24\frac{3}{8} \times 37\frac{1}{8}$ in. (62 × 94.3 cm)
*National Archives*

*Plate 46*
U. S. Custom House, Portland, Maine
Constructed 1868–72
**Alfred B. Mullett**
**Full-size details for the iron- and stonework of the stairs, ca. 1868**
J. Goldsborough Bruff, delineator
Pencil, ink, wash, and watercolor on paper
24 × 37 in. (61 × 94.1 cm)
*National Archives*

Many of the ornamental motifs used by Mullett were identical to those introduced by Ammi B. Young, perhaps because the same designer, J. Goldsborough Bruff, worked for both supervising architects. The difference in presentation is startling, however, as can be seen by comparing the single drawings required by Mullett with similar motifs included on the lithographic plate by Young (plate 36).

*Plate 47*
U. S. Custom House, Portland, Maine
Constructed 1868–72
**Alfred B. Mullett**
**Full-size details for the plasterwork of the cornice frieze in the customs room, ca. 1868**
Pencil, ink, and wash on paper
23¼ × 36¼ in. (59.1 × 92.1 cm)
*National Archives*

*Plate 48*
U. S. Custom House, Saint Paul, Minnesota
Constructed 1868–73; demolished
**Alfred B. Mullett**
**Full-size details of the ironwork for the stairs, ca. 1868**
Pencil, crayon, ink, and color washes on paper
36¼ × 23½ in. (92.1 × 59.7 cm)
*National Archives*
(Not in exhibition)

*Plate 49*
U. S. Branch Mint, San Francisco
Constructed 1869–74
**Alfred B. Mullett**
**Details of a skylight, ca. 1870**
Ink, color washes, and watercolor on paper
24½ × 37¼ in. (62.3 × 94.7 cm)
*National Archives*

*Plate 50*
U. S. Branch Mint, San Francisco
Constructed 1869–74
**Alfred B. Mullett**
**Full-size details of the wrought-iron beams for the roof, ca. 1870**
Ink, wash, and color wash on paper
37¼ × 24 in. (94.7 × 61 cm)
*National Archives*
(Not in exhibition)

Two aspects of this building by Mullett are unusual. First, it is the only one of Mullett's designs produced during his term as supervising architect which reverts to the classical style. Mullett described it as being

two stories and a basement in height, and is a simple but imposing specimen of the Roman Doric. No ornamentation has been attempted but dependence placed on the magnitude and proportion of the building for its architectural effect (*S. A. T Report*, 1868, p. 22).

Secondly, Mullett intended to demonstrate his prowess as an engineer by making it earthquake-proof. As he points out in the same report,

The destruction of the custom-house and other buildings, public and private, in San Francisco by earthquakes has rendered it necessary to take every precaution to prevent a similar catastrophe to the proposed buildings, and I am willing to risk my professional reputation upon its stability if properly carried out according to my plans (p. 22).

Mullett was totally successful; in the 1906 earthquake the mint escaped without substantial damage, although the surrounding buildings were destroyed.

*Plate 51*
U. S. Custom House and Post Office, Port Huron, Michigan
Constructed 1873–77
**Alfred B. Mullett**
**Plan and sections of the roof, ca. 1874**
Ink and color washes on paper
24¼ × 37½ in. (61.7 × 95.3 cm)
*National Archives*

*Plate 52*
State, War and Navy Building, Washington, D. C.
Constructed 1871–1888
**Alfred B. Mullett**
**Detail drawing for the ironwork of the north wing, ca. 1880**
Ink and watercolor on paper
23½ × 35⅜ in. (59.7 × 89.9 cm)
*National Archives*

Although the mammoth State, War and Navy Building was begun in 1871, when ground was broken on June 20, it would not be completed until 1888. Mullett was in charge of the work until 1874, the year he resigned as supervising architect. Nevertheless, his design remained in effect. In 1877 the supervision of the construction was assigned to Lt. Col. Thomas Lincoln Casey of the Corps of Engineers, who signed this drawing for the ironwork of the north wing (1879–82), which was the third section of the building to be completed. Casey was subsequently responsible (1876–84) for the redesign and completion of the Washington Monument and, from 1888 until his death in 1896, for supervising the construction of the Library of Congress.

This drawing is one of hundreds preserved that detail the ironwork structure employed in the interior space enclosed by the granite exterior walls of the building. All such drawings contain the same abundant detail concerning how the individual pieces are to be cast and assembled. In the lower center of the drawing, a ground plan of the north wing indicates where each type of column and pilaster will be located, and a table gives the number of pieces needed to assemble them. At

the left-hand side of the drawing, Column A is shown both in rendered form and as a section, while beneath it are depicted top views of the section of the column at four different points. These indicate at lower left, the supporting footing of the column; immediately above, a view of the floor plate and how it will be set on the footing; at top right, a view of the section of the column at point A, which shows how the floor plate will be concealed by the base of the column; and in the full section above, a view showing how the hollow shaft of the column passes continuously through all these elements. Each detail is a vital piece of information for the manufacturer of the cast-iron pieces, as well as for the assembler of the framework on the site. Most of these drawings were reproduced by photographic process for distribution to those who needed them, although for other types of drawings, particularly ones dealing with ornament, tracings were provided.

The logistical sophistication demanded in the construction of the gigantic Mullett buildings was a by-product of the knowledge gained by the "managers" and "suppliers" of the vast armies deployed during the Civil War.

*Plate 53*
U. S. Post Office and Courthouse, New York
Constructed 1869–80; demolished 1939
**Alfred B. Mullett**
**Elevation of the west front, 1869**
Pencil, ink, and wash on paper
23⅜ × 36⅛ in. (59.4 × 91.8 cm)
*National Archives*

This drawing represents Mullett's version of the "amalgamated" design put forward by the five architectural firms whose designs were the most admired in the 1867 competition for this building: Richard Morris Hunt, Renwick and Sands, Napoleon Le Brun, J. Correja, and Schulze and Schoen (figure 57). Mullett followed the lead of these designers and called for an extensive program of sculptural decoration, of which the paired figures at the attic level are certainly modeled after those of the central pavilion of the Louvre. In previous work, however, Mullett had not been inclined to embellish his buildings, and his subsequent design for the front (figure 58) omitted the sculptural decoration, as did the final building (figure 59).

*Plate 54*
U. S. Post Office and Courthouse, New York
Constructed 1869–80, demolished 1939
**Alfred B. Mullett**
**Elevation of the Broadway front, 1868**
Pencil, ink, and wash on paper
23 × 36 in. (58.5 × 91.5 cm)
*National Archives*

Excavation for the New York building began in August 1869 and was carried on all day and at night, by using calcium lights, because of the risk in excavating in a bed of sand far below the level of Broadway. Work was slowed in 1870, however, by the failure of Congress to increase the available funds. Mullett prodded Congress to act in his 1870 report by saying that unless the limit fixed by Congress was raised, it would be necessary to use timber above the main story, including the roof (*S. A. T. Report*, 1870, p. 5). The threat of a non-fireproof building apparently did the trick, for the vast building project picked up such speed that by 1871 the first story was complete. In his report for that year Mullett states:

An idea of the immense amount of work that has been done may be formed from the following statement of materials used, and labor expended, to the present time, viz: 2,476,960 bricks; 15,701 barrels cement; 144,087 feet cube granite; 2,689 yards rubble masonry; 5,206,443 pounds of wrought and cast iron. And the magnitude of the undertaking, from the fact that there are now engaged at Dix Island [Maine] 1,002 persons in the preparation of the granite alone, of whom 704 are employed in cutting the granite for the Government, and 298 in quarrying the stock and otherwise for the contractors. Three hundred and twenty-seven thousand one hundred and sixty-nine and one-half days' labor have already been expended in cutting and boxing the granite after it has been quarried; and it is estimated that three hundred thousand days' labor will

be required to complete that branch of the work alone (*S. A. T. Report*, 1871, pp. 6–7).

During the course of construction it was decided that even as large as this building would be when complete, it would not be adequate to serve the needs of both the courthouse and the post office. As Mullett reported:

The remarkable increase in the financial department of the New York post-office rendered it necessary to provide accommodations for that branch of the service in the second story of the new post-office building. To accomplish this the rooms intended for the offices of the judiciary in that story were appropriated, which of course made it necessary to provide for them elsewhere. This could only be done by the addition of a fourth story to the building, which was authorized by the act approved March 3, 1873. Orders were immediately given for the preparation of the necessary granite, which has been cut, delivered, and is now in place (*S. A. T. Report*, 1873, p. 4).

Even with this additional story Mullett expected the building to be completed and occupied by the post office by July 4, 1874, a feat that was not to be accomplished. The building was occupied by the postal service in August 1875, but it would take five more years to finish it.

Mullett clearly expected his New York building to assure his fame as an architect, and he speaks of it at some length with obvious pride and satisfaction in his annual report:

The great size of this building and its construction, which has been entirely experimental, have rendered it impossible to estimate its cost with the accuracy that would otherwise have been attained. It is, however, so far completed that it may be safely stated that its cost will not exceed $6,500,000 exclusive of fencing, grading, sewerage, machinery, furniture, and fixtures, or $7,000,000 inclusive of these items. This amount will undoubtedly appear enormous to persons who have not investigated the subject, but, when compared with the size of the building and with the cost of other great structures erected by the Government or by State or municipal authorities, it will be found to be a cheap structure. The building will be, when completed, larger than any granite or marble buildings yet commenced by the Government outside of the

District of Columbia, and is not only the largest post-office building in the world, but will have unequaled facilities and accommodations for the transaction of business. . . . The magnitude of the building may be inferred from the following statement of labor and material expended in its construction to the present time, viz: 94,000 cubic yards excavations, 8,000 cubic yards concrete, 5,500 cubic yards rubble, 15,000,000 bricks, 50,000 barrels cement, 15,000 cubic yards sand, 500,000 cubic feet granite, 6,000 tons wrought and cast iron, 350,000 feet, board-measure, rough lumber, 5,000 pounds lead, and over 1,000,000 day's labor, exclusive of that expended on contracts for iron work, &c.
I feel confident that when completed and occupied, the most prejudiced will admit that the money has been honestly and judiciously expended, and that the building is worthy of the commercial metropolis of the United States (*S. A. T. Report*, 1873, p. 5).

*Plate 55*
U. S. Post Office and Courthouse, New York
Constructed 1869–80; demolished 1939
**Alfred B. Mullett**
**Plan of the second story, 1869**
Pencil, ink, and color wash on paper
36⅛ × 23½ in. (91.8 × 59.7 cm)
*National Archives*

A fourth story could easily be added to the building because its granite perimeter walls were self-supporting. Within the building, however, Mullett had used a cast-iron support system for the basement, first, and mezzanine stories, which created vast open work spaces that allowed the different postal tasks to operate efficiently. The mezzanine work space was provided with natural light by a central skylight placed on the second story, a feature that was adopted in most of the larger post offices constructed before electricity became common in government buildings about 1890.

One feature of the building of which Mullett was especially proud was the fact that it had been planned to take advantage in the future of the "underground way" through the city, which he was convinced "must be sooner or later constructed." He introduced the same provision in the Saint Louis post office.

*Plate 56*
U. S. Custom House and Post Office, Fall River, Massachusetts
Constructed 1876–82; demolished
**William A. Potter**
**Front elevation, 1876**
George B. Phelps, delineator
Red and black ink on linen
24⅛ × 37⅞ in. (61.3 × 93.7 cm)
*National Archives*

The stamp "Return to Room 411," which appears in the corners of many drawings from the Office of the Supervising Architect, refers to the location of this bureau in the Treasury Building.

*Plate 57*
Smithsonian Institution Building, Washington, D. C.
Constructed 1847–55
**James Renwick**
**View of the north elevation of the winning design, 1848**
Watercolor on paper
16⅝ × 40⅝ in. (42 × 103 cm)
*Smithsonian Institution Archives*
(Not in exhibition)

*Plate 58*
Smithsonian Institution Building, Washington, D. C.
Constructed 1847–55
**James Renwick**
**View of the south elevation of the winning design, 1848**
Watercolor on paper
16⅝ × 40⅝ in. (42 × 103 cm)
*Smithsonian Institution Archives*
(Not in exhibition)

These two renderings apparently were made after the competition, as they represent the final choice of the building committee. Renwick had submitted for their choice another design, also in the Norman style, but with symmetrical towers. The committee, no doubt at the urging of Owen, chose the more irregular design. An important document accompanying these renderings was a cardboard model of the Smithsonian—one of the earliest models known for an American building—whose

early existence is confirmed by a daguer-
reotype view. Both documents are in the
Smithsonian Institution Archives.

*Plate 59*
Library of Congress, Washington, D. C.
**Smithmeyer & Pelz**
**Winning design in the 1873 competition**
P. J. Pelz and V. Hagmann, delineators
Ink on paper
$17\frac{7}{8} \times 31\frac{3}{4}$ in. (45.4 × 80.7 cm)
*Library of Congress*
(Not in exhibition)

*Plate 60*
Library of Congress, Washington, D. C.
**Samuel Sloan**
**Front elevation of design entered in the
1873 competition**
Ink on paper
$15 \times 34\frac{1}{2}$ in. (38.1 × 87.7 cm)
*Library of Congress*

*Plate 61*
Library of Congress, Washington, D. C.
**Adolph E. Melander**
**View of art gallery featured in design
entered in the 1873 competition**
Ink on paper
$27\frac{1}{8} \times 20\frac{3}{4}$ in. (69 × 52.8 cm)
*Library of Congress*

*Plate 62*
Library of Congress, Washington, D. C.
**Leon Beaver**
**Perspective view of design entered in the
1873 competition**
Pencil, ink, and washes on paper
$26 \times 30$ in. (66.1 × 76.2 cm)
*Library of Congress*

*Plate 63*
Library of Congress, Washington, D. C.
**Alexander R. Esty**
**Perspective view of design, ca. 1875**
Manly N. Cutter, delineator
Ink on paper
$21\frac{1}{4} \times 32\frac{5}{8}$ in. (54 × 82.9 cm)
*Library of Congress* (Not in exhibition)

*Plate 64*
Library of Congress, Washington, D. C.
**Smithmeyer & Pelz**
**Perspective view of "Victorian Gothic"
design, 1874**
Ink and wash on paper
$28\frac{3}{8} \times 48\frac{7}{8}$ in. (72.1 × 124.2 cm)
*Library of Congress*
(Replaced in exhibition by a front
elevation of this design)

*Plate 65*
Library of Congress, Washington, D. C.
**Smithmeyer & Pelz**
**Lateral section of "German Renaissance"
design, ca. 1875–80**
Pencil and ink on paper
$17 \times 23\frac{5}{8}$ in. (43.2 × 60.1 cm)
*Library of Congress*

*Plate 66*
Library of Congress, Washington, D. C.
Constructed 1886–97
**Smithmeyer & Pelz**
**Perspective view of 1885 design**
P. J. Pelz, delineator
Watercolor over heliotype
$20\frac{3}{4} \times 28\frac{3}{8}$ in. (52.8 × 72.1 cm)
*Library of Congress*

The heliotype was produced by a photo-
mechanical process that allowed architects to obtain multiple copies of a drawing. Because the heliotype provided a
monochromatic copy of very delicate detail, it was often used as the base for
further development of the design, or for
illustrating the different aspects of a
building's design. In this case, Pelz added
watercolor washes to the heliotype to
articulate the sculptural qualities of the
architecture, whereas in another view,
Smithmeyer & Pelz used the medium to
focus attention on the rustication of the
building. The heliotype process was also
used for the publication of architectural
designs during this period.

*Plate 67*
U. S. Courthouse and Post Office,
Covington, Kentucky
Constructed 1875–79; demolished
**James G. Hill**
**Detail of hardware for connecting beams
of the courtroom trusses, ca. 1876**
Ink, wash, and watercolor on paper
$24\frac{1}{4} \times 37\frac{3}{8}$ in. (61.5 × 95 cm)
*National Archives*

Although this building was designed by
William A. Potter, the detailed working
drawings were apparently made after his
brief one-year tenure and therefore bear
the stamp of his successor, James G. Hill.

*Plate 68*
U. S. Courthouse and Post Office,
Covington, Kentucky
Constructed 1875–79; demolished
**James G. Hill**
**Elevation of wooden trusses, ca. 1876**
Ink and watercolor on paper
$23\frac{3}{4} \times 37$ in. (60.4 × 94.1 cm)
*National Archives*

See note to plate 67.

*Plate 69*
U. S. Courthouse and Post Office,
Covington, Kentucky
Constructed 1875–79; demolished
**James G. Hill**
**Details of roof ornament, ca. 1876**
Ink and watercolor on paper
$23\frac{3}{4} \times 37$ in. (60.4 × 94 cm)
*National Archives*

See note to plate 67.

*Plate 70*
U. S. Courthouse and Post Office,
Jackson, Mississippi
Constructed 1882–85; demolished 1932
**James G. Hill**
**Design published in the S. A. T. Report,
1882**
R. H. Atkinson, delineator
(Not in exhibition)

*Plate 71*
U. S. Post Office, Minneapolis
Not commenced
**James G. Hill**
**Design published in the S. A. T. Report,
1883**
R. H. Atkinson, delineator
(Not in exhibition)

The post office building for Minneapolis
was constructed in 1884–89 from a totally
different design by Mifflin E. Bell.

*Plate 72*
U. S. Post Office, Hannibal, Missouri
Constructed 1884–88
**Mifflin E. Bell**
**Design published in the S. A. T. Report,
1884**
(Not in exhibition)

During this period most of the designs for
buildings published in the annual reports
were delineated as they would be seen in
the existing architectural setting of the
community and animated by incidents of
daily life. In this scene the billboard
carried by the man close to the corner of
the post office bears the monogram of the
delineator.

*Plate 73*
U. S. Courthouse and Post Office,
Louisville, Kentucky
Constructed 1884–93; demolished 1942
**Mifflin E. Bell**
**Design published in the S. A. T. Report,
1884**
(Not in exhibition)

The nine years required to complete this
building was not an unusual occurrence
during the last quarter of the nineteenth
century, and the Office of the Supervising
Architect was frequently criticized because these buildings did "not progress as
rapidly as they should." Supervising
architect Bell addressed this problem in
his annual report:

The public generally suppose that the stoppage
of work is the fault of this Department, and in
consequence, severe criticism is very fre-

quently passed upon its management, when the criticism properly belongs upon Congress. So long, also, as Congress ignores this Department in the passage of bills making an appropriation for a building, without considering its requirements or its necessities, so long will it be a very expensive system to the Government to prepare plans at one session which have to be made all over again, after another session, because Congress has revised its first legislation and extended limits of cost, sometimes fully doubling the amount of the original limit. In many cases plans for a building have been made, and after contracts have been let, Congress has extended the limits, necessitating serious modification of plans and disadvantageous adjustment of contracts (S. A. T. Report, 1885, p. 4).

Bell returned to this problem the following year, by pointing out the higher cost of drawings for federal buildings over the past decade:

A computation of the cost to the Government of the plans prepared by this Department during a period dating from July 1, 1875, to December 31, 1885, and involving the disbursing of $41,489,303.84 for public buildings in various parts of the country, fixes the cost at 2.9 per cent. The usual price paid to architects in private practice is $2\frac{1}{2}$ per cent (S. A. T. Report, 1886, pp. 3–4).

Bell also pointed out that any consideration of the cost of government buildings had to take into account the enormous correspondence connected with supervising the construction of buildings across the country which involved "the receiving and answering of nearly 3,000 letters each month in the year."

*Plate 74*
U. S. Courthouse and Post Office,
El Paso, Texas
Constructed 1889–93; demolished
**William A. Freret**
**Front elevation, ca. 1890**
Cabinet sketch
Ink and wash on paper
$17\frac{7}{8} \times 21\frac{7}{8}$ in. ($45 \times 56$ cm)
*National Archives*

The Moorish style introduced by Freret was not reserved solely for buildings in the

southwest but was also intended to be used on buildings in other parts of the country, such as the post office in Lancaster in the center of the Amish area of Pennsylvania. Some of Freret's buildings, however, were radically changed in the course of their construction by his successors, and their Moorish character was transformed, as occurred at the El Paso post office.

A design such as this, which is signed by three officers of the cabinet—the secretary of the treasury, the postmaster general, and the secretary of the interior—is known as a "cabinet sketch." This system came into being as a result of a provision written into the Public Buildings Appropriation bill of March 3, 1875, which required that these cabinet officers approve the designs of the supervising architect before working drawings were begun. This was the first step taken by Congress in an attempt to impose some measure of control over the kind of buildings designed for a particular town.

*Plate 75*
U. S. Courthouse and Post Office,
Houston, Texas
Constructed 1887–91; demolished
**William A. Freret**
**Side elevation, ca. 1888**
Pencil, ink, color wash and watercolor on paper
$24 \times 36\frac{1}{8}$ in. ($61 \times 91.8$ cm)
*National Archives*

One of the changes Freret introduced during his short term as supervising architect was the reduction of "the number of full-size working drawings by substituting $\frac{3}{4}$-inch details and, where practicable, by the use of standard sheets for the interior finish, plumbing, stairs, etc." He also reported that "costly drawings for ornamentation are now replaced by accurate and artistic plaster models prepared directly under the supervision of the office." He claims that by these two methods he has reduced the cost of preparing drawings by nearly fifty percent, adding that the drawings previously prepared were "more elaborate than the needs of the service demanded, or than was customary in pri-

vate practice" (S. A. T. Report, 1888, p. 1).

Freret also pointed out that the business of the supervising architect's office had increased by nearly three hundred percent during the past five years and since Congress continued to authorize ever more buildings (thirty new ones in 1888), it had been necessary, in order to expedite the work, to enter into contracts with private parties for the preparation of drawings. In a long defense of taking this course of action Freret cited the cost of earlier drawings commissioned from private designers, and noted that the ones he commissioned were far less expensive. Even more illuminating, however, is a table he prepared which showed that for some buildings constructed between 1883 and 1885 the drawings made in the Office of the Supervising Architect averaged 2.2 percent of the building's total cost. In contrast, the cost of drawings contracted for from the private sector in December 1888 averaged 0.72 percent (S. A. T. Report, 1888, p. 6).

Freret was also forced to turn to outside contractors because the Civil Service Commission (under whose regulations the entire office force had been included in June of that year) was unable to find employees who fit the requirements of the department. In a letter of August 24, 1888, to the Commission requesting ten "quick and reliable draughtsmen," Freret had listed the desired qualifications:

They must be capable of preparing designs for buildings of monumental character, both in elevation and perspective, in either India ink or color, and be able to furnish complete working drawings for such buildings, including details for stone, brick, metal, and wood-work.

They must have a general knowledge of the history of architecture, and be capable of demonstrating by free-hand sketches their knowledge of the different styles of architecture, and be able to design in all styles, though they may have a preference for one certain style.

They must be good constructionists, and be able to calculate and prepare drawings for all classes of foundations, trusses, columns, roofs, etc.; a knowledge of graphic statics is desirable.

For the meaning of the stamp "Return to Room 411," see note to plate 56.

*Plate 76*
U. S. Post Office, Sacramento, California
Constructed 1890–94; demolished
**James H. Windrim**
**Details of stonework, 1890**
John R. Niernsée, delineator
Ink, wash, and watercolor on paper
$24\frac{1}{4} \times 37\frac{1}{4}$ in. ($61.5 \times 94.3$ cm)
*National Archives*

The method for preparing drawings introduced by Freret was condemned by his successor, James H. Windrim, immediately upon taking office:

A method had been introduced in the office of preparing the general and detail drawings for buildings at a scale of one-sixteenth and one-eighth inch per foot, and the drawings were further reduced by photolithographic process. The imperfect illustrations of the essential plans for public buildings permitted a discretion in executing works to be done under them, instead of commanding by clear expression a specific obligation to the Government. The method was adopted for reasons of supposed economy and expedition of work; the drawings illustrating public works should be full and explicit in detail, in order that those who are to execute the work may by them be clearly instructed as to their obligations. At present the general drawings are made at a uniform scale of one-fourth inch per foot, accompanied by the requisite full-sized details of the work; necessary duplicates are made in the photographic gallery in this office, in sufficient number for the need of the service (S. A. T. Report, 1889, p. 5).

*Plate 77*
U. S. Post Office, Lafayette, Indiana
Constructed 1892–94; demolished 1931
**Willoughby J. Edbrooke**
**Front elevation, 1891**
Frederick C. Graether, delineator
Pencil, ink, and color washes on paper
$23\frac{1}{4} \times 36\frac{1}{4}$ in. ($59.1 \times 92.1$ cm)
*National Archives*

*Plate 78*
U. S. Post Office and Courthouse,
Kansas City, Missouri
Constructed 1892–1900; demolished
**Willoughby J. Edbrooke**
**Transverse section, 1892**
Cabinet sketch
Pencil, ink, wash, and color washes on
paper 18½ × 23⅞ in. (47 × 61 cm)
*National Archives*

The dome seen in this design was vastly
increased in size during the course of
construction.
   For the meaning of the stamp "Return
to Room 411," see note to plate 56.

*Plate 79*
U. S. Post Office, Fargo, North Dakota
Constructed 1892–97; demolished 1929
**Willoughby J. Edbrooke**
**Front elevation, 1893**
George R. Pohl, delineator
Cabinet sketch
Pencil, ink, wash, and watercolor on paper
18½ × 23⅜ in. (47 × 59.4 cm)
*National Archives*

Edbrooke's venture into the Beaux-Arts
style resulted, in this case at least, in a
building that could easily have been mis-
taken for the home of a wealthy family.

*Plate 80*
U. S. Post Office, Taunton, Massachusetts
Constructed 1893–97; demolished 1930
**Jeremiah O'Rourke**
**Perspective view, 1893**
George R. Pohl, delineator
Ink on paper
18½ × 24 in. (47 × 61 cm)
*National Archives*

Although great emphasis was placed both
by Congress and the supervising architect
on achieving public buildings of high dura-
bility, most of the buildings built during
this period existed for only about thirty to
fifty years. The Taunton post office, for
example, was razed in 1930, but many
were replaced during the building programs of the PWA and WPA during the
mid- and late 1930s.

*Plate 81*
U. S. Post Office, Newburgh, New York
Constructed 1895–98; demolished
**Jeremiah O'Rourke**
**Side elevation, 1894**
Cabinet sketch
Pencil, ink, and watercolor on paper
18⅜ × 23⅞ in. (46.7 × 60.7 cm)
*National Archives*

*Plate 82*
U. S. Post Office, Clarksville, Tennessee
Constructed 1897–98
**William Martin Aiken**
**Elevations, 1896**
Cabinet sketch
Pencil, ink, wash, and watercolor on
paper
18⅛ × 23⅝ in. (46.1 × 60.1 cm)
*National Archives*

Despite the dependence of this design, and
the next one, on elaborate decoration,
Aiken described the practice established in
the Office of the Supervising Architect
since he took over as follows: "In the
drawings and specifications for all buildings, since April, 1895, the prime consideration has been thorough but simple
construction, using the most substantial
and fireproof materials permissible within
the limit of appropriation, elaboration
of design being of secondary importance"
(*S. A. T. Report*, 1897, p. 6).

*Plate 83*
U. S. Courthouse and Post Office,
Paterson, New Jersey
Constructed 1897–99
**William Martin Aiken**
**Half-elevation and details of gables, 1897**
Oscar Wenderoth, delineator
Ink and watercolor on paper
24⅝ × 36¾ in. (62.6 × 93.4 cm)
*National Archives*

*Plate 84*
U. S. Post Office, Cedar Rapids, Iowa
Constructed 1892–95
**Willoughby J. Edbrooke**
**Plan of concrete foundation, 1892**
Chauncey G. Graham, delineator
Ink and color washes on paper
23⅜ × 36 in. (59.4 × 91.5 cm)
*National Archives*
(Not in exhibition)

The delicate washes placed over the different areas of this foundation drawing—
whose purpose was simply to convey basic
construction information—transform it
into an aesthetically attractive object,
thus continuing the pattern set by Mullett
some twenty-five years earlier. Simpler
and cheaper forms for conveying such
information had been developed in private
practice long before this time.

*Plate 85*
U. S. Courthouse and Post Office,
Pittsburgh
Constructed 1881–91; demolished
**Details of the ironwork for the stairs, 1890**
George R. Pohl, delineator
Pencil and ink on paper
24⅛ × 37 in. (61.3 × 94.1 cm)
*National Archives*

*Plate 86*
U. S. Appraisers' Stores, San Francisco
Constructed 1874–81; demolished
**Design of a steam freight-elevator by Otis**
**Bros. & Co., 1881**
Ink on linen
37½ × 14⅜ in. (95.3 × 36.7 cm)
*National Archives*

*Plate 87*
U. S. Courthouse and Post Office,
Charleston, South Carolina
Constructed 1889–96
**Jeremiah O'Rourke**
**Detail of elevator grille and main stairway,**
**1894**
John Young, delineator
Pencil, ink, and watercolor on paper
22⅛ × 35 in. (56.3 × 89 cm)
*National Archives*

The need for elevator cages joined with the
continued use of public stairways provided the architects of this period with
a marvelous opportunity for designing
highly decorative cast- and wrought-iron
entryways. Although most of them have
been destroyed, this example in
Charleston still survives.

*Plate 88*
U. S. Courthouse and Post Office,
Charleston, South Carolina
Constructed 1889–96
**William Martin Aiken**
**Design of an elevator car by the Graves**
**Elevator Co., 1896**
Pencil, ink, watercolor, and gouache on
paper
18¾ × 12¾ in. (47.7 × 32.5 cm)
*National Archives*

The first major use of the elevator in a
government building occurred during the
construction of the State, War and Navy
Building in Washington, D. C. Although
not included in the south wing, which was
constructed between 1871 and 1875, provisions were made for introducing it into
the east wing, under construction from
1872 to 1879. The elevator cages and cabs
were highly ornamental in all parts of the
building, but the cabs for the east wing
designed by Richard Ezdorf were the most
exceptional, with rich wood paneling,
upholstered benches, and chandeliers.

*Plate 89*
U. S. Courthouse and Post Office,
Altoona, Pennsylvania
Constructed 1900; demolished
**James Knox Taylor**
**Perspective view and plans, 1900**
Harry C. Wilkinson, delineator
Pencil, ink, and gouache on paper
18⅜ × 24 in. (47 × 61 cm)
*National Archives*

In preparing these perspective views,
which were primarily used for publication
either in the supervising architect's annual report or in architectural periodicals,
the delineator was often guided by photo-

graphs of the proposed site which allowed him to give accurate details concerning the surroundings of the future building.

*Plate 90*
U. S. Post Office, Muskegon, Michigan
Constructed 1904; demolished
**James Knox Taylor**
**Front and side elevations, 1904**
Edward Freré Champney, delineator
Cabinet sketch
Pencil, ink, watercolor, and gouache on paper
$13 \times 28\frac{3}{8}$ in. ($33 \times 72.1$ cm)
*National Archives*

*Plate 91*
U. S. Branch Mint, Denver, Colorado
Constructed 1896–1904
**James Knox Taylor**
**Design for a chandelier by the Mitchell Vance Co., 1904**
Graphite, ink, watercolor, and gouache on paper
6 ft. $4\frac{1}{2}$ in. $\times$ 3 ft. $11\frac{1}{2}$ in. ($194.4 \times 120.7$ cm)
*National Archives*

Although this amazing rendering is signed by Taylor, the signature merely records his approval, not his authorship. This drawing is one of a set of eighteen that details in the same manner each type of lighting fixture that would be used in the building. It appears that the set was not made in the Office of the Supervising Architect, but by the company that would actually manufacture the fixtures, the Mitchell Vance Co., whose stamp appears on each drawing. Whether these working drawings were based on designs provided by the supervising architect is not known.

*Plate 92*
U. S. Post Office, Oakland, California
Constructed 1900–1901; demolished
**James Knox Taylor**
**Front elevation, 1901**
H. Pratt, delineator
Ink on linen
$23\frac{1}{4} \times 37\frac{1}{2}$ in. ($59.1 \times 95.3$ cm)
*National Archives*
(Not in exhibition)

*Plate 93*
U. S. Courthouse and Post Office, Los Angeles
Constructed 1906; demolished
**James Knox Taylor**
**Design for a staircase, 1906**
Myron P. Potter, delineator
Ink on linen
$25\frac{1}{8} \times 37\frac{1}{8}$ in. ($63.9 \times 94.3$ cm)
*National Archives*

Under Taylor's direction, the Office of the Supervising Architect no longer produced detailed renderings for every part of the building. The pencil, ink, and watercolor renderings of the previous years were replaced by line drawings which could be easily reproduced by one of several photographic methods now available, including, but apparently not particularly favored, the blueprint.

The more sophisticated drawings indicate the increased capability of the on-site superintendents to supervise the translation of drawings such as this one into executed work. After these positions were made subject to the provisions of the Civil Service Commission, they became increasingly filled by professionals instead of political appointees. In some cases where the design of a building or a room was intended to be symmetrical, only one-half of the elevation would be detailed, with the other half shown only in outline and bearing the simple instruction "repeat other side." The possibility of relying on subordinates at the site who could carry out such dicta greatly reduced the need for detailed drawings and enabled Taylor to maintain the incredible pace of the building program of these years.

*Plate 94*
U. S. Courthouse and Post Office, Los Angeles
Constructed 1906; demolished
**James Knox Taylor**
**Design for the Main Street entrance, 1906**
Walter B. Olmsted, delineator
Ink on linen
$37\frac{1}{4} \times 25\frac{1}{4}$ in. ($94.6 \times 64.2$ cm)
*National Archives*

*Plate 95*
U. S. Post Office, Wichita Falls, Texas
Constructed 1910; demolished
**James Knox Taylor**
**Elevation, section, and plans, 1910**
Richard L. Watmough, delineator
Cabinet sketch
Pencil, ink, and washes on board
$23\frac{3}{4} \times 19\frac{7}{8}$ in. ($60.4 \times 50.5$ cm)
*National Archives*

In the case of post offices intended for small towns Taylor gradually resorted to preparing only a single cabinet sketch, containing all the information needed for approval. He did not stint, however, on providing these towns with the most elegant and up-to-date buildings. The post office built in Wichita Falls, Texas, in 1910 provided its citizens with an object of admiration similar to the newest addition to the nation's capital, the Pan American Union Building which had been dedicated that same year.

*Plate 96*
**Daniel H. Burnham**
**Proposal for locating a monument to Abraham Lincoln in front of Union Station, Washington, D. C., 1908–9**
Pencil and watercolor on paper
$20 \times 17$ in. ($50.8 \times 43.2$ cm)
*United States Capitol, Architect of the Capitol*

This drawing is one of some two hundred and fifty-eight sketches, plans, and renderings made in Burnham's office which deal with the Union Station–Capitol Hill area, and which deserve fuller study and evaluation. One of these sketches—which seems to be by Burnham himself—shows the Capitol ringed by possible memorials. The inscription it bears, *loci monumentorum*, gives an insight into how the classical past was not just a source of motifs or compositions for the Beaux-Arts architect, but a part of his everyday thinking and expression.

How these drawings came into the collection of the Architect of the Capitol is not known. All crammed into one paper bag, they were discovered by the author while working with drawings related to the U. S. Capitol. Eight of these drawings related to the Lincoln monument were published for the first time in the chapter on Union Station in the Dunlap Society's publication on Washington, D. C. In addition to the cache of drawings in the collection of the Architect of the Capitol, there are in the archival records of the Commission of Fine Arts (National Archives, R. G. 66) photographs of other related drawings whose whereabouts are presently unknown. Six of these photographs are also included in the Dunlap Society publication. As they deal primarily with overall scenes of the plaza, they may well record larger renderings intended for presentation.

*Plate 97*
**Daniel H. Burnham**
**View toward the Capitol from a proposed monument to Abraham Lincoln in front of Union Station, Washington, D. C., 1908–9**
Pencil and watercolor on paper
$13 \times 26$ in. ($33 \times 66.1$ cm)
*United States Capitol, Architect of the Capitol*

The area between Union Station and the Capitol remained undeveloped until 1927 when an extensive landscape design by David Lynn, Architect of the Capitol, and the firm of Bennet, Parsons & Frost, was adopted and gradually put into effect during the 1930s.

*Plate 98*
**Daniel H. Burnham**
**Proposal for locating a circular monument to Abraham Lincoln on Delaware Avenue leading to the Capitol, Washington, D. C., 1908–9**
Pencil on paper
$13\frac{5}{8} \times 17\frac{7}{8}$ in. ($34.6 \times 45.4$ cm)
*United States Capitol, Architect of the Capitol*

The drawings for the first phase of the competition for the Lincoln Memorial have not been seen since they were displayed before the Lincoln Memorial Commission in December 1911/January 1912. This part of the competition included Pope's designs for the sites on the northern side of the city at Meridian Hill and on the Soldiers' Home grounds, as well as designs by both Henry Bacon and Pope for the Potomac site.

All the drawings submitted to the Lincoln Memorial Commission by Pope and Bacon during 1911–12 were stored for a number of years in Ford's Theater and later moved to a fifth-floor service area in the Department of Interior building. In 1939, when they were transferred to the National Archives, they were already described as being much damaged by having been shifted from one store room to another. These moves were particularly difficult because of their heavy frames, the glass of which was in many instances broken.

As no provision had been made for storing architectural drawings in the building designed in 1930 (ironically, by Pope) to house the newly established National Archives, the collection of drawings for the Lincoln Memorial and many other architectural renderings were placed in the Cartographic Division, since map material presented some of the same problems of housing. The Cartographic Division, however, did not have the space or resources for adequately storing this material, as a result of which the drawings remained generally inaccessible. They were "re-discovered" during the research work carried out in the Cartographic Division by the Dunlap Society in 1977.

See note to plate 100.

The drawings for the final phase of the Lincoln Memorial competition have not been seen since they were examined by the Lincoln Memorial Commission in the early spring of 1912, Bacon's design having been chosen on April 16.

The vast size of this rendering and those reproduced in plates 103 and 107 created a difficult storage problem for the Cartographic Division, particularly as all three were framed and glazed. The only available place for them was on top of the above-head-high file cases in whatever could be found. As a result they "disappeared" from sight until the active presence in the stacks of the author and the Dunlap Society researchers in 1977–79 jogged the memories of staff members who began to recall having put a "great, big drawing" in some out-of-the-way corner of their ever-dwindling space some years before. One by one, over a period of months, many oversized drawings were recovered in this fashion.

With the support of James B. Rhoads, then Archivist of the United States, extra funds were obtained, and twenty-nine of the most important drawings were restored at the New England Document Conservation Center in 1980–81. They are now housed in the excellent new facilities of the Cartographic and Architectural Records Branch on Pickett Street in Alexandria, Virginia.

All three proposals exhibited by Bacon to the Lincoln Memorial Commission in 1912 re-emerged during the author's work at the National Archives during 1977–79. They also underwent restoration along with the designs by Pope (see note to plate 102).

All seven of Pope's dramatic alternate designs, which were also restored in 1980–81 (see note to plate 102), were published in the chapter on the Lincoln Memorial in the Dunlap Society's publication on Washington, D. C.

See note to plate 104.

See note to plate 104.

*Plate 107*
Arlington Memorial Bridge.
Washington, D. C.
Constructed 1926–32
**McKim, Mead and White**
**Design for the bridge connecting the**
**Lincoln Memorial and Arlington**
**Cemetery, 1923**
Pencil, ink, and wash on paper
3 ft. 6 in. × 11 ft. 2 in. (106.4 × 340.4 cm)
*National Archives*

This rendering was the largest discovered
during the author's research in the archives during 1977–79 (see note to plate
102). It was found on the top of a high tier
of map cases immediately below the steam
pipes. Because it was still framed (although
both frame and glass were broken), it took
six men to remove it from its storage
place. With it were other large framed
renderings by McKim, Mead and White
for the Arlington Memorial Bridge. All
were so badly stained by water, conservation was deemed impracticable except
for the one reproduced here and two
others. One of these renderings (3 ft. ×
5 ft. 6 in.) depicts the Lincoln Memorial
from the Potomac with the circular steps
of the "watergate"—an entrance approach
from the river—the architect had proposed which was subsequently built, but
without the rows of sphinxes he had
wanted to place along each side of the
stairway.

## SELECTED BIBLIOGRAPHY

*A title given in brackets indicates that there*
*is no specific reference to the publication in*
*the text, but that the work belongs to the*
*corpus of literature that has contributed to*
*the material presented here.*

*American Architect and Building News*,
1887
"Mr. W. A. Freret, of New Orleans,
Appointed Supervising Architect."
*American Architect and Building News*,
vol. 22, no. 605 (July 30, 1887), p. 45.

*American Architect and Building News*,
1894
"The Correspondence between the
Secretary of the Treasury and the
President of the American Institute of
Architects." *American Architect and
Building News*, vol. 44, no. 954 (April 7,
1894), pp. 9–12.

Anonymous 1795
*Essai sur la ville de Washington, par
un citoyen des Etats-Unis.* New York:
L'Impremerie de J. Delafond, 1795.

Anonymous 1815
"Remarks on the Progress and Present
State of the Fine Arts in the United
States." *Analectic Magazine*, vol. 6
(November 1815), pp. 363–73.

Anonymous 1829/30
"Architecture in the United States."
Parts 1–4. *American Journal of Science
and Arts*, vol. 17, no. 1 (1830 [wrapper
gives date October 1829]), pp. 99–110;
no. 2 (1830 [wrapper gives date January
1830]), pp. 249–73; vol. 18, no. 1 (1830
[wrapper gives date April 1830]), pp.
11–26; no. 2 (1830 [wrapper gives date
July 1830]), pp. 212–37.

Anonymous 1836
Cleveland, H. R., Jr. Review of
*The American Builder's General Price
Book and Estimator*, by James Gallier.
*North American Review*, vol. 42, no. 93
(October 1836), pp. 356–84.

Beaux-Arts
[Egbert, Donald Drew. *The Beaux-Arts
Tradition in French Architecture.*
Princeton: Princeton University Press,
1980.]

Berret
Berret, James G. *In Relation to General Washington's Plan of the "Federal City"* . . . [Speech] Delivered before the Art Union Association of Washington City, March 31, 1859. Washington, D. C.: Thos. McGill, Printer, 1859.

Boston, U. S. Custom House
[Wodehouse, Lawrence. "Architectural Projects in the Greek Revival Style by Ammi B. Young." *Old-Time New England*, vol. 60, no. 3 (January–March 1970), pp. 73–85.]
   The Boston Custom House is discussed on pp. 74–80.

Boston *City Record*
*Bowen's Boston News-Letter, and City Record*, November 5, 1825, p. 7.

*Bridge Commission*
U. S. Congress. *Report of the Arlington Memorial Bridge Commission*. 68th Cong., 1st sess., 1924. S. Doc. 95. Washington, D. C.: Government Printing Office, 1924.

Brooks
Brooks, Noah. *Mr. Lincoln's Washington: Selections from the Writings of Noah Brooks, Civil War Correspondent*. Edited by P. J. Standenraus. South Brunswick, N. J.: Thomas Yoseloff, 1967.

Brown 1894
Brown, Glenn. "Government Buildings Compared with Private Buildings." *American Architect and Building News*, vol. 44, no. 954 (April 7, 1894), pp. 2–9.

Brown 1896/97
Brown, Glenn. "History of the United States Capitol." *American Architect and Building News*, vol. 52, no. 1063 (May 9, 1896), pp. 51–54; no. 1065 (May 23, 1896), pp. 75–77; no. 1068 (June 13, 1896), pp. 99–102; vol. 53, no. 1071 (July 4, 1896), pp. 3–5; no. 1074 (July 25, 1896), pp. 27–30; no. 1080 (September 5, 1896), pp. 75–78; vol. 54, no. 1084 (October 3, 1896), pp. 3–6; no. 1087 (October 24, 1896), pp. 27–29; no. 1093 (December 5, 1896), pp. 81–83; vol. 55, no. 1097 (January 2, 1897), pp. 3–6; no. 1104 (February 20, 1897), pp. 59–60.

Brown 1900–1903
Brown, Glenn. *History of the United States Capitol*. 2 vols. Washington, D. C.: Government Printing Office, 1900–1903.

Burnham and Millet
Burnham, Daniel Hudson, and Francis Davis Millet. *The World's Columbian Exposition: The Book of the Builders, Being the Chronicle of the Origin and Plan of the World's Fair*. Chicago: Columbian Memorial Publication Society, 1894.

Burnham Letters
Chicago. Art Institute of Chicago Library. Daniel H. Burnham Papers.
   *See also* Hines.

Caemmerer
[Caemmerer, Hans Paul. *The Life of Pierre Charles L'Enfant, Planner of the City Beautiful*. Washington, D. C.: National Republic Publishing Co., 1950. Reprint. New York: Da Capo Press, 1970.]

*Capitol Centennial Celebration*
Walker, General Duncan S., ed. *Celebration of the One Hundredth Anniversary of the Laying of the Corner Stone of the Capitol of the United States, with Accounts of the Laying of the Original Corner Stone, in 1793, and of the Corner Stone of the Extension, in 1851*. Washington, D. C.: Government Printing Office, 1896.

Clark
Clark, Congressman Frank. "Public Buildings." *Congressional Record*. 64th Cong. 1st sess., January 17, 1916, H. R. 17188.

*Columbian Mirror*
Account of the Laying of the Cornerstone of the Capitol of the United States, datelined George-Town, September 21. *Columbian Mirror and Alexandria Gazette*, vol. 1, no. 89 (September 25, 1793), pp. 1–2.

Commissioners Correspondence
National Archives. Office of Public Buildings and Public Parks. Record Group 42. Letters to and from the Commissioners and Proceedings of Meetings from 1791 to 1802.

Craig
Craig, Lois, and the Staff of the Federal Architecture Project. *The Federal Presence: Architecture, Politics, and Symbols in the United States Government Building*. Cambridge: MIT Press, ca. 1978. Reprint. *The Federal Presence: Architecture, Politics, and National Design*. Cambridge: MIT Press, 1984.
   The only survey of the building activity of the federal government published so far, the book presents abundant visual material and pertinent contemporary critical assessments of buildings constructed between 1789 and the 1970s.

Dakin, James
*See* Scully.

*Dial*
"Notes on Art and Architecture." *Dial*, vol. 4 (July 1843), pp. 107–15.

*Documentary History*
U. S. Congress. House. Commission on Construction of House Office Building. *Documentary History of the Construction and Development of the United States Capitol Building and Grounds*. 58th Cong., 2d sess. H. Rept. 646. Washington, D. C.: Government Printing Office, 1904.

Dunlap
Dunlap, William. "On the Influence of the Arts of Design; and the True Modes of Encouraging and Perfecting Them." *American Monthly Magazine*, vol. 7 (February 1836), pp. 113–23.

Erie Bank
Library of Congress. Prints and Photographs Division. Historical American Buildings Survey. Data sheet No. Pa.-53. "Old Customs House, Erie, Erie County, Pennsylvania." By Annie Scott Baxter. 1936.

*Final Report*
*Final Report of the Architect [T. U. Walter] to the Building Committee of the Girard College for Orphans*. Philadelphia, 1848.
   *See also* Walter.

Frary
[Frary, I. T. *They Built the Capitol*. Richmond, Va.: Garrett & Massie, 1940.]
   Exceptional for the detailed chronology, pp. 263–313.

Gallier
Gallier, James. *Autobiography of James Gallier, Architect*. Paris: E. Brière, 1864.

Gilman
Gilman, Arthur. Review of *Rural Architecture*, by Edward Shaw. *North American Review*, vol. 58 (April 1844), pp. 436–80.

Grandjean de Montigny
Grandjean de Montigny, Auguste Henri Victor. *Architecture toscane: palais, maisons, et autres édifices de la Toscane*. Paris, 1815.

Greenough 1843
Greenough, Horatio. "Remarks on American Art." *United States Magazine and Democratic Review*, vol. 13 (August 1843), pp. 206–10.

Greenough 1851
Greenough, Horatio. *Aesthetics at Washington, No. 1* . . . . Washington, D. C.: J. T. Towers, 1851.

Hallet
[Bennett, Wells. "Stephen Hallet and His Designs for the National Capitol, 1790–94." *Journal of the American Institute of Architects*, vol. 4 (July–October 1916), pp. 290–95, 324–30, 376–83, 411–18.]

Hamlin 1944
Hamlin, Talbot. *Greek Revival Architecture in America*. New York: Oxford University Press, 1944. Reprint. New York: Dover, 1964.
   This book remains the best account yet of this period of American architecture. Especially valuable is the annotated, selective bibliography prepared by Sarah H. J. Simpson Hamlin, which offers an extensive sampling of contemporary critical writings on architecture.

Hamlin 1955
Hamlin, Talbot. *Benjamin Henry Latrobe*. New York: Oxford University Press, 1955.
　　*See also* Latrobe; Norton.

Hines
Hines, Thomas. *Burnham of Chicago: Architect and Planner*. Chicago: University of Chicago Press, 1974; Phoenix Edition, 1979.
　　*See also* Burnham Letters; Burnham and Millet.

Hone
*The Diary of Philip Hone 1828–1851*. Edited with an introduction by Allan Nevins. New York: Dodd, Mead, 1927; new and enlarged edition, 1936.

Howard
Howard, Alexandra Cushing. "Stephen Hallet and William Thornton at the U. S. Capitol, 1791–1797." Master's Thesis, University of Virginia, 1974.

Jefferson Correspondence
Padover, Saul K., ed. *Thomas Jefferson and the National Capitol*. Washington, D. C.: Government Printing Office, 1946.

Kersaint
Kersaint, Armand-Guy Coetnempren de. *Discours sur les monuments publics*. Paris, 1792.

Kimball and Bennett
Kimball, Fiske, and Wells Bennett. "William Thornton and the Design of the United States Capitol." *Art Studies*, vol. 1 (1923), pp. 76–92.

Kite
[Kite, Elizabeth. *L'Enfant and Washington, 1791–1792*. Baltimore: Johns Hopkins Press, 1929. Reprint. New York: Arno Press, 1970.]
　　Although the author notes that certain documents have been abridged, there are additional instances, not so indicated, where documents have not been transcribed fully.

Landau
[Landau, Sarah Bradford. *Edward T. and William A. Potter, American Victorian Architects*. New York: Garland, 1979.]

Latrobe
*The Journal of Latrobe, Being the Notes and Sketches of an Architect, Naturalist, and Traveler in the United States from 1796 to 1820*. New York: D. Appleton, 1905. Reprint. New York: Burt Franklin, 1971.
　　*See also* Hamlin 1955; Norton.

L'Enfant 1791
"L'Enfant's Reports to President Washington, Bearing Dates of March 26, June 22, and August 19, 1791." *Records of the Columbia Historical Society*, vol. 2 (1899), pp. 26–48.

L'Enfant 1800
"The L'Enfant Memorials." *Records of the Columbia Historical Society*, vol. 2 (1899), pp. 72–110. – Herman Kahn. "Appendix to Pierre L'Enfant's Letter to the Commissioners, May 30, 1800." Ibid., vol. 44–45 (1944), pp. 191–213.
　　From May 30, 1800, to January 30, 1824, L'Enfant consistently petitioned first the commissioners and then Congress for payment for his services. The 1899 "Memorials" publishes three of these documents: L'Enfant's petition of August 30, 1800, to the commissioners, his petition of December 7, 1800, to Congress, and his appendix to this letter. Kahn publishes the appendix to the first letter L'Enfant addressed to the commissioners, of May 30, 1800, to which he received no reply and thus sent an identical version on August 30. However, many unpublished petitions, drafts, and supplementary material exist in: Library of Congress, Manuscript Division, L'Enfant-Digges-Morgan Collection, 4 vols.; National Archives, Office of Public Buildings and Public Parks, Record Group 42; National Archives, Records of the House and Records of the Senate, Record Group 233. The author is preparing an analysis of all these documents for future publication.
　　*See also* Caemmerer; Kite.

Le Tarouilly
Le Tarouilly, Paul Marie. *Edifices de Rome moderne, ou recueil des palais, maisons, églises, couvents, et autres monuments publics et particuliers les plus remarquables de la ville de Rome*. 3 vols. Liège, 1840; Paris, 1850–57.

Library of Congress
[Cole, John Y. "The Main Building of the Library of Congress: A Chronology, 1871–1980." In Helen-Anne Hilker, *Ten First Street, Southeast: Congress Builds a Library, 1886–1897*, pp. 39–43. Exhibition catalogue. Washington, D. C.: Library of Congress, 1980.]

Lincoln M. C. Report
U. S. Congress. *Lincoln Memorial Commission Report*. 62d Cong., 3d sess., 1913. S. Doc. 965. Washington, D. C.: Government Printing Office, 1913.
　　Contains reports in seven appendixes that trace the search for the proper site and design for the memorial.

Lowry
Lowry, Bates, ed. *The Architecture of Washington, D. C.* 2 vols. Washington, D. C.: Dunlap Society, 1976–79; distributed by Princeton University Press. Microfiche.

Macmillan Encyclopedia
[*Macmillan Encyclopedia of Architects*. Adolf K. Placzek, editor in chief. 4 vols. New York: Free Press, 1982.]

Massachusetts Magazine
"Description of the Federal Edifice at New York." *Massachusetts Magazine*, vol. 1, no. 6 (June 1789), pp. 331–33.

McMillan Plan
U. S. Congress, Senate. Committee on the District of Columbia. *Report of the Senate Committee on the District of Columbia on the Improvement of the Park System of the District of Columbia*. 57th Cong., 1st sess., 1902. S. Rept. 166.

Mills
Mills, Robert. "The Architectural Works of Robert Mills." In Helen M. P. Gallagher, *Robert Mills, Architect of the Washington Monument, 1781–1855*, pp. 168–71. New York: Columbia University Press, 1935.

Mullett
[Wodehouse, Lawrence. "Alfred B. Mullett and His French Style Government Buildings." *Journal of the Society of Architectural Historians*, vol. 31, no. 1 (March 1972), pp. 22–37.]

National Archives
National Archives. Records of the Public Buildings Service. Record Group 121.

New Orleans, U. S. Custom House
[Arthur, Stanley C. *A History of the U. S. Custom House, New Orleans*. Rev. and 2d ed. Work Projects Administration of Louisiana. New Orleans: Survey of Federal Archives in Louisiana, 1940.]

New York, U. S. Custom House
　　*See* Torres 1961.

New York, U. S. Post Office
　　*See* New York Times.

New York City Procession
[Simpson, Sarah H. J. "The Federal Procession in the City of New York." *New-York Historical Society Quarterly Bulletin*, vol. 9, no. 2 (July 1925), pp. 39–57.]

New-York Journal
Description of Federal Hall in New York City. *New-York Journal or the Weekly Register*, March 26, 1789. Reprinted in Louis Torres, "Federal Hall Revisited." *Journal of the Society of Architectural Historians*, vol. 29, no. 4 (December 1970), p. 329.

New York Times
"The New Post Office." *New York Times*, June 7, 1867; June 17, 1868; October 29, 1873.

Norris, John S.
　　*See* Savannah, U. S. Custom House.

Norton
[Norton, Paul F. *Latrobe, Jefferson and the National Capitol.* New York: Garland, 1977.]
    *See also* Hamlin 1955; Latrobe.

Owen
Owen, Robert Dale. *Hints on Public Architecture, Containing . . . Views and Plans of the Smithsonian Institution.* New York: George P. Putnam, 1849. Reprint. New York: Da Capo Press, 1978.

Palladio
Palladio, Andrea. *The Four Books of Architecture.* London: Isaac Ware, 1738. Reprint. With an introduction by Adolf K. Placzek. New York: Dover, 1965.

Partridge
[Partridge, William T. *L'Enfant's Methods and Features of His Plan for the Federal City.* Excerpt from "Annual Report, National Capital Park and Planning Commission, 1930." Washington, D. C.: National Capital Park and Planning Commission, 1975.]

*Port Folio*
Tucker, George. "Thoughts of a Hermit . . . On Architecture." *Port Folio,* n.s. vol. 4 (1814), pp. 559–69.

Reps
[Reps, John W. *Monumental Washington: The Planning and Development of the Capital Center.* Princeton, N.J.: Princeton University Press, 1967.]

Roberdeau Correspondence
Library of Congress. Manuscript Division. L'Enfant-Digges-Morgan Collection. 4 vols.

*S. A. T. Report*
United States. Supervising Architect of the Treasury Department. *Annual Report.* 1854–1917.
    *See also* Smith; Thayer.

Savannah, U. S. Custom House
[Morrison, Mary Lane. *John S. Norris. Architect in Savannah, 1846–1860.* N.p.: Beehive Press, 1980.]

Schuyler 1894A
Schuyler, Montgomery. "Last Words about the Fair." *Architectural Record,* vol. 3 (January–March 1894), pp. 271–301.

Schuyler 1894B
Schuyler, Montgomery. "The Government's Failure as a Builder." *Forum,* vol. 17 (July 1894), pp. 609–21.

Scully
Scully, Arthur, Jr. *James Dakin, Architect: His Career in New York and the South.* Baton Rouge: Louisiana State University Press, 1973.

Smith
[Smith, Darrell Hevenor. *The Office of the Supervising Architect of the Treasury: Its History, Activities, and Organization.* Baltimore: Johns Hopkins Press, 1923.]
    *See also* S. A. T. Report; Thayer.

Stokes, Isaac Newton Phelps. *The Iconography of Manhattan Island, 1498–1909.* 6 vols. New York: Robert H. Dodd, 1915–28. Reprint. New York: Arno Press, 1967.
    For the history of the new City Hall built 1699–1704 and its subsequent alterations, see vol. 1, pp. 186–87, pl. 32-B and p. 272 for plate description; vol. 3, Addenda plate 4-A and p. 863 for plate description; vol. 4, Chronology, pp. 419–20, 728. For the building's transformation into Federal Hall, see vol. 3, Frontispiece I and pp. 537–39 for plate description; vol. 5, Chronology, p. 1232. For the Federal Procession of July 23, 1788, see vol. 5, Chronology, p. 1229.

Thayer
[Thayer, R. H., comp. *History, Organization, and Functions of the Office of the Supervising Architect of the Treasury Department.* Washington, D. C.: Government Printing Office, 1886.]
    *See also* S. A. T. Report; Smith.

Thornton Papers
Library of Congress. Manuscript Division. The J. Henley Smith Collection of the Papers of William Thornton.

Tindall
[Tindall, William. *Standard History of the City of Washington from a Study of the Original Sources.* Knoxville, Tenn.: H. W. Crew, 1914.]

Torres 1961
Torres, Louis. "Samuel Thomson and the Old Custom House." *Journal of the Society of Architectural Historians,* vol. 20, no. 4 (December 1961), pp. 185–90.

Torres 1970
Torres, Louis. "Federal Hall Revisited." *Journal of the Society of Architectural Historians,* vol. 29, no. 4 (December 1970), pp. 327–38.

Trumbull
Trumbull, John. *The Autobiography of Colonel John Trumbull, Patriot-Artist, 1756–1843.* Edited by Theodore Sizer. New Haven: Yale University Press, 1953.

Tuthill
Tuthill, Mrs. L. C. *History of Architecture, from the Earliest Times; Its Present Condition in Europe and the United States.* Philadelphia: Lindsay and Blakiston, 1848.

*Universal Asylum*
"Description of the City of Washington." *Universal Asylum and Columbian Magazine,* vol. 5 (March 1792), p. 155.

*Views in Philadelphia*
*Views in Philadelphia and Its Environs, from Original Drawings Taken in 1827–30.* Philadelphia: C. G. Childs, 1830.

Walter
[Ennis, Robert Brooks. *Thomas Ustick Walter, Architect.* Handlist of an exhibition held at the Athenaeum of Philadelphia, October 29–December 28, 1979.]
    *See also* Final Report.

Washington Correspondence
"The Writings of George Washington Relating to the National Capital." *Records of the Columbia Historical Society,* vol. 17 (1914), pp. 3–232.

Webster
Webster, Daniel. *Mr. Webster's Address at the Laying of the Corner Stone of the Addition to the Capitol, July 4th, 1851.* Washington, D. C.: Gideon & Co., Print., 1851. Reprinted in *Documentary History,* pp. 137–52.

Wodehouse
[Wodehouse, Lawrence. *American Architects from the Civil War to the First World War: A Guide to Information Sources.* Detroit: Gale Research Co., 1976.]